P9-DXN-334

To Save America

To Save America

★ ★ ★

STOPPING OBAMA'S SECULAR-SOCIALIST MACHINE

By Newt Gingrich

with Joe DeSantis

Since 1947
REGNERY
PUBLISHING, INC.

An Eagle Publishing Company • Washington, DC

Cataloging-in-Publication data on file with the Library of Congress
ISBN 978-1-59698-596-4

Published in the United States by
Regnery Publishing, Inc.
One Massachusetts Avenue, NW
Washington, DC 20001
www.regnery.com

Manufactured in the United States of America
10 9 8 7 6 5 4 3 2 1

Books are available in quantity for promotional or premium use. Write to Director of Special Sales, Regnery Publishing, Inc., One Massachusetts Avenue NW, Washington, DC 20001, for information on discounts and terms or call (202) 216-0600.

Distributed to the trade by:
Perseus Distribution
387 Park Avenue South
New York, NY 10016

*To my wife Callista, whose support and love
have made the adventure of our life together
exciting, enjoyable, and fulfilling.*

TABLE OF CONTENTS

Introduction

This is a book I never expected to write.

After the victory of freedom over Communist tyranny, of religious liberty over secular police states, and of American pride over the malaise and cynicism of the 1970s, I fully expected America to follow an upward curve of consistent improvement.

I did not expect the Left to ignore the lessons of history and move further into ideological extremism. I did not expect them to react to their meager popular support by seeking to impose a corrupt, Chicago-style political machine on the entire country.

After leaving Congress in 1999 with a balanced budget and a booming economy, I certainly did not foresee Republican failure so vast that it allowed left-wing radicals to take over the House, Senate, and Presidency.

America as we know it is now facing a mortal threat.

The Left have expanded their power through their control of academia, the elite news media, union leaders, trial lawyers, the bureaucracy, the courts, and lobbyists at the state and federal levels. They share a vision of a secular, socialist America run for the interests of the members of the political machine that keeps them in power. It will be an America where government dominates the people rather than represents them. In short, they want to use government power to change who we are and how we think.

This danger to America is greater than anything I dreamed possible after we won the Cold War and the Soviet Union disappeared in December 1991. We stand at a crossroads: either we will save our country or we will lose it.

AN ALIEN IDEOLOGY

The left-wing Democrats who currently control the White House, the House of Representatives, the Senate, and many state capitols are committed to a secular-socialist ideology that is alien to America's history and traditions.

Traditional America values hard work, entrepreneurship, innovation, and merit-based upward mobility. But the secular-socialist machine rewards its members, punishes "overachievers," kills jobs by over-taxing small businesses, and even exploits your death to tax the savings you hope to pass on to your children and grandchildren.

Traditional America was based on a profound belief that "we are endowed by our Creator with certain unalienable rights." But secular socialists are so opposed to God in public life that they can't tolerate school prayer or even allow a cross to stand in the middle of the Mojave Desert.

Our government traditionally regarded the protection of American lives as its top priority. Our primary concern with captured terrorists (or pirates, the old equivalent of terrorists) was interrogating them and using that information to stop further attacks.

The secular socialists, however, want to give our enemies the same constitutional protections we afford our own citizens, effectively placing the rights of terrorists ahead of the lives of Americans. With the Left in charge, when a foreign terrorist tried to blow up an airplane over Detroit, he was read his Miranda rights (which, as a foreign enemy combatant, he was not actually entitled to have). Taxpayers were forced to pay for the terrorist's lawyer, who most likely advised his client not to answer questions except as leverage to get a plea bargain.

Americans traditionally believed in American exceptionalism— that America has a special mission to protect and spread freedom. For many in the secular-socialist Left, however, the only thing exceptional about America is our supposed viciousness. They believe America is an exploitive, imperialist aggressor, and that the U.S. military is a nefarious tool of corporate interests. Some on the Left even hope for America's wartime defeat as a means to stop us from promoting American values across the world.

Historically, America was a low-tax, high-job-growth, small-business-oriented society in which families, charities, local governments, and the private sector were much more important to daily life than was the federal government. But the secular socialists believe the only reliable institution is a bureaucratic, centralized, supremely powerful government. Their answer to virtually every problem is higher taxes, more spending, and bigger bureaucracies, because they don't believe Americans can be trusted to make the "right" decisions.

Americans traditionally believed that elected officials served the people and were obligated to listen to them. "No taxation without representation" was really a battle cry insisting that free people have the right to temporarily loan power to elected officials. In contrast, because the secular-socialist Left cannot win by proclaiming their real goals, they resort to dishonesty to ram through their agenda. They represent the worst aspects of a Chicago-style political machine combined with the greatest political corruption ever seen in modern America.

Given this enormous gulf between historic America and the secular socialists, it's clear that if the Left stay in power, they will transform America into a radically different nation—a union-dominated, bureaucratically controlled, high-tax, low-growth country. Powerful politicians will impose their will on an exhausted, submissive citizenry, who will look to government bureaucrats for guidance and permission to succeed in life. Naturally, there will be no place for God in this new, purely secular society.

As my daughter, the columnist Jackie Cushman, wrote, "We were told to vote for change we could believe in and found we had elected people who wanted to change what we believe."

The America in which we grew up is vastly different from the America the secular-socialist Left want to create. And that's why saving America is the fundamental challenge of our time. The secular-socialist machine represents as great a threat to America as Nazi Germany or the Soviet Union once did.

This diagnosis may strike some readers as alarmist. But this book will show just how radical, how corrupt, and how ruthless the Left have become. You will also see why the term "secular-socialist machine" is the only honest way to describe the Left's ideology and the way they operate today.

Time has not run out, but it is running short. It's up to those of us who love our country to save America from the destructive, irreversible transformation that the Left have in store for us.

CHAPTER ONE

Who We Are

For the first time since the Civil War, we as Americans have to ask the most fundamental question possible: "Who are we?" In 1861 that question related to whether the American Experiment was to be dissolved, whether one-half of our country was to perpetuate the institution of slavery, or whether we, as a united country, were going to abolish it.

Today, we face a challenge equally grave: whether the United States as we know it will cease to exist. I'm not talking—not yet—about the threat of terrorism, or of the growing power of China, or about any other external threat. I'm talking about losing what defines us as Americans.

Most of us know who we are. We know that America is an exceptional country with a unique genius for combining freedom and order, strength and compassion, religious faith and religious tolerance. But today we have given power in Washington and in state capitols nationwide to a radical left-wing elite that does not believe in American exceptionalism. Barack Obama has told us so. When he was asked by a *Financial Times* reporter whether he believed in American exceptionalism, he replied, "I believe in American exceptionalism, just as I suspect that the Brits believe in British exceptionalism and the Greeks believe in Greek exceptionalism."

In other words, everything we cherish about America, our president thinks is not so very special, not so very different from any other country. That's why he and his supporters feel free to change our country as they see fit, to use all the levers of federal power to annex our healthcare system to the federal government, to act as if the bureaucracy—not the private sector—is the great job creator, to make America a more socialist, more secular society.

To put it plainly, America is facing an existential threat—and it comes from a movement that fundamentally rejects the traditional American conception of who we are. No longer, in the Left's view, are we the Americans of the frontier, the sturdy, independent farmers; no longer are we America the capitalist colossus serving as the arsenal of democracy; no longer are we the America that believes our liberty is an unalienable right that comes from God. All this, the secular socialist wants to deny—and is denying—in favor of a secular, bureaucratic society guided by government elites.

Overall, the fundamental definition of what it means to be American is being undermined and distorted by the values, attitudes, and actions of the secular-socialist machine.

This brings us back to the essential question: who are we? By this, I mean what are America's basic values and traditions, and what ideals have successfully guided us in the past? By contrasting these historic American attitudes with the alien, destructive values the Left are now imposing on us, we can develop solid principles that should guide our efforts to rescue our country from secular socialism.

The fundamental difference between historic American ideals and those of the secular-socialist Left can be seen in ten conflicting values:

1. Work versus theft
2. Productivity versus union work rules and bureaucracy
3. Elected representation versus bureaucrats and judges
4. Honesty versus corruption
5. Low taxes with limited government versus high taxes with big government
6. Private property versus government controls
7. Localism versus Washington control
8. American energy versus environmental extremism
9. Conflict resolution versus litigation
10. Religious belief versus secular oppression

Any one of these conflicts represents clashing values on the most basic level. Taken collectively, they indicate two irreconcilable worldviews that, in the long run, cannot coexist in the American system. Eventually one of these value systems will defeat and replace the other—and that time will come sooner rather than later. If we lose this struggle, the America of our fathers and forefathers will be forever lost, giving way to a secular-socialist machine that will never relinquish power of its own accord.

1. Work Versus Theft

The work ethic is so central to the American experience that it was already being emphasized over 400 years ago, in 1607, during the very first summer of English-speaking colonization in Jamestown, Virginia. When wealthy aristocrats told Captain John Smith they did not have to work, he replied with a dictate reminiscent of St. Paul's second epistle to the Thessalonians: "This is a new world and we can't afford to carry people who won't work. If you don't work you won't eat."

Thus, from its earliest days, America was based on a simple proposition: people should work hard, and in return they could keep the fruits of their labor.

There is a vivid contrast between a free, work-oriented society and the dependency-dishonesty model of Soviet Communism—and to some extent of the left-wing welfare state. Soviet workers had a motto: "We pretend to work and they pretend to pay us." Americans had a remarkably different slogan: "An honest day's work for an honest day's pay." America today is still filled with small businesses, self-employed people, professionals, and others who live by that principle every day.

Because we are self-reliant and operate in markets where people won't pay us if we cheat, Americans have created an environment where honesty pays. In contrast, the secular-socialist machine, with its commitment to a socialist vision of wealth redistribution, has undermined the very concept of "an honest day's work," especially through its union power. In fact, it spreads the opposite ethic: game the system to get as many benefits as you can while working as little as possible.

A typical example is the Long Island Railroad. According to a September 2008 *New York Times* investigation, nearly every career employee of the Long Island Railroad is approved for disability payments shortly after retiring.[1] In one recent year, 97 percent of all new retirees applied for and received disability, part of a scam that has cost taxpayers at least $250 million since 2000.

Here's another example: at the heavily unionized Big 3 auto makers in Detroit—General Motors, Ford, and Chrysler—thousands of workers were paid not to work. They were part of a United Auto Workers "jobs bank" plan to keep them as dues paying members even if they did nothing productive. According to Mark Perry, an economics professor at the University of Michigan-Flint, the jobs bank program cost the Big 3 automakers more than $4 billion between 2005 and 2008.[2] With these kind of union "deals," is it any wonder the auto companies got in such trouble?

The Post Office, which is suffering from a $7 billion deficit, has a similar program called "standby time" that pays a large group of employees more than a million dollars a week to do nothing.[3] Union rules prevent the Post Office from laying off redundant workers.

Worse, New York City has "rubber rooms" to house teachers who are so incompetent they can't be allowed to teach children. Yet because of their union contract, it takes up to *seven years* to fire them, so in the meantime they are paid to sit in a room and do nothing. This act of theft—taking something for nothing—costs New York City schools about $65 million a year, which should be spent on educating children.[4]

Or consider today's typical mode of school attendance certification. Students are officially counted two or three times a year, and the results determine how much the school gets paid for the rest of the year. On these counting days, some schools hold "pizza days" or adopt other gimmicks to encourage maximum attendance. After that, attendance can be dramatically lower because it does not affect the school's payments.

Clearly, we need reforms to restore the traditional work ethic. And it can be done. Just imagine a reform movement that insists:

1. You should only get disability if you really deserve it.
2. You should only get paid if you actually work.
3. Teachers who can't be allowed near students should be removed from the payroll.
4. Every teacher should report actual attendance electronically every hour (a method McDonald's uses to report every sale in its 37,000 stores worldwide), and

schools will only get paid for students who actually attend class.

Think what would happen if these kinds of reforms spread throughout the entire economy—once again, we would live by "an honest day's work for an honest day's pay."

One thing's for sure: these reforms would provoke bitter resistance from those members of the machine who profit from the status quo. Their source of income might be called cheating or extortion (like New York's rubber-room teachers); it might even be considered theft in some cases (such as lying to get disability or workmen's comp). But they consider it "their" money, and they think they're entitled to it.

The people who live off your taxes without doing an honest day's work understand exactly what they're doing. They are beating the system. And if you advocate reforms that threaten their lifestyle, they'll try to beat you, too.

2. Productivity Versus Union Work Rules and Bureaucracy

From the Japanese attack at Pearl Harbor on December 7, 1941, to victory over Japan in August 1945, America won World War II in three years and eight months. That's the traditional, can-do America.

In contrast, it recently took twenty-three years to add a fifth runway to the Atlanta airport. More strikingly, we still have not rebuilt the World Trade Center more than eight years after it was destroyed. That's bureaucratic America.

The father of the modern Democratic Party, Franklin D. Roosevelt, understood the danger of paralysis posed by a unionized, bureaucratic government. In 1937, he explained how government employee unions must be held to a different standard than private ones:

All Government employees should realize that the process of collective bargaining, as usually understood, cannot be transplanted into the public service.... The very nature and purposes of Government make it impossible for administrative officials to represent fully or to bind the employer in mutual discussions with Government employee organizations. The employer is the whole people, who speak by means of laws enacted by their representatives in Congress. Accordingly, administrative officials and employees alike are governed and guided, and in many instances restricted, by laws which establish policies, procedures, or rules in personnel matters.[5]

Unfortunately, FDR's Democratic descendants have ignored his wise counsel. Today, can-do America is being steadily eroded by its bureaucratic counterpart. America is now so tied up in regulations, litigation, and bureaucratic rules that key sectors of our economy—especially energy exploration—are becoming stagnant.

Consider *New York Times* columnist Tom Friedman, who continually laments America's inability to match China's speed in developing large-scale projects. Yet, he cannot understand that the U.S. government bureaucracies he admires and the liberal policies he supports are the very heart of the problem.

For example, President Obama needed emergency stimulus money so fast that no one in Congress had time to read the $787 billion stimulus bill. Then that legislation met the federal bureaucracy. Consider the example of "fast track" green energy projects which, despite their name, still have to go through a multi-layered environmental impact and public review process. According to the website of the Bureau of Land Management (which handles green energy projects for the Department of the Interior), these projects could "potentially" be cleared for approval to receive stimulus funds by December 2010, almost *two years* after the stimulus was passed.

Still, Friedman is correct that China is developing quickly. When my wife Callista and I were in China in August 2009, it was clear the Chinese were heavily investing in building the world's largest and most efficient high-speed train system. They are determined to connect all their major cities with 215-mile-per-hour trains.[6]

That project will allow the Chinese to save energy, improve the environment, and dominate the world's high-speed train market with the most advanced manufacturing in the world. They have an investment strategy rather than a stimulus strategy. They focus on getting the job done, rather than on following bureaucratic red tape.

We could apply the same technology in the Boston-Washington corridor or along the Florida and California coastlines, but the combination of union work rules, land use studies, bureaucratic red tape, and the likelihood of litigation bottles everything up, keeping Americans trapped in obsolete, slower trains—even Amtrak's high-tech Acela is outdated by the new Chinese standards.

Similarly, the United States has enormous amounts of energy reserves.* However, American energy is trapped by litigation, regulation, and hostile bureaucracies. Even when a decision is made to open up federal land for natural gas exploration, bureaucrats slow down the permitting process. Then, when the permits are finally issued, left-wing environmental groups file lawsuits. The Left's goal is to exhaust the time and money of potential energy producers so they will develop foreign resources instead of American ones. The result is a government-created energy scarcity that increases prices, drives jobs abroad, and hurts our balance of payments.

---

* I describe America's huge energy potential in my book *Drill Here, Drill Now, Pay Less* (Washington, D.C.: Regnery, 2008), and in a movie Callista and I hosted and produced, *We Have the Power*.

Again and again the process of studying, organizing, preparing, and then regulating and litigating adds months, years, and even decades to critical American initiatives.

Yet, the secular-socialist machine will resist any effort to bring back America's traditional can-do attitude, which would reduce the machine's power. The Left have spent decades building a trap of bureaucracy, union work rules, and litigation to erode the independent, competitive, and productive instincts of the American people. And they will not relinquish their system without a fight.

3. Elected Representation Versus Bureaucrats and Judges

Elected representation is the heart of the American political system.

Since our Declaration of Independence in 1776 proclaimed that "we are endowed by our Creator with certain unalienable rights— among which are life, liberty and the pursuit of happiness," we Americans have believed we have been entrusted by God with rights that no politician, bureaucrat, or judge can revoke.

This concept of freedom came to Americans during our long, bitter dispute with the British Empire, its London bureaucracy, and its imperial and dictatorial judges. Our forefathers believed ultimate power should always reside in the people, who would loan power to elected officials and who could reclaim it from them if necessary.

The government was viewed as a servant of the people, not the other way around. New Hampshire's state motto, "Live free or die," was typical of the intensity with which Americans guarded their natural-born rights.

Characteristically, one of the first acts of the first Congress was to pass a Bill of Rights that strictly limited the power of government. The First Amendment protects the right to free speech and also prevents the government from trying to control religion.

The Second Amendment guarantees the right to bear arms—something that is not understood by many politicians today who confuse it with the right to hunt ducks, as President Clinton once did. The Founding Fathers knew better. The British were stopped at Lexington and Concord by a well-trained and well-armed local militia. The American right to bear arms turned out to be the key to retaining all other rights in the face of tyranny.

Secular socialists believe it's the government's right, and even its duty, to change the people—to make them more progressive, more secular, and more "tolerant." Thomas Jefferson believed so deeply in the opposite proposition—that it's the people's right to change their government—that he declared every generation might need its own revolution. He was speaking about a peaceful, democratic revolution, and he proved his seriousness in 1800 when a political party he helped to create, the Democratic-Republican Party, swept away the establishment and took control of the presidency and both houses of Congress.

For the first 100 years of American self-government, elected officials dominated relatively small, politically appointed bureaucracies. The Jeffersonians completely reshaped government after their 1800 victory, abolishing over half of all sitting federal judges—eighteen of thirty-five. A generation later, Andrew Jackson's election in 1828 led to a "spoils system" in which the winning candidate could dramatically reshape the bureaucracy by packing it with his supporters. And at the beginning of his presidency, Abraham Lincoln regarded one of his most important tasks to be appointing people to federal jobs. He believed the bureaucracy had to be changed to heed the will of the people as expressed through their choice of elected officials.

One occasion when unelected officials tried to impose their views on the country was the Supreme Court's 1857 Dred Scott decision. Extending slavery to the entire country, the decision was a major cause of Lincoln's reentry into politics, and it sparked the rise of a Republican Party that split the nation and led to our most devastating conflict—the Civil War.

After a century of subservience to elected representatives, the bureaucracy began accumulating power in the 1880s, when the rising professional class produced a civil service movement that aimed to modernize government. The Progressives, as they were called, believed well-educated professional bureaucrats were more capable than elected officials of rendering "correct" judgments. This view, derived from the snobbish elitism of the professional classes, gradually came to dominate our bureaucracies, courts, and our universities, leading to a much bigger, more dominating federal bureaucracy.

Today, we have moved from a world of decisive elected officials to a world of elected officials being limited and trapped by red tape, litigation, bureaucrats, and lawyers. And the American people know it. A recent Rasmussen poll revealed only 21 percent of Americans believe the U.S. government has the consent of the governed.[7]

Much of the current anger at the political establishment resembles the righteous rage Andrew Jackson and his allies felt while fighting to clean up what they perceived to be an oligarchy trying to impose a corrupt, Washington-centered, elitist system on the American people.

"I weep for the liberty of my country," said Jackson, "when I see at this early day of its successful experiment that corruption has been imputed to many members of the House of Representatives, and the rights of the people have been bartered for promises of office."

Today, the tea party movement, the explosion of insurgent primary challengers, the general anger at Washington, Sacramento, Albany, and all the other centers of unionized bureaucratic power— all these elements are coming together to force a fundamental choice in the Jeffersonian and Jacksonian tradition: will the American people continue to select representatives to whom we loan power? Or will America become a European-style country in which the permanent bureaucrats and permanent judges decide virtually everything, while the politicians merely play partisan games to entertain the public and satisfy their own ambitions?

The people's fight to take back power from the bureaucracy is a fight all the Founders would support. With Bill Forstchen and Steve Hanser, I recently completed two novels on George Washington and the American Revolution. When you immerse yourself in the stories of people who fought to create this country, you realize how passionately they believed in liberty. They really did risk everything—their lives, their fortunes, and their sacred honor—to give us a free country. And they fought for eight long years.

At Gettysburg, commemorating the first national military cemetery, Lincoln observed that Americans were involved in a great struggle to decide if we will have "government of the people, by the people, and for the people." He was prepared to fight our bloodiest war—620,000 Americans killed—to ensure the continuation of this Union where people lent power to those they elected.

Now we will discover if we have the same commitment to America that Washington and Lincoln had, the same willingness to endure, and the same courage to stand for our beliefs.

4. Honesty Versus Corruption

Historically, America's insistence on the rule of law and honest government has contrasted sharply with the tradition—and even acceptance—of corruption and dishonesty around the world.

America, of course, has had corrupt episodes—look at the Tammany Hall political machine in New York City during the 1800s, or the Democratic machine that dominates Chicago to this day. But the American people have never tolerated corruption—we've consistently tried to clean it up as soon as we learn of it, lock up the crooks, and maintain a standard of honesty.

Part of this attitude stems from the religious core of the American experience. "Thou shalt not steal," the Eighth Commandment God gave Moses during the exodus from Egypt, is an injunction taken seriously throughout American history. Furthermore, if we were "endowed by our Creator with certain unalienable rights," then stealing someone's endowment is an offense against the Creator. Finally, if we're all born with equal rights, then theft by one diminishes the rights of another.

Americans have also understood that honesty is the key underpinning of the free market. If people trust you, they're more likely to undertake bigger projects and take bigger risks with you.

The American belief that honesty is the key to a successful free market drew much of its inspiration from two very different men. The first was in some ways the first modern American—Benjamin Franklin. As a successful businessman, social entrepreneur, scientist, and politician, Franklin understood the importance of hard work, honesty, frugality, and of opposing corruption. His writings in the Almanac and in his autobiography show he was a prototypical self-made man.

The second champion of honesty was a Scottish intellectual, Adam Smith, who wrote two introductions to free-market theory. The first, *A Theory of Moral Sentiments*, outlines the importance of honesty and conscience in living the good life. His classic work arguing for free enterprise, *The Wealth of Nations,* was published in 1776, the same year as our Declaration of Independence. Note that moral philosophy came first and free markets second in Smith's writing.

Smith and his fellow writers of the Scottish Enlightenment strongly influenced the Founding Fathers. In fact, one of the most famous phrases from the Declaration of Independence—Jefferson's reference to "the pursuit of happiness"—was borrowed from the Scottish Enlightenment. In that context it meant "virtue and wisdom," not "hedonism and acquisition" as it's often interpreted today.

Abraham Lincoln's life was marked by this same sense of simple honesty, which obliged him once to walk miles to return a few cents to an overpaying customer. Furthermore, as a young man he voluntarily took on the massive debt that his unscrupulous business partner left behind when the partner skipped town. It took Lincoln years to pay it off, but he earned a growing reputation as "Honest Abe," a name that resonated with a population that valued honesty, self-sufficiency, and clean government.

Americans traditionally have believed corruption favors the privileged few at the expense of the many. The rule of law, in contrast, favors the average person because it means everyone—rich and poor alike—has the same opportunity.

Thus, the Wright brothers in their bicycle store in Dayton, Ohio, could believe they had as good a chance to invent the airplane as the top researchers at the Smithsonian Institution in Washington, D.C.

Henry Ford, working for Detroit Edison Electric Company and building his first car in his garage at night, could believe he had as good a chance to invent the mass-produced automobile as the most powerful person in the country.

But today, an un-American tolerance for corruption has spread throughout government. When Henry Paulson, a Secretary of the Treasury who had been Chairman of Goldman Sachs, pushed through a bailout that placed $13 billion of taxpayer money in the hands of Goldman Sachs, Americans knew something was wrong.

When a mortgage company gave Senator Chris Dodd a sweetheart deal for a home mortgage while the committee he was chairing had oversight of that company, Americans knew something was wrong.

When fellow congressmen tried to protect William Jefferson after police found $90,000 in cash hidden in his freezer, Americans knew something was wrong.[8]

The scale of corruption at every level of American government—from local city and county officials, to state officials such as former Illinois governor Rod Blagojevich, to members of Congress—now rivals that found in some of the worst governments around the world.

There are three forms of this corruption. First, there is the "gaming the system" mentality outlined above. It's exemplified, for example, by Americans willing to lie to get workmen's comp or disability pay, or to take money while doing no work.

Second, there is the natural corruption of big government. As Jefferson and other Founders argued, big government is *inherently* corrupt. Markets are ultimately fair because they empower individual consumers to make their own choices. Bureaucracies, in contrast, are fundamentally unfair because they empower a few insiders who inevitably drift toward cronyism and corruption. The only solution for big-government corruption is smaller government—any other solution is self-deception. As Lord Acton warned, "Power tends to corrupt, and absolute power corrupts absolutely."

Third, there is the corruption of the secular-socialist machine, which knows if it competed fairly in the political system it would be crushed by the vast majority of Americans who oppose its values. Thus, out of necessity, left-wing politicians routinely encourage vote theft, lie about their policies, and defame their opponents.

The secular-socialist machine relies on corruption for its very existence. It *has* to coerce money from union members who oppose its political policies; it *has* to rig the laws to enrich its trial lawyer allies; it *has* to cut special deals with big, rich corporations. Otherwise, the secular socialists would have no money. And that's why they fight tooth and nail against attempts to clean up corruption.

An America marked by limited government, honest politicians, and a small bureaucracy, and which focuses on fairness and the rule of law for every small business, every entrepreneur, every worker, and every retiree, is inherently a conservative, decentralized, individualistic America. It is the antithesis of a secular-socialist America dominated by political machines of big government, huge bureaucracies, and powerful politicians.

5. Low Taxes with Limited Government Versus High Taxes with Big Government

Americans have historically favored higher take home pay and lower taxes—we believe we could do a better job spending the money we earn than bureaucrats could. And unlike proponents of European-style socialist welfare states, we're willing to forego many government services in favor of lower taxes.

Paul Johnson caught the American tradition perfectly when he wrote in his classic book, *A History of the American People*, that in 1770 Americans were one of the lowest taxed people in history—and they resented every penny of it.

Americans historically came to this continent to escape from intrusive, expensive, overbearing European governments. They created an American model (stated quite explicitly by Thomas Jefferson and Andrew Jackson) comprising small government, low taxes, and enormous incentives for hard work. They believed highly-motivated Americans would invent new products, establish new companies, steadily raise the standard of living, give to charity, and do it all better than any government-dominated, high-tax system could.

For two hundred years that model has made America the envy of the world in income, productivity, innovation, and the overall standard of living. But a different approach is now undermining and crowding out that model.

Since 1932 we have gradually built a new system of too much government with too many bureaucrats taking too much of our money to decide too many things for us and impose too many things upon us. And the growth of government has empowered enormous interest groups of bureaucrats and their clients who fight ferociously to sustain a high-tax, big-bureaucracy system. Developing specific proposals to replace this system with our traditional low-tax, small-government model will be one of the greatest intellectual and entrepreneurial challenges of the next decade.

We have already made some progress, however, such as the gradual replacement of bureaucratic state schools by charter schools. A Pell grant system for K through 12 would be an even bolder model. Another positive trend is the replacement of defined benefit retirement plans with retirement systems based on defined contributions and 401k plans. The spread of Health Savings Accounts that increase transparency and empower individuals to make informed choices is another good trend.

The Left, unsurprisingly, have opposed every one of these reforms toward more personal freedom, more personal control, more personal empowerment, and more personal responsibility.

6. Private Property Versus Government Controls

Early Americans passionately believed in private property rights. In fact, Jefferson originally wrote property rights into the Declaration of Independence where the right to "the pursuit of happiness" now appears.

For early Americans, freedom was inextricably linked to property rights. If the government could take your property, confiscate your wealth, define what you could do with your own land, money, or goods, and even quarter troops in your home, then clearly you were not free but a mere subject of the state.

Thus, the Founding Fathers counted private property among the unalienable rights endowed by our Creator. They wrote the Constitution in part to protect private property rights (including the value of money and the sanctity of debt) from the mob (meaning popular demagoguery) and the mob's government.

Rejecting the sanctity of private property, the secular-socialist model has no problem with a city council or Washington bureaucrat taking your property and giving it to someone else. It has presided over a steady decline in private property rights over the last generation, highlighted by the tragic *Kelo vs. City of New London* case, in which the Supreme Court unconscionably ruled that private property can be confiscated from individuals and given to private developers if, in the judgment of local, state, or federal bureaucrats, doing so would aid economic growth and raise tax revenues.

Reasserting private property rights will be deeply resisted by every local and federal bureaucrat and every judge who likes having the power to use your property to enrich someone else. And it will be opposed by every environmental group eager to tell you what you can and cannot do with your own property.

7. Localism Versus Washington Control

There has been an enormous transfer of power from local and state governments to the Washington bureaucracies. Historically, Americans largely governed themselves. Local people mostly governed their affairs in their own communities, while states enjoyed immense freedom from the federal government. Likewise, local school boards had real power, and city councils and county commissions used their own community resources to solve problems. Washington was a distant place that had relatively little day-to-day impact on the average citizen. And that is the way our government was devised, with the Tenth Amendment decreeing that all power not specifically assigned to the federal government should reside in the states.

This intense localism led to an extraordinarily dense system of local elections that we still have today, even if the elected representatives have lost much of their power to the federal bureaucracy. There are more than 513,000 elected local, state, and federal officials in the United States, only 537 of whom are federal, or about one-tenth of one percent. In other words, 99.9 percent of all elected officials are at the local and state level.

With one in 600 Americans holding elected office at any one time, and when you consider these offices have routine turnover, it's likely that one out of every hundred Americans holds an elected office during their lifetime. This creates a common understanding of the give and take of public life, of collective decision making and of the responsibility of citizenship.

While local citizens can hold their local elected officials accountable at the next election, U.S. senators may represent so many million people that they don't even have the resources to respond to all their constituents' letters and phone calls, much less know them all personally. This situation creates an outsized influence for powerful interest groups and insiders, and a debilitating remoteness for average citizens.

A decentralized system of local power empowers local people who are most familiar with the complexities of their own communities. Today's big-government system, however, assumes bureaucrats in Washington who have never been to your town so profoundly understand the principles of good government that they should make decisions your mayor, city council, county commission, or school board cannot be trusted to make.

I often tell audiences to imagine their local mayor has a cousin in the Washington bureaucracy. According to the secular-socialist model, the cousin in Washington knows better than the mayor what's right for the local community. Now imagine that the mayor swaps jobs with his cousin. As the mayor drives toward Washington, his IQ goes up. Meanwhile the IQ of his cousin, as he drives home from Washington, drops with every passing mile. By the time the former mayor reaches Washington and takes on his new bureaucratic job, he has grown smart enough to issue orders to his cousin, the new mayor, who has grown dumb enough that he needs instructions from Washington to solve the problems of his local community.

This story shows how the principles of the current Washington-centric system are simply, irredeemably wrong.

Craig Shirley, the great biographer of Ronald Reagan, draws another analogy: megabanks versus microlending in poor neighborhoods. Shirley notes that microlending efficiently gets small amounts of money to local entrepreneurs in poor countries. Microlending requires a very inexpensive process of understanding and analyzing the borrower, analyzing the project, making and implementing a decision to lend, and sometimes advising the recipients.

Megabanks, which got into so much trouble during the Wall Street meltdown, could never successfully microlend. They're too big and too bureaucratic to understand and analyze millions of small entrepreneurs, and they could never afford the cost of analyzing so many loan applications and processing checks.

Now consider this: if big banks are too isolated and too bureaucratic to operate successfully in small, local settings, why would we think big, centralized government bureaucracies could do better?

Shifting from centralized bureaucracy to localism is a crucial reform, though the secular-socialist machine will bitterly oppose it. The Left built these big bureaucracies precisely because they knew they could never win enough local elections to change the country. When localities are empowered, they prove time and again that conservative solutions work and left-wing solutions fail.

Localism—returning power from Washington to state and local governments—will be one of the most important movements of the next decade. I frequently remind governors and state legislators they need to move power from their state capitol back to local communities just as energetically as they fight for power to return from Washington back to them.

8. American Energy Versus Environmental Extremism

There is no American energy shortage. And there is no reason America (and the world) should be vulnerable to energy blackmail by dictators from Venezuela to Saudi Arabia to Iran. What we have is a long-standing government policy to restrict our own energy production and to artificially inflate energy costs.

Most Americans are shocked to find out just how extensive our energy resources really are.

- We have a 500-year supply of coal, which will remain the lowest cost source of electricity in our lifetime barring a fantastic breakthrough in some other production method.
- Our offshore oil reserves are big, though we don't know exactly how big because the Left have prevented any geologic surveys from being conducted since 1984.
- On land, it now seems we have more oil than we thought, with indications, for example, that the Bakken formation in North Dakota is three times as large as previously estimated.
- We have three times more oil than Saudi Arabia if you count our shale oil deposits, and we have an astounding

1,100-year supply of natural gas that can now be tapped thanks to new technology.
- We have the technology to produce virtually unlimited amounts of carbon-free electricity through nuclear power.

Traditional America used all available energy to build the world's richest economy. Science and technology led the process, constantly creating new, more efficient ways to extract resources and produce energy.

Today, a traditional American approach would be to strive for energy independence through an "all of the above" policy that fully exploits our coal, oil, natural gas, and nuclear resources, while also cultivating the next generation of energy technology: biofuels, wind, hydrogen, and solar power, as well as developing new conservation methods.

Secular socialists have a different view. Through the misguided attempts of some to create an environmental utopia, and the cynical attempts of others to use our concern for the environment as a weapon against capitalism, they have restricted and regulated energy development so extensively that they have forced America, which should be an energy powerhouse, to become dependent on foreign oil, much of it from unstable or tyrannical regimes. Relentlessly demonizing energy companies, they tie up every new oil, natural gas, coal, and nuclear project in years of frivolous litigation.

The Left only allow development of alternative renewable energy like wind and solar that, while useful, will take generations to displace fossil fuels as our primary energy source. Until then, they are content for America to suffer shrinking energy supplies, rising prices, foreign dependence, and the loss of energy jobs.

Imagine if, through the traditional American approach, we achieved energy independence by unleashing the full potential of our own energy supply. Imagine the economic effect of keeping

$535 billion at home every year instead of sending it to foreign dictators for oil; that's over $5 trillion a decade—more than a third of the entire national debt. Imagine if the next building boom were in St. Louis instead of Dubai, and if a new wave of jobs washed over America instead of foreign countries.

What we see from the secular socialists today is not an energy strategy. Bowing to a Saudi king is not an energy strategy. Accepting gifts from Venezuelan dictator Hugo Chavez is not an energy strategy.

The challenge is not natural resources—America has plenty of those. The challenge is bad government imposing bad laws, bad regulations, and bad litigation.

9. Conflict Resolution Versus Litigation

To compete successfully with China and India, we must have litigation reform.

To have an effective government, we must have litigation reform.

To encourage young people to pursue medical careers, we must have litigation reform.

If we want Americans to emphasize cooperation and problem solving over acrimonious, costly conflicts, we must have litigation reform.

Most Americans agree there are too many lawyers filing too many lawsuits, especially in medicine. According to a Rasmussen poll from December 2009, 57 percent of Americans favor limiting the amount of money a jury can award a plaintiff in a medical malpractice lawsuit, while only 29 percent disagree.[9]

As Wayne Oliver, leader of the Health Justice Project at the Center for Health Transformation, has noted, an estimated $151–210 billion is wasted annually in defensive medicine, as doctors follow unnecessary procedures and conduct needless tests and services solely to avoid malpractice lawsuits.

In preparing for health reform in 2009, the Congressional Budget Office (CBO) estimated that litigation reform in medical malpractice would save the federal government $53 billion over ten years. Yet, even though Obama, Pelosi, and Reid needed money to pay for their government health program; even though doctors made malpractice reform their number one reform goal; and even though a significant majority of the American people supported litigation reform, it was impossible for the Democrats to support it.

For the Left, this isn't about ideology; it's about raw power. The simple fact is that trial lawyers are one of the primary components of the secular-socialist machine and major financiers of the Democratic Party. The lawyers understand their income directly depends on their ability to sue. And the Democrats will never cross such important supporters on such a crucial issue.

For most doctors and businesses, litigation reform is important but it's not dire. But for the trial lawyers—the reactionary defenders of the old order—this is a life-or-death issue. Their status, their incomes, their ambitions to someday own a large private plane and a baseball or football team, or to buy a Senate seat or a governorship—all these dreams could be destroyed if litigation reform led to fewer lawsuits and smaller awards.

Anyone who doubts how tough this fight will be should talk with a colleague of mine at the Center for Health Transformation, Dr. John Gill, who helped lead the Texas malpractice reform effort. After winning a seven-year fight to get the Texas legislature to approve malpractice reform, he and his colleagues came to a dramatic conclusion: the only way to ensure trial lawyers didn't undermine the law was to get it written into the Texas state constitution. And that's just what they did; the people of Texas approved tort reform in a public referendum.

10. Religious Belief Versus Secular Oppression

Secularism is the heart of the secular-socialist movement. I'm not talking about secularism simply as a lack of religious conviction. I mean secularism as an explicitly anti-religious outlook expressed in policies designed to ban all religious expression from the public square.

Seeking to create a man-centered world, leftist elites invoke secularism as a pleasant-sounding term to disguise their egocentric worldview. In their minds, there are no God-given rules for us to follow. There are no Ten Commandments, or really any commandments of any kind.

Secular elites, particularly in academia, the media, and the courts, are engaged in a steady assault on religious belief. They believe religious expression should be private, marginal, and irrelevant. It's okay to be religious as long as the religion has no meaning. It's fine to be vaguely spiritual as long as you don't try to translate it into some kind of historic religion, especially Christianity.

The Left originally appealed for tolerance for minority views. Now they demand obedience to these minority views.

The secularizing pattern, beginning with the 1963 Supreme Court decision outlawing school prayer, has built such momentum that two Connecticut Democratic legislators introduced a bill that would have effectively driven the Catholic Church out of their state.

Furthermore, in the 2010 U.S. Senate special election in Massachusetts (a colony founded by Puritans searching for religious liberty), Democratic nominee and state attorney general Martha Coakley suggested Catholics shouldn't serve in emergency rooms because they might hold unacceptable pro-life views. In a similar attempt at exclusion, the Left are trying to restrict the activities of faith-based social service agencies that believe marriage is between a man and a woman.

Religious expression is also under attack in our courts: a plaintiff in Southern California has filed a lawsuit seeking to knock down a cross erected in 1934 in the middle of the Mojave Desert. Other lawsuits are trying to stop us from uttering the phrase "one nation under God" as part of the Pledge of Allegiance.

Traditionally, America has been a religious society based on the fundamental belief that there is something out there larger than ourselves. Our subordination to God sets boundaries for what we can or should do to ourselves and others. It also creates expectations for us to live up to; a belief in God turns a wasted life into a betrayal of God's gifts.

If we are endowed by our Creator with the right to pursue happiness, we also have a responsibility to use God's gifts to pursue happiness (remembering that happiness in this context means wisdom and virtue).

There is a profound reason Alcoholics Anonymous' 12-step program stresses the importance of God. Simply read the twelve steps and imagine what little would be left if God were removed from this process of saving and rebuilding lives.

THE TWELVE STEPS OF ALCOHOLICS ANONYMOUS[10]

1. We admitted we were powerless over alcohol—that our lives had become unmanageable.

2. Came to believe that a Power greater than ourselves could restore us to sanity.

3. Made a decision to turn our will and our lives over to the care of God *as we understood Him.*

4. Made a searching and fearless moral inventory of ourselves.

5. Admitted to God, to ourselves, and to another human being the exact nature of our wrongs.

6. Were entirely ready to have God remove all these defects of character.

7. Humbly asked Him to remove our shortcomings.

8. Made a list of all persons we had harmed, and became willing to make amends to them all.
9. Made direct amends to such people wherever possible, except when to do so would injure them or others.
10. Continued to take personal inventory and when we were wrong promptly admitted it.
11. Sought through prayer and meditation to improve our conscious contact with God, *as we understood Him*, praying only for knowledge of His will for us and the power to carry that out.
12. Having had a spiritual awakening as the result of these Steps, we tried to carry this message to alcoholics, and to practice these principles in all our affairs.

A federal official once proposed that a federal anti-addiction program be developed based on Alcoholics Anonymous—but "without all the God stuff." That shows the depth of anti-religious antipathy in elite circles: AA may be the world's most successful addiction recovery program, but the government apparently could improve it by banishing God.

Chuck Colson, with his extraordinarily effective prison ministry, faces similar opposition from secular elites. The prison ministry system undoubtedly works; it has enabled thousands of people to leave prison as profoundly changed men and women, able to lead decent, productive lives. But many elites would rather condemn prisoners to hopeless lives of secular despair than risk saving them through religious faith. Sadly, simply due to this kind of prejudice, there is significant resistance to prison ministry activities.

Chasing religion from the public square inevitably lowers public morality. That's because a belief in God limits our tendencies toward hedonism, exploiting others, and abusing power. If you are subordinate to God then by definition you are subordinate to rules that transcend your own ego and your own personal appetites.

The Founding Fathers overwhelmingly agreed that religion was crucial in sustaining the culture of responsibility needed to keep the country free.* The Northwest Ordinance of 1787 says, "Religion, morality, and knowledge, being necessary to good government and the happiness of mankind, schools and the means of education shall forever be encouraged."

Note the order: first comes religion. Then comes morality. Knowledge is the last goal.

The move toward secularism has harmed American society. Look at the problems affecting today's teenagers, compared to the same data for 1963, the year the Supreme Court banned school prayer.

- Drug addiction is up.
- Teenage pregnancy is up.
- Drinking is up.
- Violence is up.
- Rape in schools is up.
- Assaults on teachers are up.
- The display of disrespectful attitudes is up.

Did the elimination of school prayer help our schools? No. To the contrary, the decline of morality in school and in society overall has given rise to a destructive pattern that the late Senator Pat Moynihan captured perfectly in his article, "Defining Deviancy Down."

The secular-socialist effort to drive God and morality to one hour a week in Church, Synagogue, Mosque, or Temple, but to preserve

---

* See our book *Rediscovering God in America* and the two movies of that name for more details on this theme.

the other 167 hours a week for secularism, has deeply weakened our capacity to distinguish right from wrong and to sacrifice short-term gratification for a commitment to permanent moral principles.

Perhaps more than any other area, the Left will fight any rise in religious expression. Secularism is their guiding philosophy, which they enforce with ruthless intolerance. If they find a cross in the middle of the Mojave Desert unacceptable, imagine how they will fight the restoration of God to the public square.

Through any means necessary, from violent street protests to the insidious expansion of bureaucratic power, the Left have spent the last four decades tightening their grasp over America and its most important institutions—the federal bureaucracy, academia, Hollywood, Big Labor, and even big business. From that dominating position, they have propagated a completely foreign set of secular-socialist values. Rejecting American traditions of hard work, self-sufficiency, and honesty, they encourage Americans to learn how to game the system—sucking the maximum resources out of our country while contributing the minimum.

Once people accept this outlook, they quickly realize the bigger government gets, the more opportunity there is to game it. A small government with relatively few resources and strict oversight is difficult to cheat. In a leviathan like the Left want to create, however, with more bureaucrats controlling more money, it's much easier to buy favors and abuse programs. This is a lesson we should learn from Europe, where the massive, largely unaccountable EU bureaucracy is mired in waste, fraud, and inefficiency.

The struggle between America's historic value system and that of secular socialism will be intense. The Left did not fight this long just to give up when they're so close to victory: creating a socialist system where a voting majority, dependent on the state's largess, will permanently vote for the party of big government. And so Americans who prefer traditional America to the socialist vision are left with one option: to stand up and fight.

In the following chapters, I'll explain the goals and methods of the secular-socialist machine in more detail, and propose policies and strategies to help save America from its manipulations.

CHAPTER TWO

Why "Secular-Socialist Machine" Is the Only Way to Describe the Left

While it may sound alarmist, the best way to describe the opponents of American liberty is this: they are a secular-socialist machine.

Many people, especially on the Left, will reject this term. So let me explain why it's the only honest description of the way Barack Obama, Nancy Pelosi, Harry Reid, and the many left-wing power figures and organizations operate.

The "Left" is a term stemming from the seating of political parties in the National Assembly during the French Revolution. The radicals were seated on the left and the conservatives on the right. Today, the Left comprise a range of opinion favoring various levels of state control over society and over the economy. So the Obama-Pelosi-Reid agenda is indeed leftist, but it is also a unique collection of policies and attitudes that deserves a more specific description.

"Liberalism" also fails to capture the values and beliefs that animate this agenda. Originally describing the nineteenth-century movement for free markets and limited government, liberalism later came to signify President Roosevelt's New Deal. FDR's liberalism, however, was so much more accepting of God (see his national radio prayer on D-Day, for example), so much more pro-work, and so much more concerned with defending America (FDR tried German saboteurs by military tribunal and executed them within six weeks of their capture), that the modern Left can honestly be characterized as a radical break from FDR's worldview.

Today, it's not liberalism but secular socialism that drives the Left's policies, which are enacted through a political machine. Because defining the Left in these terms will be controversial, we should briefly examine the interlocking relationship of secularism, socialism, and machine politics.

SECULARISM:
ONE COUNTRY WITHOUT GOD

Describing the Left as "secular" will be controversial for two reasons. First, when you discuss a left-wing politician's secular policies, many on the Left, abetted by the mainstream media, will indignantly insist you are accusing them of being atheists or apostates. Don't take the bait. We cannot know what is in the hearts of other men and women, and any speculation is an exercise in hubris and futility.

Instead, our central argument lies in the second reason for controversy. It is one rooted in historic fact and American history, which makes it a winning argument for us. But it requires a calm, steady, and repeated explanation of the facts to counter the bed of lies that has obscured our understanding of the "separation of church and state" and "religious freedom."

Among some Americans, particularly the academic elite, it has become unchallenged conventional wisdom that the First Amendment's establishment clause—"Congress shall make no law respecting an establishment of religion"—means the U.S. government must purge all religion from public life. To understand just how wrong this interpretation is, we need to discuss what the term "secular" actually means.

The Latin root of "secular" is "saeculum," which meant "an age," or roughly, a human lifespan. It is closely related to the word "century," or 100 years. The connection from this original meaning to the term's modern understanding as "non-religious" is its emphasis on the "current" and "the now" rather than being concerned with an afterlife.

A purely secular outlook does not acknowledge God. It does not consider the implications of one's actions beyond the impact they make within one's own life. It does not recognize any higher moral order beyond that which human beings have rationally developed.

The argument that the Constitution's establishment clause requires a purely secular government is fatally flawed because America's historic conception of rights is clearly dependent upon a higher moral order than the laws of man.

For example, the Declaration of Independence, America's founding political document, boldly proclaims, "We hold these truths to be self-evident, that all men are created equal, that they are endowed by their creator with certain unalienable rights, that among these are life, liberty, and the pursuit of happiness."

This extraordinary sentence makes some key assumptions: that God is sovereign over the affairs of the universe; that God created man; and that man must obey an order of justice God Himself has instituted.

How then can a purely secular worldview account for the original American understanding of our rights and freedoms?

It cannot.

The secular-socialist Left bitterly oppose anyone who speaks the truth about the central role of "our Creator" in the Founders' formulation of our rights and freedoms. When confronted with the facts, they often resort to ad hominem attacks, arguing that if you oppose militant secularism in the public square, then you must be endorsing a theocracy. This is a ludicrous, insulting charge, especially when so many people throughout the world today are enslaved by religious dictatorships.

When forging the Constitution, the Founding Fathers did not see the need to choose between the fraternal twin oppressions of a militantly secular government or a state-sponsored and imposed religion. Their new, American model was a country with no official national religion where everyone could worship as they pleased. But they were also careful not to shut out religion from public life. The Founders saw religion as vital to the survival of republican government because they believed the maintenance of liberty requires virtue.

That's why, in addition to the establishment clause ("Congress shall make no law respecting the establishment of religion...."), the First Amendment also contains the free exercise clause ("...or prevent the free exercise thereof").

That's why George Washington declared, "Of all the dispositions and habits which lead to political prosperity, religion and morality are indispensible supports."

That's why John Adams said, "We have no government armed with power capable of contending with human passions unbridled by morality and religion. Avarice, ambition, revenge, or gallantry, would break the strongest cords of our Constitution as a whale goes through a net."

And that's why Thomas Jefferson, probably the least religious of the Founding Fathers, stated, "Reading, reflection, and time have convinced me that the interests of society require the observation of those moral precepts...in which all religions agree."

It's worth focusing on Jefferson, because he is the Founding Father most cited by militant secularists. Jefferson, of course, wrote the phrase "separation of church and state," which appeared in an 1802 letter to the Danbury Baptists. For fifty years, a deeply anti-religious court system has used this phrase to justify banning school prayer, tearing down crosses on public land, and even threatening the Boy Scouts, whose program includes a multi-denominational religious component.

The importance of this five-word phrase from one of Jefferson's private letters has been exaggerated and its meaning completely distorted. In fact, if you look at Jefferson's public actions as vice president and later as president of the United States, it's clear he did not intend the establishment clause to ban religion from the public square.

The most obvious example is that two days after he penned the letter to the Danbury Baptists, Jefferson attended church in the U.S. Capitol building. These services were acceptable to Jefferson (and James Madison, who also attended) because they were voluntary and non-discriminatory; many different preachers, and eventually priests, from various denominations led services. Jefferson also allowed other executive branch buildings to be used in a similar manner.

It's hard to square Jefferson's support for church services in the U.S. Capitol building with the secular insistence that all matters of faith be banned from public life.

Instead, it's clear that Jefferson, like the rest of the Founders, wanted a government that allowed for public religious expression, but did not endorse any particular denomination. Doing so would preserve the rights of Americans of all faiths (and of no faith), while recognizing the importance of religion and morality to the Republic's survival.

The plain facts of our nation's history have not stopped anti-religious bigots in the judiciary, academia, and in elected office from insisting that religious belief is inherently divisive and that the discussion of public affairs can only occur in secular terms. Consider the oppressive effect of this secular worldview in our public schools:

- School officials prevented a New Jersey student from reading his favorite story to the class because it came from the Bible.
- A Pennsylvania school suspended a teacher's assistant because she wore a necklace with a cross.[1]
- A Colorado high school valedictorian was refused a diploma unless she apologized for mentioning Jesus in her commencement speech.[2]

Such absurdities, of course, hardly display the "tolerance" that the Left claim to value above all else. And recent court cases are even more disturbing:

- A federal court in California found that the leasing of parcels of parkland to the Boy Scouts was unconstitutional. While the case was stayed pending a related decision, the fact that the plaintiffs were found to have standing to bring the suit, in the words of six dissenting judges on the Ninth Circuit, "creates a new legal landscape in which almost anyone who is offended by anything has standing to air his or her displeasure in court."[3]
- The American Civil Liberties Union (ACLU) is arguing on behalf of a parks service employee to remove the 76-year-old World War I Memorial Cross in the Mojave National Preserve.[4] The cross has been covered with a plywood box until the Supreme Court decides the case. An organization I founded called Renewing American Leadership, headed by Rick Tyler, has filed an amicus

brief along with Citizens United in support of maintaining the cross. To be clear, the Mojave cross is in the
middle of the desert, eight and a half miles away from
any major roadway. Imagine for a second the mindset
of a militant secularist who is so terrified and offended
by a cross in the middle of a desert.

- In DeFuniak Springs, Florida, a judge ordered that a
copy of the Ten Commandments in the courthouse be
covered during a murder trial because he did not want
the jurors to see the commandment "Do not kill."[5]

- In June 2002, the Ninth Circuit Court of Appeals found
the words "under God" in the pledge of allegiance to be
unconstitutional. The Supreme Court dismissed the
case in 2004 upon procedural grounds rather than on its
merits. In early 2010 the issue was brought up again in
the Ninth Circuit, and this time the court ruled in favor
of keeping "under God." Michael Newdow, the atheist
behind this string of lawsuits, has vowed to appeal the
ruling.[6]

The wall of separation these secularists seek to enforce is really one
between the historic America and the radically different America
they want to create—an America without God, traditional values,
or knowledge of its own history.

SOCIALISM:
SPREADING THE FAILURE AROUND

Describing the Left as socialist will also be controversial because
the Left hate accurate language about their goals. But any fair assessment of the Obama-Pelosi-Reid economic policies shows they are
indisputably socialist.

Broadly defined, socialist policies favor increased central planning of the economy by politicians and bureaucrats instead of allowing entrepreneurs, businesses, and customers to make decisions in the free market. Socialists also favor government attempts to collectivize the means of production and to divvy up the national wealth. Socialists favor these methods because they insist on equality of *results*, rather than the traditional American belief in equality *under the law*. Therefore, they champion a strong central government to impose equality of outcomes, as Joe the Plumber found out during the 2008 campaign when he was told by then-candidate Obama that taxes needed to be raised in order to "spread the wealth around."

It's hard to imagine, but as late as the 1970s, before the Reagan revolution and the collapse of the Soviet Union, socialism had not yet been thoroughly discredited in the United States. Meanwhile, conservatism, while growing in force, was not yet the dominant ideology in America or even in the Republican Party. American politics was stuck in a cycle arguing between slower and faster routes toward big government. Favoring the fast route, many Democratic Party leaders sought to impose a form of socialism on America.

With that in mind, it's important to recognize that most of today's powerful Democratic congressional committee chairmen were first elected in the 1970s. In other words, today's Democratic leaders joined Congress at a time when socialist, big-government solutions were in the mainstream in their party.

Coupled with the current Speaker of the House, who is a legitimate representative of the left-wing values of her home district in San Francisco, is it any wonder the new Democratic majorities have aggressively pursued big-government, socialist policies?

Look at the signature bills considered by the House and Senate under President Obama, the committee chairmen responsible for their development, and when these chairmen were elected to Congress.

• **The Employee Free Choice Act** (*Education and Labor Committee: Chairman George Miller, 1974*) Last year, the House passed the EFCA card check legislation that would strip American workers of the right to a secret ballot when deciding whether to join a union. It would also institute "binding arbitration" that takes power away from U.S. employers and employees and gives it to new arbitration bureaucracies. The political rationale for this bill is that unions—long-time power centers of the global socialist movement and a powerful Democratic constituency—have been shrinking in size and influence over the past fifty years (with the notable exception of public employee unions). This bill is a clear attempt to reinvigorate them with new powers, even if workers don't agree.

• **Cap and Trade** (*Energy and Commerce Committee: Chairman Henry Waxman, 1974; Energy Independence and Global Warming Committee: Chairman Edward Markey, 1976*) The House passed a huge energy tax increase on the American people in the guise of a cap-and-trade scheme. The bill would concentrate the authority to choose the recipients of carbon permits—and by extension, the power to determine which U.S. firms will be allowed to produce, innovate, and grow—into a centralized bureaucracy. This is clearly a step toward central economic planning.

It's also worth noting that the Senate's failure to pass this bill has provoked threats from the Obama administration to have the Environmental Protection Agency regulate carbon as a pollutant, a move that would centralize economic power in bureaucracies even more than cap and trade would have done. Additionally, the Copenhagen Conference on global warming produced a commitment from participants, including the United States, to initiate a vast transfer of wealth from developed nations to poor ones. It's socialism on a global scale.

• **Stimulus Bill** (*Appropriations Committee: Chairman Dave Obey, 1969*) Congress circumvented the normal appropriations process and hastily passed this convoluted legislation that mandated which agencies, firms, and individuals would (and, implicitly, would not) receive taxpayer dollars. Five-hundred thirty-five individuals exercised complete control over $787 billion in taxpayer funds. Another step toward centralized economic planning, the stimulus has only sent a fraction of the money to "shovel ready" infrastructure and other jobs projects. Far more has gone into state and federal bureaucracies, perhaps irreversibly growing the size and power of government at the federal, state, and local level.

• **Healthcare Overhaul** (*Energy and Commerce Committee: Chairman Henry Waxman, 1974; Ways and Means Committee: Chairman Charles Rangel, 1970; Education and Labor Committee: Chairman George Miller, 1974; Senate Finance Committee: Chairman Max Baucus, 1978*) The healthcare bill signed into law in March 2010 will turn healthcare into a de-facto nationalized utility by forcing all Americans to buy health insurance and micromanaging insurance companies from the Department of Health and Human Services. Fortunately, many of the most destructive elements of this bill do not take effect until 2014, so there is still time to repeal it and start over with market-based, patient-oriented health reform.

With this 1970s-era cohort in charge, it's unsurprising the major legislation passed by this Congress has increased centralized economic
planning. Another example is the government takeover of General
Motors, engineered by a "car czar" who is not subject to congressional approval.

And then there's the Left's redistribution of taxpayer money for
massive housing subsidies through Fannie Mae and Freddie Mac. "I
want to roll the dice a little bit more in this situation towards subsi-
dized housing," said Democratic congressman Barney Frank in
2003. Of course, this gamble helped spark the housing crash, but
that hasn't stopped the Left. In fact, in December 2009, the Obama
administration lifted the $400 billion cap on Treasury funding to
Fannie and Freddie, a big step toward nationalizing the home loan
market.

For these archaic, left-wing Democrats, their return to power with
the Democratic House and Senate majorities of 2007, along with the
2008 election of a new, left-wing president, is their last chance to
achieve their dream of instituting socialism in America.

The policies of the Left are clearly socialist. They would have
government define and dominate every aspect of energy production in America. They would have government define and
dominate healthcare—one-sixth of the U.S. economy. (The first
healthcare overhaul bill to pass the House gave the Secretary of
Health and Human Services the power to unilaterally reduce benefits, increase premiums, and establish waiting lines for high risk
patients.) They have taken over AIG, America's largest insurer.
They took over General Motors and Chrysler. They dominate
banking. They have a "pay czar" in the White House to dictate
salaries at ostensibly private companies. These actions are consistent with a socialist vision of America where the government
defines and dominates the private sector.

WHY THE SECULAR-SOCIALIST
LEFT HAS TO LIE

If you are a political candidate with unpopular secular-socialist beliefs, you simply cannot be candid about what you want to accomplish. Therefore, secular socialists learn very early they have to misinform and mislead in order to get elected.

Additionally, if you're a secular socialist, you have to maintain your power in ways the public inherently dislikes: paying off supporters by putting earmarks in appropriations bills; holding secret conferences to write bills; making absurd deals to pick up enough votes to pass legislation; and appointing really bizarre people to top government jobs. You learn to hide what you are doing, deny what you are doing, and if caught, try to deceive the people about what you've done.

Finally, if you're part of a movement that believes it knows better than the American people what's best for them, you inherently scorn the values and judgment of the people you intend to change. Since the vast majority of Americans have the "wrong" values and the "wrong" attitude, they have to be misled into voting for the enlightened elite who will remake them into the right attitudes and the right values.

Thus, in order to achieve its historic mission of transforming America, the secular-socialist movement must resort to dishonesty in communicating with the American people.

ALINSKY'S RULES FOR DISHONESTY

Perhaps nobody has been more clear about the Left's need for dishonesty than Saul Alinsky.

One of the twentieth century's most influential radicals, Alinksy is considered the godfather of community organizing. His two most famous works, *Reveille for Radicals* and *Rules for Radicals*, were published in the late sixties and early seventies. In these works, Alinsky draws a distinction between meek, garden-variety liberals and brave, revolutionary radicals. "While liberals are most adept at breaking their own necks with their tongues," Alinsky writes, "radicals are most adept at breaking the necks of conservatives."

Many of his "rules" are guidelines for engaging in immoral, dangerous, political dishonesty. Echoing the maxims of Vladimir Lenin, the architect of Soviet Communism, Alinsky justifies almost any immoral act, especially outright dishonesty and hypocrisy, if it's done while pursuing revolution. Alinksy writes, "[The organizer] does not have a fixed truth—truth to him is relative and changing; everything to him is relative and changing. He is a political relativist."

David Horowitz, in his small book *Barack Obama's Rules for Revolution: The Alinsky Model,* cogently explains the significance of Alinsky's teachings to the modern Left.[7] In particular, he cites what he calls the "most important" chapter in *Rules for Radicals,* "Means and Ends," whose "rules" include the following:

- "In war the end justifies almost any means."
- "Concern with ethics increases with the number of means available and vice versa."
- "The less important the end to be desired, the more one can afford to engage in ethical evaluation of means."
- "You do what you can with what you have and clothe it with moral garments." (Later, Alinsky discusses the Communist Leon Trotsky's summation of Lenin's speeches: "They have the guns and therefore we are at peace and for reformation through the ballot. When we have the guns then it will be through the bullet.")

For Alinsky, a radical's primary goals must be acquiring power and destroying the current system. What replaces it is of secondary concern. He teaches that you amass power by organizing people based on their naked self-interest, not on any idealism or common vision for the future. In fact, he argues that clearly naming or describing such a vision—and spelling out clearly how to get there—only alienates some people and therefore divides your potential power base.

Now consider Alinksy's eleventh rule of Means and Ends:

> Goals must be phrased in general terms like "Liberty," "Equality," "Fraternity," "Of the Common Welfare," "Pursuit of Happiness," or "Bread and Peace." Whitman put it: "The goal once named cannot be countermanded." It has been previously noted that the wise man of action knows that frequently in the stream of actions of means toward ends, whole new and unexpected ends are among the major results of the action.[8]

"Change We Can Believe In" fits nicely into that list of bromides. Horowitz aptly sums up Alinsky's teachings:

> In contrast to liberals, who in Alinsky's eyes are constantly tripping over their principles, the rule for radicals is that the ends justify the means. This was true for the Jacobins, for the Communists, for the fascists and now for the post-Communist left.... The very nature of this future [they desire]—a world without poverty, without war, without racism, and without "sexism"—is so desirable, so noble, so perfect in contrast to everything that exists as to justify any and every means to achieve it.
>
> ... The German philosopher Nietzsche had a phrase for this: "Idealism kills." And of course, the great atrocities of the modern era, whether Nazi or Communist, were com-

mitted by people who believed in a future that would save mankind.[9]

If you think it's unfair to hold the current leaders of the Democratic Party responsible for the teachings of a deceased left-wing radical, consider that in his early days in Chicago, Barack Obama taught courses on Alinsky's techniques for community organizing groups. So his endorsement of these tactics of fundamental dishonesty is a matter of a public record.

President Obama's own website displayed a picture of a younger Obama teaching in a Chicago classroom. On the chalkboard behind him are written the phrases "Power Analysis" and "Relationships Built on Self Interest."

In an interview with Ryan Lizza of the *New Republic*, Obama said, "The key to creating successful organizations was making sure people's self-interest was met, and not just basing it on pie-in-the-sky idealism. So there were some basic principles that remained powerful then, and in fact I still believe in."

Saul Alinsky's son, L. David Alinksy, writing in the *Boston Globe*, marveled at how many of his father's methods were evident at the Democratic National Convention. It was clear, he wrote, that "Obama learned his lesson well."[10]

THE PERVERSION OF LANGUAGE

Another primary weapon in the secular-socialist arsenal is the deliberate misuse of language. George Orwell, one of the most insightful analysts of tyranny and politics in the first half of the twentieth century, explained the danger of corrupted language in "Politics and the English Language." In that brilliant essay, Orwell warns, "If thought corrupts language, language can also corrupt thought." He explains,

In our time, political speech and writing are largely the defense of the indefensible. Political language has to consist largely of euphemism, question-begging and sheer cloudy vagueness. Such phraseology is needed if one wants to name things without calling up mental pictures of them. Consider for instance some comfortable English professor defending Russian totalitarianism. He cannot say outright, "I believe in killing off your opponents when you can get good results by doing so." Probably, therefore, he will say something like this:

"While freely conceding that the Soviet regime exhibits certain features which the humanitarian may be inclined to deplore, we must, I think, agree that a certain curtailment of the right to political opposition is an unavoidable concomitant of transitional periods, and that the rigors which the Russian people have been called upon to undergo have been amply justified in the sphere of concrete achievement."

When there is a gap between one's real and one's declared aims, one turns as it were instinctively to long words and exhausted idioms, like a cuttlefish spurting out ink.[11]

Remember Orwell's warning the next time you listen to a secular-socialist politician, academic, or TV analyst employ euphemisms and other rhetorical tricks that allow them to avoid calling things by their proper names. Consider these examples:

- The "Employee Free Choice Act" strips the right to a secret ballot for workers voting on whether to join a union, exposing them to coercion tactics from union thugs, thus *threatening* their freedom to choose.
- The Obama administration announced it would refer to terrorist attacks as "man-made disasters" and the war on

Islamic terrorists would be called "overseas contingency operations."

- Supporters of the cap-and-trade energy tax bill, which would cast a tangled web of new bureaucracies and regulations over our economy, say their bill is "market-driven."
- Supporters of the so-called "public option" in health insurance claimed it will introduce "competition," even though more than 1,000 health insurance companies are already competing against each other in America. In reality, the public option would allow the government to gradually drive private insurers from the market altogether.
- President Obama claimed the stimulus bill had no "earmarks or the usual pork barrel spending." This assertion, however, relies on an extremely narrow definition of an "earmark" as an outlay for a specific project or company. Although they cleverly avoided this level of specificity in the stimulus, Democrats packed the bill with spending on narrowly defined programs. For instance, in the $8 billion set aside for high speed railway, there was a specific outlay for a Los Angeles–to–Las Vegas maglev. There was also $1 billion for a zero emissions energy plant in Illinois, of which there was only one in development. These are earmarks in all but name—and everyone knows it, including President Obama.

HOW SECULAR SOCIALISM BUILDS THE MACHINE

It would be hard to overstate the degree to which the modern Left appeal to the self-interest of their various interest groups rather than to any sort of unifying vision for the future. There's a reason for that:

while secular socialism is the intellectual mindset of the left-wing party bosses and politicians, it is not the worldview of the vast majority of Americans. It would be impossible to build a governing majority around such an alien ideology.

But secular socialists know the bigger and more powerful government gets, the more politicians can use its power to benefit their supporters. In other words, secular socialism doesn't win power because it's a compelling vision for the future; it's just a convenient way to pay off members of their coalition and bribe new ones into joining. And the more power secular-socialist politicians have, both in elected positions and in the bureaucracies, the better these coalition members can be fed from the public trough.

The secular-socialist machine is diverse. Trial lawyers are among the biggest donors to left-wing Democrats, who return the favor by preventing tort reform. This allows the lawyers to continue suing doctors and businessmen and women for huge sums of money that the lawyers then donate to left-wing Democrats.

Union bosses are another key machine component. They donate money to secular socialists from compulsory member dues and "encourage" their members to man phone banks and conduct get-out-the-vote operations. They expect their candidates, once in power, to change laws to give union organizers even more leverage against the businesses they are bankrupting, as well as to prevent reform of our union-dominated public bureaucracies, like education.

"Social justice" groups like the corrupt ACORN organization have received public dollars to perform voter registration drives that are really just operations to turn out voters for far-left Democrats, who gratefully steer more money toward groups like ACORN. Although ACORN's long history of fraud has finally put it out of business, the group's branches are now reorganizing to continue the same scam under new names.

And finally, big business hedges its bets by funding big-government supporters in both parties, hoping they will craft legislation that gives big business an advantage over its competitors.

There is one name for this kind of cynical cronyism and crass political manipulation: machine politics.

The way the Left govern in Sacramento, Albany, in many local governments, and especially in Washington is clearly indicative of a machine. When a $787 billion stimulus package can pass in days with no elected official having read the bill, it is evidence of a machine. When a 300-page amendment can be attached at 3:00 am to a bill passed at 4:00 that afternoon with no hearings and no amendments (the maneuver that bought enough votes to pass the Waxman-Markey energy tax), it is evidence of a machine. When 4,500 pages of healthcare bills affecting one-sixth of the economy are negotiated in secret, bypassing the normal open bill resolution process, it is evidence of a machine. When New York City mayor Bloomberg reports, as he did on *Meet the Press*, that no senators or congressmen he had talked with knew what was in the health bill they had voted for, it is clearly evidence of a machine.

Today, the Obama-Pelosi-Reid Left are indisputably secular, they are socialist, and they operate as a machine. Therefore, "secular-socialist machine" is the most accurate way—in fact, the *only* accurate way—of describing the movement that now controls our government.

WHY SECULAR SOCIALISM NEEDS A MACHINE

Once the Left's values and goals are clear, their secular-socialist agenda will be crushed in free and fair elections. To avoid this repudiation, they have to build a political machine that is too powerful to be defeated by popular anger. That is the Chicago model of "unrepresentative government."

Union funding for politicians who will eliminate the right to a secret ballot when voting to form a union is a classic example of machine politics. This effort stems from the difficulty unions have had winning secret ballot elections in recent years. One solution would be to improve the union model so it could win secret ballot elections. But union leaders instinctively adopted a coercive strategy: eliminating secret ballots and relying on public commitments, which makes it easier to apply social pressure to coerce workers into joining unions.

Similarly, every test of voluntary payments to unions for political activism has resulted in a catastrophic drop in donations—as much as 96 percent in some cases. The unions' answer: make the payments mandatory so people have to fork over the money to be in the union, and they have to be in the union to keep their job.

Similar kinds of social and economic coercion are found in other fields. In Hollywood, if you are openly on the Right you probably won't get a job. And in many universities, conservatives will never get tenure.

This coercive brand of machine politics is the key to the Left's attempts to gain power and remake the American people. The secular-socialist machine does not seek to serve the American people; it wants to force us into accepting the values and obeying the institutions of secular, big-government bureaucracies and their unionized employees.

WHY THE MACHINE HAS TO RELY ON THE PHILOSOPHY OF SECULARISM

Transplanting secular-socialist values into people through government action requires a malleable view of human nature and a government-centric concept of citizens' rights.

To socialists, people are inherently bad and capitalism is always exploitive. Only strong government can take money from the rich, give it to the poor, and reeducate the ignorant or misinformed through government-sponsored programs. (Read the education philosophies of Bill Ayers or John Dewey to understand the Left's mania for incorporating public education into the secular-socialist machine.)

This socialist worldview is the exact opposite of our Founding Fathers' outlook. As we've seen, the Founders believed our rights come from God, that our behavior should be shaped by a culture infused with religious values, and that government shoud be a carefully limited servant of the people.

A religious worldview inherently limits the purview of government. Even the concept of sin limits government by suggesting that external constraints of right and wrong should guide us no matter what the state says.

In short, our core religious values hinder the secular socialists from realizing a government-dominated, politician-defined world of limited citizenship and unlimited bureaucracy. Thus, the culture of secularism has to replace the culture of religion if socialism is to survive.

WHY SECULAR SOCIALISM IS CONDUCIVE TO DICTATORSHIP

For secular socialists, the government's overarching goal is to condition people to accept alien behaviors and values. In practice, this outlook inherently produces creeping dictatorial bureaucracy and, ultimately, totalitarianism. George Orwell, despite being an avowed socialist, warned of this tendency in his essay "Why I Write":

> My recent novel [*1984*] is NOT intended as an attack on
> Socialism or on the British Labour Party (of which I am a

supporter) but as a show-up of the perversions to which a
centralised economy is liable and which have already been
partly realised in Communism and Fascism.... I believe also
that totalitarian ideas have taken root in the minds of intel-
lectuals everywhere, and I have tried to draw these ideas out
to their logical consequences. The scene of the book is laid
in Britain in order to emphasize that the English-speaking
races are not innately better than anyone else and that totalitarianism, *if not fought against,* could triumph anywhere.[12]

For those who ridiculed warnings that "death panels" would accom-
pany a government-run health system, Orwell should stand as a stark
reminder that the expansion of government power may be a small
step on the long march to tyranny and domination by bureaucrats
and politicians.

In *The Road to Serfdom,* Friedrich Hayek, an influential critic of
centralized government and a major influence on President Reagan
and Prime Minister Thatcher, similarly warned that "[government]
planning leads to dictatorship because dictatorship is the most effective instrument of coercion and the enforcement of ideals." He
added, "The more the state 'plans' the more difficult planning
becomes for the individual."

Hayek clearly explains why the utopian fantasies of the secular-
socialist machine are a direct threat to our freedom. Defeating this
machine, and thwarting its furious attempts to impose alien values
on us, is not a partisan matter between Democrats and Republicans;
it's an effort to save America.

CHAPTER THREE

The Lies They Told Us (Because They Had To)

How does the secular-socialist machine gain power? That's easy: they lie to us.

But at some point in 2009, the American people realized they were not getting the truth from President Barack Obama, House speaker Nancy Pelosi, and Senate majority leader Harry Reid.

Perhaps it became clear in December during Congress's first round of voting on healthcare "reform." After an embarrassing and shocking parade of political payoffs to achieve the necessary votes, House and Senate leaders met with White House officials to draft a final bill.

President Obama, Speaker Pelosi, and Leader Reid bypassed the normal conference committee for the bill, opting instead to hash out the details behind closed doors. There, they struck a corrupt deal with their union boss donors that would exempt union members from paying taxes on certain healthcare plans while non-union Americans would still get taxed.

Not only did this flagrant venality mock the very idea of equal protection under the law, but the process that created it was the polar opposite of the way President Obama and Speaker Pelosi had promised to govern.

When Democrats won control of the House of Representatives in November 2006, Speaker Pelosi pledged, "This leadership team will create the most honest, most open, and most ethical Congress in history."

They promised to give members of Congress—and the American people—twenty-four hours to review bills before voting on them, to conduct rigorous internal ethics investigations, and to reform the earmark process to stop taxpayer-financed political payoffs.

Similarly, candidate Obama passionately vowed to make Washington more bipartisan, more transparent, and more accountable to the American people. Condemning backdoor negotiations, he called for "bringing all parties together and broadcasting [healthcare] negotiations on C-SPAN so that the American people can see what the choices are."

He made this pledge at least eight times during the campaign, and the pledges were compiled in an online video. In one clip, he explains that he is personally responsible for making this happen, insisting, "One of my jobs as President will be to guide this process."

C-SPAN founder Brian Lamb asked congressional leaders to live up to those pledges so the American people could see how their representatives decide the vital issue of healthcare. But President Obama, Nancy Pelosi, and Harry Reid refused. And no wonder; TV cameras would have exposed exactly the sort of corrupt bargaining on behalf of major political donors that candidate Obama had pledged to "shame"—his word—congressional leaders from making.

Thanks to that video, President Obama's C-SPAN flip-flop may have been the most vivid example of the Democratic leadership's unwillingness to uphold campaign promises, much less the ideals of this country. That instance of hypocrisy, however, is just the tip of the iceberg.

"THE MOST HONEST AND ETHICAL CONGRESS IN HISTORY"

Any honest assessment of the campaign promises made by the current Democratic Congress reveals a stunning gap between words and deeds. Despite the Democrats' much-heralded promises of transparency, accountability, and higher ethical standards, the current Congress has featured unprecedented corruption and secrecy.

During Obama's presidency, we have seen Democrats ram massive, complex legislation through the House and Senate and sign it into law so fast that members—as well as the American people—had no time to read it.

We've also seen Nancy Pelosi protect Democratic congressmen under criminal investigation. One such congressman, Charles Rangel from New York, who has taken a "leave of absence" from his position as head of the committee that writes our tax laws, is under an ethics committee investigation for alleged tax dodging, filing deficient financial disclosure forms, and other charges. Although the committee "admonished" him—its weakest reprimand—for taking corporate-sponsored trips to the Caribbean, Pelosi declined to join many of her Democratic colleagues in calling for Rangel to step down as chairman of the Ways and Means Committee. In fact, in an interview with ABC News' *This Week*, Pelosi conceded that the admonishment of Rangel was "not good," but stressed that Rangel's actions were "not something that jeopardized our country in any way." Is this the new ethical standard we were promised—that corruption is acceptable as long as it doesn't "jeopardize" the country?

In fact, under the Democrats, we've seen the very apparatuses used to police ethics in Congress made more and more feckless. For example, even though they created the Independent Office of Congressional Ethics, the Democrats failed to give it subpoena power and have ignored its findings.

Meanwhile, under Democratic control, the ethics committee seems surprisingly eager to clear members of Congress of wrongdoing. The committee cleared two members of Congress who, according to the panel, tacitly tied requests for campaign donations to earmarks that would have benefited the donors. Five others—four congressmen and one delegate—who took the same Caribbean trips as Congressman Rangel were cleared after claiming they did not realize the trips were sponsored by corporations, even though they repeatedly took pictures in front of corporate logos. The ethics committee has even issued guidelines for congressmen on how to get around new rules that prohibit lobbyists from throwing parties in their honor: make sure the parties are honoring more than one member of Congress.

Most significant, in order to get President Obama's initiatives approved in Congress, the Democratic leadership used the American people's money to buy the votes of key senators and congressmen and to pay back their own political allies, behavior that the Founding Fathers rightly called corruption and for which they rebelled against Britain.

Look, for example, at the shameless bribes used to get wavering Democratic senators to vote for the healthcare bill. These bribes were so outrageous—even by Washington standards—they each earned a nickname:

- **The Louisiana Purchase**—Senator Landrieu was promised an additional $300 million in Medicaid funding for Louisiana.

• **The Cornhusker Kickback**—Perhaps inspired by his Louisiana colleague, Senator Ben Nelson secured exemptions for Nebraska's Medicaid payments worth around $100 million. Along with Michigan senator Carl Levin, he also got a carve-out from the insurance fees for his state's Blue Cross/Blue Shield programs. Moreover, insurance fees for Medigap policies sold by Mutual of Omaha and other Nebraska companies were reduced. As California governor Arnold Schwarzenneger put it, "[Nelson] got the corn, we got the husk."

• **The U-Con**—Senator Chris Dodd was promised $100 million for a medical center in Connecticut.

• **Gator Aid**—Senator Bill Nelson inserted a grandfather clause that would protect Florida's Medicare Advantage program, a *$2.5–3 billion* buyoff.

• **Handout Montana**—Senator Max Baucus obtained Medicare coverage for any mineworkers in Libby, Montana, who were exposed to asbestos.

Additionally, Democratic senators from Nebraska, Vermont, Massachusetts, Michigan, Connecticut, Montana, South Dakota, North Dakota, and Hawaii secured bonuses in the Medicare payments for hospitals in their states worth more than $2 billion.

Although the so-called "reconciliation bill" stripped out some of these abuses, they were only removed due to widespread public outrage—the politicians, who make deals like this all the time, were slow to realize the American people were paying close attention.

When asked about this extraordinary abuse of taxpayer dollars, Senate majority leader Harry Reid suggested senators who didn't get a payoff were not doing their job. "I don't know if there is a senator that doesn't have something in this bill that is important to them," he said. "And if they don't have something in it important to them, then it doesn't speak well of them."

At some point in American history, a Senate majority leader may have made a bolder statement extolling corruption and vote-buying—but I'm unaware of it.

THE DISCONNECT BETWEEN CANDIDATE OBAMA AND PRESIDENT OBAMA

The lies and corruption of the Pelosi-Reid Congress are extraordinary, but they pale in comparison to the gaping disconnect between the promises of candidate Obama and the governing of President Obama.

Hidden beneath the pleasant campaign facade of Senator Obama was a ruthless willingness to replace "the audacity of hope" with "the audacity of raw, ruthless power." He has brought the corrupt, Chicago-style politics he learned in his youth to the White House. Combined with Pelosi and Reid, Obama has created a powerful political machine in Washington unlike anything seen in my lifetime.

The creation of this machine was enabled by the elite media, which was so fawningly supportive of candidate Obama and so unwilling to dig into his past, render critical judgment, or ask critical questions, that the Obama team arrogantly came to believe it could break any promise and get away with it.

President Obama hides his duplicity behind secrecy, clever language, and legalisms. Like President Reagan, Obama possesses captivating, eloquent rhetorical gifts. While Reagan used rhetoric to clarify and educate, however, Obama uses his skills to confuse and deflect. These are profoundly different models of leadership. But then, clarity was Reagan's ally, since he was a conservative who articulated the values of the American people. In contrast, as an apologist for the secular-socialist Left, Obama knows clarity is his opponent; the less the American people understand about what he's doing, the better.

That's why Obama's most honest comments have been those when he went "off message." In an interview with the *San Francisco Chronicle* he said, "So if somebody wants to build a coal-powered plant, they can; it's just that it will bankrupt them because they're going to be charged a huge sum for all that greenhouse gas that's being emitted." This was a striking, unscripted comment; Obama's normal campaign rhetoric did not include promises to bankrupt our own coal industry.

And who can forget that at a private fundraiser in liberal San Francisco, Obama declared that small-town folk "get bitter, they cling to guns or religion or antipathy to people who aren't like them or anti-immigrant sentiment or anti-trade sentiment as a way to explain their frustrations."

These are two examples of Obama's fundamental deception of the American people. While he promised a new dawn of abundant energy, he actually planned to declare war on the coal industry; and while he publicly praised the goodness of the American people, he really thinks we're a bunch of angry, racist, gun-toting, religious extremists.

Perhaps more than anything else, Obama campaigned on the unshakeable vow to make Washington more transparent and accountable. Yet, after a full year of Obama's presidency, Washington is more corrupt and secretive than ever. For example, major federal agencies have become much less cooperative with Freedom of Information Act requests. According to the Associated Press, the agencies cited legal exceptions to avoid disclosure more than 70,000 times during the first budget year of Obama's presidency, compared to roughly 47,000 times during Bush's last budget year.

It's almost impossible to count this administration's broken promises. What follows is merely a greatest hits compilation.

BIPARTISANSHIP

On election night, in a moving speech at Grant Park describing a reunified America, President-elect Obama said:

> Let us resist the temptation to fall back on the same partisanship and pettiness and immaturity that has poisoned our politics for so long. Let us remember that it was a man from this state who first carried the banner of the Republican Party to the White House—a party founded on the values of self-reliance, individual liberty, and national unity. Those are values we all share, and while the Democratic Party has won a great victory tonight, we do so with a measure of humility and determination to heal the divides that have held back our progress. As Lincoln said to a nation far more divided than ours, "We are not enemies, but friends . . . though passion may have strained it must not break our bonds of affection." And to those Americans whose support I have yet to earn—I may not have won your vote, but I hear your voices, I need your help, and I will be your president, too.[1]

Tragically, President Obama promptly turned massive power over to Nancy Pelosi and Harry Reid, both of whom wrote legislation so stunningly partisan that virtually no Republicans have voted with them on any major bills.

The pork-filled, economically illiterate stimulus bill earned zero House Republican votes. Similarly, the first round of healthcare reform voting earned no Republican votes in the Senate and just one in the House. Then, instead of drafting a conference report that would have guaranteed at least some Republican input, the White House, Reid, and Pelosi decided to hammer out a final healthcare bill behind closed doors. Then, when Scott Brown's election in Massachusetts cost the Democrats their 60-vote Senate majority, they opted to ram the Senate bill through the House with no Republicans voting in favor. In fact, the only bipartisan position on the health bill was in opposition to it.

SECRET SIGNING STATEMENTS

We find more broken promises and deliberate obfuscations in President Obama's policy on presidential signing statements.

Presidential signing statements have been used for more than 180 years by presidents of both parties, though they've been used more often since Ronald Reagan's tenure. Some of these statements are merely symbolic declarations about the importance of the legislation being signed. But presidents also use signing statements to declare their intention to ignore certain parts of the legislation, or to interpret them a certain way, often because they believe those parts are unconstitutional or pose other problems. Their oath to uphold the constitution, presidents argue, requires them to do so.

Accusing then President Bush of abusing signing statements, candidate Obama pledged in a 2007 *Boston Globe* op-ed not to use them to "nullify or undermine congressional instructions as enacted into law." At a campaign rally, a citizen asked Obama, "When Congress offers you a bill do you promise not to use presidential signings to get your way?" He responded unequivocally, "Yes . . . we aren't going to use signing statements as a way to do an end run around Congress."

After taking office, however, President Obama suddenly became enamored with signing statements. In fact, in 2009 Obama used signing statements to object to specific legislative provisions seventeen times, one of which earned a 429-to-2 rebuke from Congress. Could there possibly be a more blatant example of Obama doing the exact "end run around Congress" that he'd vowed not to do?

President Obama stopped issuing these statements after some Democrats objected that he was breaking his campaign pledge. Promise salvaged?

Actually, no—it just got worse. According to a January 2010 *New York Times* article, the Obama administration still ignores parts of legislation they sign; they just stopped issuing signing statements announcing their intention to do so. Instead, the administration feels justified in ignoring objectionable provisions as long as they have previously expressed concern about them in a "statement of administration policy." Thus, Americans no longer have any idea which provisions of a bill the administration will ignore or selectively enforce.

Furthermore, the article notes President Obama has at least once relied on an opinion from his Office of Legal Counsel to justify treating a provision of a bill he'd signed as advisory, rather than binding. As the article points out, opinions from this office are often secret.

So what President Obama has done, effectively, is to create a precedent for secret signing statements.

Is this an end to the alleged abuse of presidential signing statements? Is this the transparency and accountability we were promised?

Hardly.

LOBBYING: BUSINESS AS USUAL

Initially, President Obama appeared serious about his famous pledge to toughen ethics rules to prevent the influence of lobbyists in his administration. The day after he took office, January 21, 2009, he signed an Executive Order barring industry lobbyists entering his administration from working on "regulations or contracts directly and substantially related to their prior employer for two years."

The order, however, included a giant loophole, or "waiver," that could nullify the rule if its application "is inconsistent" with its purpose, or if "it is in the public interest," which "shall include, but not be limited to, exigent circumstances relating to national security or the economy." Thanks to President Obama's famous gift for language, nearly any appointee to any position could probably qualify for the waiver.

And indeed, just hours after signing the order, the president moved to nominate William J. Lynn III as deputy secretary of defense. For the six years prior to his nomination, Lynn was a registered lobbyist for Raytheon, a major defense contractor. As Senator Charles Grassley wrote to the president:

> Mr. Lynn's lobbying reports clearly indicate that he lobbied extensively on a very broad range of DOD programs and issues in both the House and Senate and at the Department of Defense. If confirmed, Mr. Lynn would become the top operations manager in the Pentagon. He would be the final approval authority on most—if not all—contract, program and budget decisions. Surely, a number of Raytheon issues would come across his desk.... Based upon President Obama's statements made during the presidential campaign and leading up to and following the signing of the Executive Order, I simply cannot comprehend how this particular lobbyist could be nominated to fill such a key position at DOD overseeing procurement matters, much less be granted a waiver from the ethical limitations listed in the Executive Order.[2]

The administration cited Lynn's superb qualifications to justify his ethics waiver. And indeed, Lynne had an extensive resume. In the 1980s, he worked for Senator Ted Kennedy on defense issues. Then, he worked on budgetary matters while serving in various roles in President Clinton's Defense Department, becoming Clinton's undersecretary of defense (comptroller) in 1997. After leaving the Clinton administration, Lynn became Raytheon's executive vice president in 2002.

The problem with Lynn's resume is that, rather than justifying Obama's waiver, it undermines the rationale for it. Lynn's career is a perfect illustration of the "revolving door" between government and lobbying that has led to so much corruption over the past decade. Lynn cashed in on his government service by using his contacts and expertise to give Raytheon an advantage in securing more government contracts and taxpayer money. Then, once he made lots of money, he returned to government service, bringing the biases and interests of his former employer.

President Obama has granted at least two other ethics waivers: one went to Jocelyn Frye, the director of policy and projects in the Office of the First Lady, who was previously a lobbyist for the National Partnership for Women and Families; and the other was given to Cecilia Muñoz, director of intergovernmental affairs in the Executive Office of the President, who previously lobbied for the National Council of La Raza.

Still, you might be tempted to cut President Obama a break. After all, he has appointed over 800 people and given only three waivers.

But it turns out there is another loophole within his Executive Order, a loophole within a loophole if you will: former lobbyists can simply agree to recuse themselves from matters related to their lobbying activities. Worse, there is no public record of these recusals, though the media has unearthed some examples.

Take Mark Patterson, chief of staff to Treasury Secretary Tim Geithner. Prior to joining the Obama administration, Patterson was a lobbyist for investment giant Goldman Sachs. It's simply impossible to imagine the chief of staff to the Treasury secretary recusing himself from every discussion involving Goldman, given the firm's central role in the financial industry.

Thus, similar to the signing statements, once the president was criticized for breaking his word on the ban on lobbyists, he resorted to a secret process to hide his hypocrisy, this time, in effect, with secret waivers for former lobbyists.[3]

TERRORISTS' LAWYERS IN THE JUSTICE DEPARTMENT

Perhaps the most shocking example of the Obama administration's lack of transparency is the case of the nine lawyers hired by the Department of Justice who had previously represented or advocated on behalf of terrorists.

These nine lawyers were among the over 400 members of the so-called "Gitmo Bar" who volunteered to represent terrorist detainees at Guantanamo. Most of the terrorists defended by these lawyers were alien enemy combatants challenging their detention, not defendants in a criminal trial, and thus they had no legal right to representation. Those few who were under trial for war crimes in a military commission were already entitled to competent military counsel. Nevertheless, the Gitmo Bar volunteered its services to the terrorists.

All these lawyers would undoubtedly deny having sympathy for al Qaeda, but the actions of some of them went far beyond simply challenging a detention policy they thought was unjust or unconstitutional. The most outrageous example was detailed in August 2009 in the *Washington Post*, which reported that lawyers representing Khalid Sheikh Mohammed and other 9/11 conspirators worked with a left-wing organization called the John Adams Project to provide photographs of CIA officers to their clients in an attempt to identify those officers who had interrogated them when they were captured overseas. The lawyers were apparently unconcerned by the potential threat to our CIA officers and their families from being identified by name to al Qaeda and Taliban terrorists.

A Freedom of Information Act request filed by Debra Burlingame of Keep America Safe and Thomas Joscelyn of the Foundation for Defense of Democracies revealed other unconscionable acts by Gitmo Bar lawyers. Writing in the *Wall Street Journal*, Burlingame and Joscelyn revealed that some lawyers provided their terrorist clients with extremely inflammatory anti-American literature for them to share with other inmates. One of these was an 18-page color brochure from Amnesty International accusing America and her allies of "anti-Arab, anti-Islamic, and other racist abuse." Another document was the transcript of a speech comparing American military physicians at Guantanamo to the Nazi doctors of the concentration camps. One lawyer was even caught drawing a map of the detention camp for his client, including the location of guard towers; others posted photos of Guantanamo security badges on the Internet.

Given these appalling actions, it's perfectly reasonable for the American people to want to know which lawyers hired by the Justice Department had previously represented terrorists, and if they are now setting security policy in the Obama administration. However, when senators asked Attorney General Eric Holder to identify those lawyers and their current roles in the Justice Department, he at first refused, and then dribbled out small bits of information. After several months, Keep America Safe began running ads demanding that he disclose the names of all the terrorists' lawyers. The ensuing controversy led news organizations to finally uncover the names.

The revelations embarrassed the Obama administration. One of the lawyers now working in the Department of Justice's security division is Jennifer Daskal, formerly of Human Rights Watch, who in 2006 campaigned for the UN Human Rights Committee to condemn the United States for its actions in the "so-called 'war on terrorism.'" Daskal has also argued for closing Guantanamo and releasing those terrorists we cannot try in civilian courts, despite acknowledging "these men may...join the battlefield to fight U.S. soldiers and our allies another day."

The Obama administration has the right to appoint anyone they want to fill spots at the Justice Department (assuming they can get Senate confirmation when needed) and to set policy as they see fit. But why the constant attempt at secrecy? If they want to appoint radicals and terrorist lawyers, why not just level with the American people about it?

The answer, of course, is that the American people would never accept what they're doing.

TIME FOR REVIEWING LEGISLATION

There's more.

On the *very first* bill he signed, President Obama broke his pledge to give the American people five days to review bills sent for his signature. According to a *Washington Times* analysis of data from the Library of Congress, President Obama failed to live up to his 5-day pledge on 32 of the 117 bills he signed in 2009. These included the 1,000-page, $787 billion stimulus package and the $400 billion omnibus spending bills for 2009 and 2010, enormous pieces of legislation filled with earmarks and political pay-offs.

Clearly, it's difficult to competently debate legislation when no one has actually read it.

THEY LIE BECAUSE THEY HAVE TO

The record of the Obama-Pelosi-Reid team is clear. Contrary to their promises to clean up Washington, the president, House speaker, and Senate majority leader have governed with a political machine mentality that is more corrupt and secretive than anything we have seen in modern American politics.

Perhaps this shouldn't have surprised us. After all, it's clear the Left cannot tell the American people the truth about their goals and the way they operate.

Imagine if candidate Obama, along with Nancy Pelosi and Harry Reid, had in 2008 declared,

> We are going to pass a $787 billion spending bill that no member of Congress had time to read, explode the deficit to unsustainable levels, seize control of private car companies, push for a massive energy tax, socialize the health system, sign an enormous number of earmarks, negotiate in secret with senators whom we will bribe to vote for a health bill their constituents oppose, and give the Environmental Protection Agency massive bureaucratic power to intimidate American businesses while dictating pay and bonus policy to dozens of companies. Oh, and our Justice Department will consistently favor protecting the rights of terrorists over the lives of Americans.

I'm not a fortune teller, but I can confidently predict that platform is not going to win any elections. Since the secular-socialist Left cannot tell the truth and survive, it uses deception and machine politics to gain power, with the goal of subverting and destroying traditional America—our economic system, our relationship to government, and our values.

CHAPTER FOUR

The Secular-Socialist Machine in Action

One of the most disturbing developments in modern American political life has been the rise of an anti-democratic political machine that increasingly controls Washington, many state capitols, and many cities and counties.

A political machine does not care about popular opinion. In fact, its very reason for being is to crush such opinion by the weight of organized money and manpower. And when it can't crush public opinion, it seeks simply to outlast it.

Patience is a key element to a political machine's survival. People get angry at politicians and they vote (as in the 2009 California spending and taxing referendum) or they turn out for tea parties (as hundreds of thousands did that spring). But they tend to quickly go back to their daily routines. Having expressed themselves, they think politicians will listen. And while we are engaged in our daily business, we forget that the business of a political machine is surviving in power.

A political machine understands that an attack on any part of the machine is an attack on the whole machine. Therefore, even the most innocuous reform, if it affects the machine, can produce a furious counterattack as the machine brings to bear its full financial power and its organizational strength.

California provides a perfect example. In the early 1900s, the progressive movement led by Hiram Johnson shattered the old railroad-dominated political machine and inaugurated a period of genuinely popular government in the Golden State, with citizens gaining unprecedented power via the ballot initiative and the referendum. For well over a half century, California experienced constant reform and widespread popular involvement in government.

But when Californians passed Proposition 13—the anti-tax, anti-spending referendum of 1978—the Left realized popular political participation was undermining their goals. Thus, they created the California political machine—an interlocking coalition of interest groups that rely on government money and government-imposed rules to enrich their members at the expense of the rest of society. Beginning with Democratic State Assembly speaker Willie Brown in 1980, the Left have controlled California through a money-driven special-interest system that is impervious to popular opposition.

In November 2003, Arnold Schwarzenegger was elected governor in response to public anger over California's machine politics as personified by his predecessor, Gray Davis. In an unusual recall election, Schwarzenegger ran as an outsider, beholden to no one, who would clean house in a state that was in a deep fiscal hole. Schwarzenegger had a string of early successes in office, but he was unprepared for the ferocity he would encounter when he tried to enact reforms that threatened the Sacramento political machine.

In June 2005, Schwarzenegger called a special election and backed four propositions that were the centerpieces of his reform efforts. Two of these were controversial from the start. Proposition 76 would have authorized the governor to slow the rate of increase of state spending on education and other public services, while Proposition 77 would have transferred redistricting—the periodic redrawing of electoral districts—from the legislature to a panel of three retired judges appointed by the legislature.

Education spending is always a heated topic, so it was no shock that a June 2005 poll showed 35 percent supported Proposition 76 while 42 percent opposed it. Proposition 77, surprisingly, was also contentious (perhaps because of a distrust of judges), with the same poll showing 35 percent for it and 46 percent opposed.

However, Proposition 74—increasing the amount of time it takes for teachers to gain tenure from two to five years—and Proposition 75—requiring unions to obtain their members' permission to use any portion of union dues for political donations—were initially very popular, earning 61 percent and 57 percent approval, respectively.

These two measures threatened the power of unions and would have substantially weakened the Sacramento political machine. So the machine responded with total war.

It was the most expensive special election in history, costing by some accounts more than $300 million. Unions alone spent more than $100 million in advertising and voter mobilization efforts. The result: all eight ballot initiatives were defeated, including the four backed by Schwarzenegger. Despite their initial popularity, propositions 74 and 75 lost by ten points or more. Propositions 76 and 77 were beaten by even larger margins.

A *Los Angeles Times* op-ed by broadcaster John Ziegler aptly summed up the result. It was titled "How the Liars Won":

> The entire special election was dictated by 30 second TV ads. .... The vast majority of the commercials—which, for merely a couple of hundred million dollars, took over our television sets for the final weeks of the campaign—treated the truth as a mere technicality and the facts as just an obstacle to a goal apparently inspired by Oakland Raiders owner Al Davis' famous mantra, "Just Win Baby."
>
> ...In general the news media seems to have created a matrix through which we were supposed to view all political discourse with such extreme cynicism that it is presumed that no one is telling the truth. So if one side claims that $2 + 2 = 4$ and the other claims $2 + 2 = 100$, there appears to be a consensus that the real answer must be somewhere in the middle. Ask yourself who prevails in that scenario? Obviously, it is the liars who win big because the truth, by its very nature, cannot be exaggerated.

Of course, we've already learned just how little the truth matters to the secular-socialist machine.

BRIBERY AND PAYOFFS OF THE SECULAR-SOCIALIST MACHINE

The governance of a machine is always infused with lies and corruption.

The machine that currently runs Washington, D.C., is no exception. Having promised honest and accountable government, the administration picked a Secretary of the Treasury, Timothy Geithner, who failed to pay his taxes. Then, Obama's officials announced grandly they will do no business with companies that fail to pay their taxes.

Similarly, it made perfect sense for Christopher Dodd, chairman of the Senate committee overseeing mortgage lenders, to take a sweetheart deal from a mortgage lender. After all, if you're going to work hard to get power, shouldn't you get something back for your troubles?

After people become corrupt, it's natural for them to bribe others in the same manner. That's why rule-breaking, writing payoffs into legislative bills, and fawning over special interests is the modus operandi of the secular-socialist machine.

The machine uses government resources to enhance its power, pay off allies, and buy off others. We've seen political machines in America in the past, mostly at the municipal level. But the modern era is even more dangerous due to the emergence of a huge government in Washington with enormous power and resources. This has enabled secular socialists to use payoffs and special favors on a grand scale in order to construct a *national* political machine. And in order to maintain their machine, secular socialists have to pillage government assets to reward their friends and allies.

This machine is now running the country. The only question is whether it will become permanent, or the American people will dislodge it.

ONCE, WE WOULD HAVE CALLED IT A SCANDAL

A prime example of the machine in action can be seen in the automobile bailout and in the ensuing bankruptcy proceedings for Chrysler. Although the Democrats and the mainstream media tried to treat this extraordinary intervention as routine, it wasn't. In fact, there was a time when we would have called it a scandal.

In 1921, for example, oil tycoon Harry Sinclair gave several prize head of cattle and around $269,000 to President Harding's secretary of the interior, Albert Fall. In return, Sinclair got the exclusive rights to drill in an oil field in Wyoming. Sinclair's no-bid contract exploded into the Teapot Dome scandal, the most notorious example of political corruption in America prior to Watergate.

Now, consider the Chrysler bankruptcy. Between 2000 and 2008, the United Auto Workers (UAW) union gave $23,675,562 to the Democratic Party and its candidates while giving just $193,540 to Republicans. In 2008 alone, the UAW gave $4,161,567 to the Democratic Party, including Barack Obama.

In return, in a rigged proceeding in which the federal government disregarded bankruptcy law in order to engineer a desired political outcome, the unions were made the primary beneficiaries of the Chrysler bankruptcy. The Obama Treasury Department strong-armed Chrysler's creditors into a deal in which the UAW was given 55 percent ownership of the company while Chrysler's secured creditors—investors who normally receive priority in bankruptcy proceedings—were left with just 29 cents on the dollar. These secured creditors included the state of Indiana's teacher pension fund which, according to Indiana State Treasurer Richard Mourdock, lost at least $4.6 million in the bankruptcy.

As rotten as it was, the Chrysler bankruptcy was just a prelude to the General Motors bankruptcy, again brokered by the Obama administration. And once again, the big losers were the bondholders, who included substitute teachers in Florida and retired tool and dye supervisors in Michigan. Holding $27 billion in GM debt, they are receiving a 10 percent stake in the new company. In contrast, the UAW, which is owed about $20 billion from GM, is walking away with 17.5 percent of the company and a cool $9 billion in cash.

According to a *Barron's* magazine analysis, while the bondholders will be lucky to recover 15 cents on the dollar, the UAW can expect to recover up to 60–70 cents on the dollar—four to five times what the bondholders will receive. As the magazine noted, "Never has an American union done so well at the expense of shareholders and creditors."

Bankruptcy was once a legal process in which an insolvent company, an impartial judge, and creditors cooperated in good faith to make the best of a bad situation. Under the secular-socialist machine, the Chrysler and GM bankruptcies became a naked opportunity for political patronage.

In the end, the losers weren't just the secured creditors and the taxpayers who footed the bill for all these bailouts, but the rule of law itself.

COERCIVE TACTICS OF THE SECULAR-SOCIALIST MACHINE

Perhaps the most disturbing aspect of President Obama's first year in office is the machine's brazen willingness to use the power of the state to coerce and intimidate his opponents while rewarding his political allies.

A perfect example was the investigation launched by the Centers of Medicare and Medicaid Services into the insurance company Humana for having the gall to send its members a letter describing how the healthcare bill would negatively affect their benefits.

Another stunning example was reported by FOX News' Andrew Napolitano, who had to hide the name of the people and the institution involved because of threats made by the administration. Napolitano revealed that in spring 2009, a major bank that had accepted a relatively small amount of TARP money wanted to return the money to the government. The Obama administration, however, refused to accept it and threatened "adverse" consequences if the bank's chairman pursued the matter. This report is particularly troubling considering the administration's attempts shortly thereafter to convert TARP recipients' preferred stock into common stock, which would give the government voting rights on the banks' management or policy.

Finally, who can forget the administration's war against FOX News? As opposition grew to their efforts to nationalize healthcare, administration officials began calling on other news organizations to shun FOX for producing, as then-White House communications director Anita Dunn put it, "opinion journalism masquerading as news." The White House even refused to provide guests to *FOX News Sunday* for having the temerity to fact-check assertions made by administration officials. Other news organizations, rightly concluding they could be the next target, refused to ostracize FOX, and the administration eventually backed down.

This wasn't the first time Team Obama tried to intimidate a news program. In August 2008, the Obama campaign encouraged supporters to call and email a Chicago radio station—WGN AM—to protest the appearance on the station of conservative journalist Stanley Kurtz, who had been investigating Obama's ties to former Weather Underground terrorist Bill Ayers.

HOLDING THE CONSTITUTION HOSTAGE

Perhaps the worst example of the machine's intimidation tactics is President Obama's unconstitutional use of the Environmental Protection Agency to blackmail Congress into passing his cap-and-tax energy bill.

In summer 2009, the House of Representatives narrowly passed the job-killing cap-and-trade energy tax bill. But because the bill needed sixty votes, including those of senators from coal producing states, it was obviously going nowhere in the Senate.

So at the end of 2009, the administration tried to bully the Senate into passing the bill. They cited a 2007 Supreme Court ruling that the EPA could regulate carbon dioxide as a pollutant under the Clean Air Act. The Bush Administration had refused to do so, realizing it would create a morass of new regulations and bureaucracy. But as the UN's annual climate change conference began in Copenhagen on December 7, Obama's EPA chief, Lisa Jackson, announced the EPA now considers six greenhouse gases, including carbon dioxide and methane, dangerous to the environment and public health, and that the EPA would begin drawing up new regulations to arbitrarily reduce them.

The announcement deliberately coincided with the climate change conference, which aims to establish an international treaty to reduce greenhouse gas emissions. Of course, the president cannot implement a treaty by himself; he needs the approval of two-thirds of the U.S. Senate. So the EPA's announcement was actually a threat to circumvent the Senate's constitutional prerogatives. Obama was indicating he would commit the United States to carbon-cutting goals reached at Copenhagen, and if the Senate refused to approve a carbon-cutting treaty or to pass cap and trade, Obama would simply use the EPA to regulate carbon whether the Senate likes it or not.

Senator John Kerry, a co-sponsor of the Senate cap-and-trade bill, aptly summed it up: "The message to Congress is crystal clear: get moving."

This is a breathtakingly anti-democratic and unconstitutional arrogation of power by the president. Even Democratic senator Jim Webb warned Obama in a public letter that "only specific legislation agreed upon in the Congress, or a treaty ratified by the Senate, could actually create such a commitment on behalf of our country."

But for a president trained to value the acquisition of power above all else, why let the Constitution obstruct that goal?

THE MACHINE'S MILLIONAIRE BACKERS

Finally, no overview of the secular-socialist machine would be complete without acknowledging its key source of funding: a clique of left-wing millionaires operating outside the Democratic Party.

A "shadow party," as David Horowitz and Richard Poe coined it, was enabled by a rapid influx of money from a few rich liberals united in their opposition to George W. Bush and their frustration with the Democratic establishment's ineffectiveness and lack of ideological purity.

Horowitz and Poe's book *The Shadow Party*, along with Matt Bai's *The Argument*, detailed the modus operandi of this new power center. By funneling money through interlocutor organizations to left-wing groups, these benefactors created an alternative structure that compliments the Democratic Party while pushing it to the Left. Conveniently, this method allows the donors to avoid compliance with campaign finance laws that regulate political parties.

This funding enriched established far-left groups like ACORN and People for the American Way. But it also helped to create new liberal "message machines" like the Center for American Progress and Media Matters for America, organizations that quickly grew to dominate the Democratic Party, scooping up its resources and volunteers.

Having aided the Democratic victories in the 2006 mid-term elections, this shadow party was also instrumental in the overwhelming fundraising and organizing success of the Obama campaign, creating a ready network of volunteers and financing to defeat Hillary Clinton and then John McCain.

A small group of far-left tycoons presides over this entire effort: George Soros, Peter Lewis, Herb and Marion Sandler, and Stephen Bing.

Soros, who declared in 2003 that defeating President Bush was "the central focus of my life," is the key figure. Through his various organizations, he finances an array of domestic and international left-wing causes. A major supporter of international efforts to curtail gun rights, Soros funds the International Action Network on Small Arms, which is pushing for a UN arms treaty to regulate international weapons sales. The Bush administration opposed this anti-democratic power grab, but the Obama administration has vaguely indicated openness to it.

Soros also finances marijuana legalization campaigns, contributing over $15 million through his organizations to such efforts, including ballot initiatives in several states. Furthermore, he was a big supporter of campaign finance reform. There's some irony in that; Soros backed the McCain-Feingold Act, touted as a way to remove the corrupting influence of money from politics. Yet, since the act's approval in 2002, Soros himself has donated tens of millions of dollars to political action committees (PACs) and other advocacy organizations that can circumvent the act's restrictions.

Soros first united with the other big money families to flex their muscle in the 2004 presidential election, when Soros, Lewis, and the Sandlers donated more than $20 million to America Coming Together (ACT), a PAC supporting Democratic candidate John Kerry. ACT marshaled an impressive army of activists and volunteers who went door-to-door to turn out the vote for Kerry. According to Bai, it was also the first time such a small group of people had invested so much money in a single campaign.

Frustrated by Kerry's narrow loss, the left-wing money families redoubled their efforts. Influenced by former Clinton lawyer Rob Stein, who explained to them how conservative think tanks and policy journals ostensibly help shape the Republican message, they set out to create not just a parallel voter turnout organization, but also an alternative "messaging machine" to the Democratic Party.

The funding families formed a new organization, Democracy Alliance, to channel cash to liberal organizations. Soros, Lewis, and the Sandlers alone provide about 40 percent of the alliance's funding.

Democracy Alliance gives tens of millions of dollars in grants to far-left organizations. But it's impossible to know exactly who has received how much, since the alliance prohibits grant recipients from revealing its funding. This makes the alliance a major source of undisclosed and unaccountable political influence.

Despite this veil of secrecy, we know some organizations that have received Democracy Alliance funds, though not the precise amounts of the grants. According to the Capital Research Center, these include the aforementioned ACORN, as well as Media Matters for America, the Center for American Progress, the Sierra Club, Air America, and People for the American Way.

All these organizations are active supporters of the Obama-Pelosi-Reid agenda. All are now part of the secular-socialist machine.

CHAPTER FIVE

The Secular-Socialist Machine's Health Bill Disaster

With David Merritt, Vice President of National Policy for the Center for Health Transformation

Nothing captures the corruption of today's secular-socialist machine better than the Democrats' takeover of the healthcare system. It's hard to imagine a more destructive course of action than the one they pursued: using fast-paced votes and procedural tricks to pass trillion-dollar bills no one had read; scheming to pass bills without actually voting on them; dismissing deep public opposition; relying on secret negotiations among a handful of staff and politicians; bullying opposition with bare-knuckled threats; and resorting to backroom deals to buy support.

This process was a tragedy, because improving healthcare for all Americans is one of our country's most pressing priorities. The healthcare system has become an anchor on virtually every aspect of society, including personal health, the quality of care we receive, and the availability and cost of insurance.

- Health insurance premiums skyrocketed 87 percent between 2000 and 2007, while wages grew only 20 percent over that period.
- Weighted down by healthcare costs, employers are dropping employees' coverage, with only 59 percent of individuals now receiving employer-based health benefits, down from 64 percent in 2000.
- More than 7,000 Americans are killed annually by preventable medication errors, and nearly 100,000 Americans are killed every year by preventable medical errors.
- Sixty-four percent of adults are either overweight or obese, according to the Centers for Disease Control and Prevention. The number of obese children has tripled since 1980.
- Diabetes is a major factor in killing more than 220,000 Americans every year.

Democrats were right to try to fix the health system, whose deficiencies threaten America's future. We need reform so that every American has more choices of greater quality healthcare at lower cost. Everyone—policymakers, doctors, hospitals, employers, individuals—must work together to accomplish this goal.

But Obama, Pelosi, and Reid didn't choose this path of inclusion, cooperation, and expertise. They saw the large Democratic majorities in Congress and a Democratic White House as an opportunity to expand the power of the secular-socialist machine by growing government. This was their moment to build another Great Society—a permanent expansion of the welfare state that would reduce ever more Americans into government dependence and bind them to the Democratic political machine. That's just what they tried to do when the president signed health reform into law on March 23, 2010.

SECULAR SOCIALISM IN THE HEALTH BILL

The destructive, corrupt, and thuggish path the Left followed on health reform perfectly captures the extremism of the secular-socialist machine.

The Left had to resort to this corrupt process because Americans won't willingly approve a "reform" that massively increases government power, erodes individual freedom, and redefines citizens' relationship to our government. Obama's healthcare reform will do all those things: it is impossible to spend trillions of taxpayer dollars and reduce the role of government. Instead, you get new bureaucracies, more regulation, more complexity, and less control of your healthcare, just as the Left planned.

Just look at H.R. 3590. That's the bill that Senate Democrats passed on Christmas Eve—and the one the president signed into law. In 2,409 pages, the word "shall" appears 4,231 times. That's nearly two federal requirements, directives, or bureaucratic powers per page. The law has the word "tax" 208 times—and not once to cut taxes. The word "require" appears 198 times, usually referring to the people who are required to do something—not government. It adds 159 new federal agencies, offices, and programs to what is already the largest department in the federal government. Among the new offices is the Personal Care Attendants Workforce Advisory Panel and four duplicative offices on women's health (see pages 1089-1109). Women's health is obviously important, but is it necessary to have four new offices *within the same federal department?* Just to make things even more bureaucratic, there will be a new Coordinating Committee on Women's Health to oversee the four offices. And that's not all; here are some of the other "vital" new offices, councils, groups, and programs created by the healthcare bill:

- Grant program to establish state Exchanges (Section 1311(a))

- State-based American Health Benefit Exchanges (Section 1311(b))
- Exchange grants to establish consumer navigator programs (Section 1311(i))
- Private Purchasing Council for state cooperatives (Section 1322(d))
- Program to determine eligibility for Exchange participation (Section 1411)
- Federal Coordinated Health Care Office for dual eligible beneficiaries (Section 2602)
- Interagency Working Group on Health Care Quality (Section 3012)
- Program for use of patient safety organizations to reduce hospital readmission rates (Section 3025)
- Consumer Advisory Council for Independent Payment Advisory Board (Section 3403(k))
- Grant program for technical assistance to providers implementing health quality practices (Section 3501)
- Program to develop independent standards for patient decision aids for preference sensitive care (Section 3506)
- National Prevention, Health Promotion, and Public Health Council (Section 4001)
- Demonstration grant program to promote research-based dental caries disease management (Section 4102)
- Interagency Pain Research Coordinating Committee (Section 4305)
- Planning grant program for state and local healthcare workforce development activities (Section 5102(c))
- Public Health Workforce Loan Repayment Program (Section 5204)
- Grant program to provide mid-career training for health professionals (Section 5206)

- Commission on Key National Indicators (Section 5605)
- Board of Governors for Patient-Centered Outcomes Research Institute (Section 6301 (b))
- Standing methodology committee for Patient-Centered Outcomes Research Institute (Section 6301(d))
- Elder Justice Coordinating Council (Section 6703)
- Multi-state health plans offered by Office of Personnel Management (Section 10104(p))
- Advisory board for multi-state health plans (Section 10104(p))
- Interagency Access to Health Care in Alaska Task Force (Section 10501)

And what will all these new federal agencies and programs do? They will regulate, they will issue rules, they will dictate. They will empower bureaucrats to decide what care you can receive, who can give it to you, and when you can get it.

Just look at the "essential health benefits" mandated by the law (Section 1302), which contains federal requirements for every private insurance policy sold in the United States to meet a certain minimum set of benefits or coverage. Individuals and businesses usually make these decisions, but under this bill, the federal government will decide. For example, if you are a single male with no children, the legislation still requires you to have maternity benefits and well-baby and well-child care coverage. You don't want or don't need that coverage? Sorry, you have to pay for it anyway.

The legislation signed by the president contains this and countless other expansions of government control. For example, the president pushed for, and Harry Reid included, the Independent Payment Advisory Board, a new bureaucratic body of government appointees explicitly charged with reducing healthcare spending not just in Medicare, but in *the private market* as well.

The larger question is this: does anyone believe federal bureaucrats can effectively manage the largest, most complex sector of our economy? Let's face it, the federal government could not get "Cash for Clunkers" right, and that formula was simple: 1) buy a car, 2) file paperwork, 3) dealer gets paid.

Despite limitless examples of government failure, the Left expect tens of thousands of new bureaucrats to run healthcare efficiently. And the argument that this bureaucratic system won't reduce the range of your private healthcare choices is so preposterous that it's hard to believe many Democrats actually believe it.

RATIONING CARE

Instead of the miraculous cost savings the president claimed for his reform plan, healthcare rationing will be a much more likely outcome. Take comparative effectiveness research as an example. The new health reform law creates a new office of comparative effectiveness research that will study the value of one treatment or therapy to another to determine which is more effective. To be sure, this process can generate important knowledge that saves lives—we want to know which treatments are most effective, which medicines are more efficacious, and which approaches are best practices.

Secular socialism, however, has put comparative effectiveness research in the United States on the same path as in Britain: toward becoming a bureaucratic cost-control measure. The United Kingdom, which has a nationalized, single-payer health system, explicitly uses comparative effectiveness to ration medical care. Government uses this research to decide, sometimes with devastating consequences, which treatments its citizens can get.

Let's say a government uses comparative effectiveness to determine the efficacy of new drug treatments. The research reveals drug A works 70 percent of the time and drug B works 50 percent of the time. The government would then decide to cover drug A. But what if, as often happens in medicine, 30 percent of the people who did not respond to drug A did respond to drug B? Or what about the even smaller groups that may have responded best to drug X, Y, or Z? Not wanting to cover less effective drugs, the government may simply decree those people are out of luck. These are the problems patients face when the government is empowered to decide what medicine they can have.

Consider this: what happens when one drug is more effective than another but costs three times as much? Do you want government to decide that relieving your pain and suffering isn't worth the cost? That's what happens in Britain. Government approves and government decides—not patients and doctors. Here is what Britain's National Health Service (NHS) tells its citizens:

> You have the right to drugs and treatments that have been recommended by NICE [National Institute for Health and Clinical Excellence] for use in the NHS, if your doctor says they are clinically appropriate for you. You have the right to expect local decisions on funding of other drugs and treatments to be made rationally following a proper consideration of the evidence. *If the local NHS decides not to fund a drug or treatment you and your doctor feel would be right for you, they will explain that decision to you.* [emphasis added]

During the healthcare debate, House and Senate Republicans offered amendments to prohibit the federal government from using comparative effectiveness research to deny or ration care. Democrats rejected them all and moved full steam ahead. But because of the citizen backlash against the federal government using comparative effectiveness research to ration care, the bill that the president signed deceptively renames the new federal body the "Patient Centered Outcomes Research Initiative."

All this was unsurprising: in healthcare, the goal of the secular-socialist machine is to use the power of government to control Americans' health decisions. This goal is both an ideological imperative that places the power of government over the rights of citizens and a raw power grab. It is a symptom of secular socialism's creeping totalitarianism—a mindset completely opposed to historic American values.

TAXES

Economics 101 states that when government levies a tax on business, it is not the business that will ultimately pay it—consumers will. And the Left's health reform has plenty of new taxes. The $28 billion tax on drug makers won't dent the companies' revenue; the firms will just raise the price of your medications. And health insurers will recoup the new $70 billion tax on them by raising your premiums—so said Congressional Budget Office (CBO) director Douglas Elmendorf when discussing the original proposed fee on insurers: "Our judgment is that that piece of the legislation would raise insurance premiums by roughly the amount of the money collected."

Look at what the Left will do to medical technology companies. There are more than 80,000 medical devices in the United States, everything from artificial heart valves, pacemakers, and NICU incubators to thermometers and toothbrushes. The new law will impose a 2.9 percent tax on the sale of medical devices. That will raise prices for thousands of medical products because these costs will be passed on to consumers through higher prices, higher insurance premiums, or through lost wages when an employer has to pay. Thomas Barthold, chief of staff of the Joint Committee on Taxation, commented, "We have analyzed this as largely falling on the consumer."

And the law has even more tax increases, over half a trillion dollars in higher Medicare payroll taxes; new taxes on investment income; taxes on random services like indoor tanning facilities; and fees on all insurance policies to fund federal comparative effectiveness research.

All these taxes will drive up costs. Yet, while campaigning for president, Barack Obama promised that his plan "will save a typical American family up to $2,500 every year on medical expenditures."

With all the new taxes passed on to consumers, and with all the new federal programs, departments, offices, and subsidies, could he truly believe that costs will go down? Why should the American people believe that *spending* trillions of tax dollars will somehow *reduce* healthcare costs? As CBO chief Elmendorf noted in summer 2009, "In the legislation that has been reported we do not see the sort of fundamental changes that would be necessary to reduce the trajectory of federal health spending by a significant amount. And on the contrary, the legislation significantly expands the federal responsibility for healthcare costs." Sadly, little changed in the final product that was signed into law.

Despite all this, the president boldly declared to Congress, "I will not sign [a healthcare reform bill] if it adds one dime to the deficit, now or in the future, period." That promise was absurd, and the American people knew it. My friend, the pollster Frank Luntz, reported that by a 61 to 14 percent margin, more people believed scientists will discover life in outer space than believed the Democrats' healthcare plan wouldn't increase the deficit.

MEDICARE CUTS

Throughout the healthcare debate, most Americans asked a question to which they never got an honest answer: "How will reform impact me?" For seniors, it was easy to answer: you're in trouble.

To put seniors and Medicare in context, remember that the non-partisan Medicare Trustees projects Medicare will be broke in six years—two years earlier than previously estimated. That is just the beginning of the problems. Medicare is already burdened with an unfunded liability of up to $85 trillion in benefits that have been promised future generations with nothing saved to cover them.

Democrats did nothing to fix the structural problems behind this shortfall. Instead, the law simply guts the program for today's seniors to create a new healthcare entitlement. The cuts to Medicare will pay for the other aspects of the reform plan, like government subsidies and Medicaid expansion. They simply rob Peter to pay Paul while failing to fix Medicare's fundamental problems.

The chief actuary at the Centers for Medicare and Medicaid Services, which administers both programs, estimated that the law would cut Medicare by $494 billion. This breathtaking figure is the amount of money that would have gone to doctors, nurses, and other providers who deliver care and coverage to seniors. According to CMS, the new law cuts deep and wide, including home health ($39 billion); hospitals ($131 billion); skilled nursing facilities ($22 billion); and Medicare Advantage benefits ($101 billion).

Clearly, you cannot cut Medicare by more than a half a trillion dollars and not jeopardize seniors' access to care. Medicare access is already declining. The Mayo Clinic announced that on January 1, 2010, its Arizona facilities would stop seeing Medicare beneficiaries because the federal government does not pay the clinic enough to even cover its costs. According to Lynn Closway, spokeswoman for Mayo, the clinic lost $840 million in 2008 treating Medicare patients. And that's before the Democrats' half a trillion in cuts.

Jeff Korsmo, executive director of the Mayo Clinic Health Policy Center, said with these kinds of cuts, "We will have to violate our values in order to stay in business and reduce our access to government patients."

Just days before the president signed the legislation into law, Walgreens, the nation's largest retail pharmacy chain, announced it would no longer accept the new Medicaid patients in Washington state. Why? Because the government pays the store so little to fill prescriptions for Medicaid beneficiaries that it loses money. Government often tries to control costs by cutting Medicaid reimbursements to providers, cuts which Walgreens described as "extreme." With 20 million Americans being pushed into Medicaid by the new law, this is an ominous sign of things to come.

MACHINE POLITICS IN THE HEALTH BILL

On the day that President Obama was sworn into office, the White House launched a new website that included this pledge: "President Obama has committed to making his administration the most open and transparent in history."

As the debate over health reform heated up that summer, the president made another pledge:

> So I just want everybody to know, Congress will have time to read the bill. They will have time to debate the bill. They will have all of August to review the various legislative proposals. When we come back in September, I will be available to answer any question that members of Congress have. If they want to come over to the White House and go over line by line what's going on, I will be happy to do that.

Did the health reform debate live up to the president's standard? Hardly. The American people were promised a fair, bipartisan, transparent process, but instead the Democrats wrote trillion-dollar, 2,000-plus page bills in secret with no Republican input and no public oversight. Republicans repeatedly offered constructive ideas, only to be shut out and denounced as obstructionists. The one time the president actively sought out Republican ideas—the televised "Blair House summit" in February 2010—was a cynical public relations ploy to appear bipartisan at a time when Democrats had already pushed radical bills through the House and Senate on party-line votes, despite the president's campaign promises not to do so.

Already opposed to the socialist bent of the reform bills, Americans were further disgusted by the ugly machine politics the Left used to ram the bills through Congress.

We already discussed President Obama's disregard for his repeated promises to broadcast reform negotiations on C-SPAN. But there's more. The administration and its congressional allies set artificial deadlines, not for any legitimate reason, but simply to rush the bills through at maximum speed. The president long demanded the House and Senate pass their respective bills by the August 2009 recess. When that deadline was missed, new ones were set in September...then October...then Thanksgiving...then Christmas... and then Easter recess. These self-imposed, politically-driven deadlines left little time for sound policymaking, public input, or even time for members to the read the ever-changing proposals.

"READ THE BILL!"

Even if the process had been transparent and had a reasonable timeline, many lawmakers still probably wouldn't have understood the bills' mind-numbing complexity. "I don't expect to actually read the legislative language because reading the legislative language is among the more confusing things I've ever read in my life," said Delaware Democratic senator Tom Carper. Michigan Democratic congressman John Conyers put it even more bluntly: "What good is reading the bill if it's a thousand pages and you don't have two days and two lawyers to find out what it means after you read the bill?"

And he's chairman of the House Judiciary Committee, which has jurisdiction over matters like the federal courts and constitutional interpretation.

Such outrageous statements led to petition drives and grassroots protests demanding that lawmakers "Read the Bill!" There was even a high-profile website, www.readthebill.org, demanding that representatives actually know what they were voting on. Ignoring these appeals, Washington Democrats tried to recreate the panicked sense of crisis they had exploited to stampede Congress into approving the stimulus.

Things got so bad in the Senate that a group of eight Democratic senators sent Majority Leader Harry Reid a letter demanding he slow the process down and shine a light on what they were voting on. They demanded that the bill, amendments, and budget estimates be publicized seventy-two hours before any vote.

But even that modest request was too much for the Senate Finance Committee, which rejected an amendment by Republican senator Jim Bunning that would have required a 72-hour period for public review. All but one of the committee's Democrats voted to keep the process at warp speed—and the public in the dark.

The secrecy continued even after one committee passed its bill. The Senate Health, Education, Labor, and Pensions Committee voted for its health reform bill on a party-line vote over the summer, but it took *two months* for the final text to be made public. Only then was it apparent that Democratic staff had made more than seventy-five changes to the final legislative text that senators had approved.

While voting on bills that no one had read is outlandish enough, Pelosi had an even more outrageous idea. A *Washington Post* front-page headline said it all: "House may try to pass Senate health-care bill without voting on it." The plan was to bundle three bills together, including the bill that passed the Senate on Christmas Eve, whereby a vote on the combined bill would "deem" the underlying bills to have passed. Pelosi spelled out what attracted her to this strategy: "I like it because people don't have to vote on the Senate bill," she said. She wanted to spare Democrats from making a recorded vote for seedy, widely condemned payoffs like the Cornhusker Kickback and the Louisiana Purchase. After a fierce outcry from the public and even fellow House Democrats, the strategy was ultimately abandoned.

IGNORING THE AMERICAN PEOPLE

We remember the people's anger boiling over in August 2009, when Americans from all walks of life demanded answers and accountability from their representatives about healthcare reform. We saw budget hawks recoil in horror at the trillion-dollar price tags. We saw seniors outraged by the hundreds of billions of dollars in Medicare cuts. We saw people with disabilities speak out against the specter of government deciding the fate of their medical care. We saw pro-life supporters denounce proposed federal funding for abortion. We saw citizens demand that their tax dollars not pay for healthcare for illegal immigrants.

These protestors rose up in virtually every congressional district in the country. Afraid of facing their own constituents, some House Democrats stopped having townhall meetings. Others opted for safer "town calls" where they could screen participants over the phone. Virginia Democratic congressman Jim Moran even demanded to see the driver's license of one townhall attendee to verify he was a real constituent. (He was.) Meanwhile, Harry Reid compared congressmen who wanted a slower, more deliberative process to supporters of slavery.

As public anger erupted and the healthcare reform bills plunged in the polls, Washington Democrats continued their march ahead. They assumed machine politics could override the needs and desires of the American people.

Poll after poll showed Americans repudiating every aspect of the Democratic plan. Back in April 2009, an NBC/*Wall Street Journal* poll had found 33 percent of Americans favored the plan, with 26 percent opposed. By January 2010, the same poll showed support steady at 33 percent, while opposition shot up twenty points to 46 percent. Similarly, a January 2010 Rasmussen poll found just 12 percent of Americans believed the legislation would achieve the stated goal of reducing healthcare costs, while 60 percent thought it would increase costs.

The more the American people learned about the reform, the more adamantly they rejected it. Americans knew the Democrats' efforts were more about ideology than about solving real problems. Even the president said as much, telling House Democrats, "We need courage, that's what we need....We need an up or down vote—it's time to vote." Ask yourself this: why would members of Congress need courage if the American people supported what they were doing?

So why did Obama press ahead against the determined opposition of the American people? Because public opinion had nothing to do with the real goal of healthcare reform: to increase the power of the secular-socialist machine.

WHY WASN'T MEDICAL MALPRACTICE INCLUDED?

Medical malpractice reform enjoys near universal support: doctors, hospitals, businesses, insurers, and voters all want to fix tort law to eliminate frivolous lawsuits.

According to Rasmussen, by a margin of 57–29 percent, Americans want to limit the amount of money juries can award a plaintiff in medical malpractice lawsuits. Forty-seven percent believe restricting jury awards for medical malpractice lawsuits would significantly reduce the cost of healthcare in the United States, while just 28 percent disagree. And 48 percent believe it's too easy to sue for medical malpractice, while only 19 percent believe it's too hard.

Americans have long known that the threat of being sued forces doctors to practice medicine differently. They order more tests, do more procedures, and otherwise go out of their way to minimize the risk of a trial lawyer accusing them of not doing enough. Jackson Healthcare and Gallup asked doctors what percentage of their care is solely due to the threat of lawsuits. Doctors estimated 26 percent of their services—costing more than $650 billion every year—doesn't benefit the patient at all. In fact, it endangers patients by exposing them to higher risks of hospital-acquired infections, medical errors, and medication errors.

And all this unnecessary care drives up costs; even the Congressional Budget Office, one of the most risk adverse institutions in Washington, reported in September 2009 that medical liability reform would save $54 billion over ten years through lower malpractice insurance and more appropriate care. Some experts like Dr. Mark McClellan, who ran the Food and Drug Administration and the Centers for Medicare and Medicaid Services, peg the cost of defensive medicine at $120 billion *every year*.

You would think congressional Democrats, who were so desperate to fund their government takeover that they included a tax on indoor tanning services, would have jumped at the chance to save $54 billion. But tort reform went nowhere, despite wide public support from businesses to doctors to the public. President Obama only gave it a token acknowledgement after the Blair House summit, when he magnanimously suggested that Congress give $50 million to state pilot programs for tort reform. As Charles Krauthammer remarked, the president was offering "a few ridiculously insignificant demonstration projects amounting to one-half of one-hundredth of 1 percent of the cost of Obama's health-care bill." As if this proposal wasn't hollow enough, who did Obama task with overseeing tort reform? Kathleen Sebelius, Secretary of Health and Human Services—a former executive director of the Kansas Trial Lawyers Association.

Why do Democrats oppose tort reform? Former Democratic National Committee chairman Howard Dean answered that candidly at an August 2009 townhall meeting: "The reason why tort reform is not in the bill is because the people who wrote it did not want to take on the trial lawyers in addition to everybody else they were taking on, and that is the plain and simple truth."

He's right. Why would the Left take on trial lawyers, a key part of the secular-socialist machine? According to Federal Election Commission data, the Association of Trial Lawyers of America (now deceptively called the "American Association for Justice") has contributed more than $28 million to Democratic candidates since 1990—and less than $3 million to Republicans.

Nearly every aspect of the health reform debate—from process to policy—has followed this corrupt pattern: reward friends, punish and destroy enemies.

HOUSE MUSCLE

Of all the groups the Democrats demonized during the health-care debate, health insurers topped the list. Speaker Pelosi called them "evil," "immoral," and "villains." In the spirit of Joe McCarthy, Energy and Commerce Committee chairman Henry Waxman and Oversight and Investigations Subcommittee chairman Bart Stupak sent a letter to fifty-two of the nation's largest health insurance companies that contained a not-so-veiled threat.

The letter demanded detailed information about the companies' executive pay, conferences and corporate outings, and business practices. For any employees or officers making more than $500,000 a year going back to 2003, the congressmen demanded details on salaries, bonuses, pensions, and other compensation. They also insisted that insurance companies disclose the identity of all board members and their compensation.

Imagine that: two powerful Democrats launched an investigation of health insurance companies during a national debate over health insurance reform. Although Stupak later threatened to oppose the final reform bill because it allowed federal funding of abortion, he was always a strong advocate of Democratic reform and ultimately helped to deliver the key votes to pass it in the House. The message of the letter he and Waxman wrote to insurers was clear, if unstated: get on board with "reform," or we'll embarrass and investigate you until you do.

They were using raw political power to silence their opponents, plain and simple. If not, why did they single out insurance companies? Why didn't they ask the same questions of others, like physician groups, hospitals, and drug companies? It's no coincidence that the main lobbying organizations of the groups being left alone by Congress supported the Democrats' reform, while the insurance industry largely opposed it.

THIS IS USUALLY CALLED A BRIBE

To win final passage of his bill in the Senate, Harry Reid didn't use muscle. He used political payoffs. We already discussed the most egregious ones: Ben Nelson's Cornhusker Kickback, Senator Mary Landrieu's Louisiana Purchase, and the rest. The Democrats' own Russ Feingold, senator from Wisconsin, commented simply, "These 'sweeteners' are unjustifiable."

But perhaps the most outrageous of all sweetheart deals was struck by the congressional leaders, the White House, and organized labor. Union leaders adamantly opposed a provision in the Senate bill that would have levied a 40 percent tax on high-value health insurance plans, also known as "Cadillac" plans. These types of insurance plans, common among labor unions, are expensive because they cover so many services at very low costs to the individual.

This tax was a critical piece of the Senate bill that would have raised $149 billion, according to the CBO. But congressional Democrats could hardly afford to alienate such an important part of their machine as organized labor. So congressional Democrats struck a deal giving unions, along with state and local government workers, a 5-year exemption from the tax. Non-union plans would still pay, of course. AFL-CIO president Richard Trumka bragged that the payoff was worth $60 billion. Unsurprisingly, after securing the deal, Trumpka triumphantly announced union officials would support Obama's reform. Going even further, the final law pushed back the effective date of the tax to 2018 and raised the threshold so that only a few of the richest plans would be hit.

People know that deals happen every day in Washington. But the Left's health reform was something different—a parade of brazen political payoffs to ensure victory for a radical, deeply unpopular reform. In the world of the secular-socialist machine, it's called negotiating. In the real world, it's called bribery.

This naked display of the secular-socialist ideology and machine politics led to a stunning electoral upset in the special election to the U.S. Senate in Massachusetts. According to an exit poll by Tony Fabrizio of Fabrizio, McLaughlin & Associates, 39 percent of those who voted for the winner, Republican Scott Brown, did so specifically because of his opposition to the Democrats' health reform plan—and this occurred in one of the most heavily Democratic states in the country. This was for the Senate seat that had been held since 1962 by Ted Kennedy, who called universal healthcare the "cause of my life." It could not have been a clearer repudiation of the machine's healthcare machinations—and the Democrats ignored it anyway.

Repealing Obamacare and replacing it with a market-oriented, patient-focused, commonsense healthcare vision will be a central fight of the 2010 and 2012 elections. As I said earlier, reforming healthcare is one of the most critical problems we face. Our system kills people. It eats money. It threatens the future of our country. We have to fix it. I founded the Center for Health Transformation to create and advocate for the right ways to do that. You will find real health solutions in chapter fifteen of this book.

CHAPTER SIX

The Secular-Socialist Machine and ACORN's Vote Fraud

Since the secular-socialist machine has to lie about its misuse of government money and power, it is a short step to engineering dishonest elections. Voter fraud, along with corruption and deceptive language, form a triad of dishonesty that the machine relies upon to maintain power among a people who decisively oppose its goals.

With a vested interest in rigged elections, the Left have opposed efforts to curb voter fraud, such as state laws requiring a valid ID to vote as well as measures to cull deceased voters, felons, and former residents from voter rolls. The movement also actively *engages* in vote fraud, often using homeless people. We see this chicanery in local elections—such as Xavier Suarez's theft of the Miami electoral race with over 4,500 absentee ballots submitted by bribed homeless people—and on the national level—such as an Al Gore supporter bribing homeless people with cigarettes to vote in Minnesota during the 2000 presidential election.

The Left have also passed laws that make vote fraud easier. The first legislation signed by President Clinton was the 1993 Motor Voter law, which required states to offer the ability to register to vote without identification to anyone who shows up to an official office to use government services. States were also required to allow for mail-in voter registration—a method particularly susceptible to fraud—and they were prevented from clearing names from their voter rolls for at least eight years of those who had moved or died.

As a result, voter registration has jumped 20 percent, but improper registrations have also exploded. An *Indianapolis Star* investigation in 2000 reported that as many as one in five names on Indiana's voter rolls was invalid.

By abolishing ID requirements, Motor Voter has allowed illegal aliens to register to vote. A 1996 investigation in Orange County, California, found that more than 4,000 illegal voters may have cast ballots in the congressional race between Robert Dornan and Loretta Sanchez. Dornan lost by less than 1,000 votes.

Every time responsible legislators introduce bills to approve ID requirements for voting or to allow states to keep their voter rolls up to date, the secular-socialist machine responds with charges of racism. For instance, a 2005 Georgia law requiring an ID to cast a ballot was challenged in court by left-wing organizations that claimed it disenfranchised the poor and minorities. During the course of two years of litigation, however, the plaintiffs could not find a *single* eligible voter in Georgia who was disenfranchised by the Georgia law.

The sad truth about the spurious cries of racism is that the real disenfranchisement of American voters comes *from* voter fraud, not from efforts to *prevent* it. After all, every fraudulent vote cancels out the vote of an honest citizen.

ACORN: TAKING YOUR TAXES TO STEAL YOUR VOTE

Of all the parts of the secular-socialist machine engaging in vote fraud, ACORN (Association of Community Organizers for Reform Now) is the most notorious. Its criminal behavior and thuggish tactics are a perfectly logical product of the secular-socialist rejection of the virtue of honesty. It makes a mockery of the American ideal of "one person, one vote."

ACORN's agenda is, as Sol Stern wrote in *City Journal*, "anti-capitalism, central planning, victimology and government handouts." As documented in Michelle Malkin's *Culture of Corruption*, in addition to conducting fraudulent voter registration efforts—for which ACORN workers have repeatedly been indicted—the group pickets the houses of bankers and uses other forms of intimidation to pressure banks to give home loans to the poor (who can't afford them). As recently as 2009, the group staged an illegal break-in of a foreclosed home as a PR stunt.

Nate Toler, who worked for ACORN until late 2006 on voter registration drives and on a campaign against Wal-Mart, spoke to the *Wall Street Journal* about the organization's dishonesty. "The internal motto is, 'We don't care if it's a lie, just so long as it stirs up the conversation.'" On ACORN's voter registration efforts, he said, "There's no quality control on purpose, no checks and balances."

Similarly, Mac Stuart, a former Florida ACORN employee, has accused the group of failing to deliver registration cards marked "Republican," accepting applications from felons, and falsifying information.

Wall Street Journal columnist John Fund has written arguably the definitive work on vote fraud and vote theft in America. In *Stealing Elections* he outlines the multi-faceted strategies the secular-socialist machine employs to fraudulently register voters and to strike down anti-fraud laws. Fund's many ACORN-related examples demonstrate the group's shocking disrespect for the law. In July 2007, for example, prosecutors indicted seven Seattle ACORN workers for turning in falsified registration forms. As Fund explains,

> The list of "voters" registered in Washington included former House Speaker Dennis Hastert, *New York Times* columnists Frank Rich and Tom Friedman, and actress Katie Holmes, as well as nonexistent people with nonsensical names such as Stormi Bays and Fruto Boy. The addresses used for the fake names were local homeless shelters.[1]

Fund then notes the rules that enable this fraud: "Given that the state doesn't require the showing of any identification before voting, it is entirely possible that people could have voted illegally using some of those names."

Overall, of 1,805 names submitted by ACORN in King County, over 97 percent were found to be invalid. Washington's secretary of state called it "the worst case of voter registration fraud" in the state's history.

There's more.

In spring 2008, county registrar's offices in Louisiana noticed a huge increase in the number of suspicious and outright fraudulent voter registration forms. In Shreveport, the registrar's office reported that only 2,200 of its 6,000 forms were valid. The mischief was traced back to ACORN and to a national Democratic Party effort called Voting Is Power. After they were caught, instead of promising to clean up their act, Democrats hurled meaningless accusations at the registrar's offices. "Instead of throwing up complaints, they should be working to get as many people as possible registered," said Matt Miller, a spokesman for the Democratic Senatorial Campaign Committee.

That was no isolated incident. In Kansas City, Missouri, four ACORN employees pleaded guilty to registration fraud in November 2006. Forty percent of the 35,000 registrations submitted by

ACORN there were found to be fraudulent.

And in St. Louis, Missouri, eight ACORN workers pleaded guilty to federal election fraud in April 2008. City officials claimed more than 1,000 of the addresses on the registration forms submitted by ACORN during that election cycle didn't exist.

What makes these stories even more outrageous is that ACORN has been a steady recipient of government funding throughout its 40-year history. Until recently, taxpayer dollars accounted for up to 40 percent of its budget. According to the *Washington Examiner*, ACORN received $53 million in federal funds between 1994 and 2009. Most of this money was supposed to fund housing assistance programs, but it would be naïve to think none of this money actually went to ACORN's other activities, like its corrupt voting drives.

In fact, we *know* ACORN manipulated its funds in this way. In 1994, the ACORN Housing Corporation (AHC) received a $1.1 million grant from AmeriCorps, the federal volunteer agency. ACORN claimed the AHC was a separate entity from ACORN, but the grant was cancelled a year later after the inspector general for AmeriCorps found that "AHC used AmeriCorps grant funds to benefit ACORN either directly or indirectly," including its lobbying activities and growing its membership roles.

And yet, the flow of government money to ACORN continued anyway.

OBAMA AND ACORN

Despite its long association with voter fraud efforts, the Obama White House enlisted ACORN as an official partner of the U.S. Census Bureau to help recruit more than a million census-takers for 2010. Judicial Watch, a government watchdog group, noted that "the Census Bureau offered ACORN the opportunity to 'recruit Census workers' who would participate in the count. Moreover, as an 'executive level, partner, ACORN has the ability to 'organize and/or serve as a member on a Complete Count Committee,' which, according to Census documents, helps 'develop and implement locally based outreach and recruitment campaigns.'"

That the White House should enlist an organization specializing in voter fraud to help organize the census should not be surprising, considering President Obama's long history with the group. As detailed in *Stealing Elections*, in 1993 Obama ran a voter registration drive in Illinois that helped to get Democrat Carol Moseley Braun elected to the U.S. Senate. Obama conducted that campaign for Project Vote, an ACORN-affiliated group that later worked for Obama's presidential campaign.

Obama served as ACORN's attorney in 1995, when the group sued Illinois governor Jim Edgar to implement the Motor Voter law in Illinois. Obama also trained ACORN members in community organizing tactics and provided ACORN with funding as a board member of the Woods Fund, a foundation that funds left-wing organizations and causes.

In 1996, Obama filled out a questionnaire in advance of his Illinois state senate run. When asked which groups would support his campaign, he listed ACORN first. And as a U.S. Senator, he echoed ACORN'S criticism of voter ID laws. As Obama said himself in a February 2008 speech to ACORN leaders,

> I've been fighting alongside ACORN on issues you care about my entire career. Even before I was an elected official, when I ran Project Vote voter registration drive in Illinois, ACORN was smack dab in the middle of it, and we appreciate your work.

Before he became president, Obama proudly and publicly declared that ACORN-style "community organizing" groups would influence his administration. When asked at a December 2007 Democratic campaign forum for community organizers whether he'd meet with a delegation of community groups at the beginning of his presidency, Obama replied,

> Before I even get inaugurated, during the transition, we're going to be calling all of you in to help us shape the agenda. We're going to be having meetings all across the country with community organizations so that you have input into the agenda of the next presidency of the United States of America.

Once in power, the Obama administration went to remarkable lengths to protect ACORN, as seen in its handling of complaints of ACORN voter registration fraud during the 2008 election in two Connecticut cities, Stamford and Bridgeport. According to complaints submitted by the towns' Republican registrars of voters, ACORN submitted hundreds of invalid registrations including, for example, a 7-year-old who was registered using a forged signature and a fake birth certificate. Based on FBI documents, Judicial Watch disclosed that soon after Obama took office, his Justice Department closed down an official investigation of the cases, claiming ACORN had not done anything illegal.

Judicial Watch president Tom Fitton did not mince words about how the investigation was quashed:

> These documents reflect systematic voter registration fraud by ACORN. It is a scandal that there has been no comprehensive criminal investigation and prosecution by the Justice Department into this evident criminal conduct. Given President Obama's close connections to ACORN, including his campaign's hiring of the ACORN's Project Vote organization, it seems rather obvious why Attorney

General Holder has failed to seriously investigate these and other alleged ACORN criminal activities.[2]

THE RESILIENCY OF
THE SECULAR-SOCIALIST MACHINE

Many observers thought ACORN's rampant law-breaking was finally over in September 2009, when an undercover filmmaker released footage of employees from multiple ACORN offices advising him, while posing as a pimp, and his partner, who posed as a prostitute, how to set up a child prostitution ring. Responding to public outrage, Congress overwhelmingly approved a law barring ACORN from receiving federal money. (A judge later overturned the law, though Congress did not give ACORN any more funds.) The uproar also cost ACORN its role in the 2010 census.

ACORN seemed to be on the ropes. In Ohio, as part of a legal settlement, the group agreed to cease operating in the entire state. The *Columbus Dispatch* reported,

> ACORN was active in Ohio in the 2006 and 2008 elections, working to register thousands of low-income people to vote and get them to the polls. The group's efforts were marred by irregularities, including one case in which ACORN workers allegedly induced a Cleveland man to register to vote 72 times, offering cigarettes as an incentive.[3]

The victory, however, was short-lived, showing just how resilient the secular-socialist machine is. While the national ACORN organization has shut down, many of the group's branches have simply re-formed under new names while using the same tactics to pursue the same agenda.

In addition to federal money, the "new" groups will be eligible to receive money from the states—and that's a lot. As the *Washington Times* reported in February 2010, shortly before ACORN disbanded, ACORN was eligible for up to $4 billion in HUD Community Development Block Grants (CDBGs) that are doled out by state and local governments. Matthew Vadum, a senior editor at Capital Research Center, told the *Times* it's difficult to track the money once it goes through state and local governments. "Nobody knows how much ACORN, which has hundreds of different affiliates, has actually received over the years in CDBG funding," he said.

In other words, it's business as usual for the machine.

CHAPTER SEVEN

Why Big Business and the Secular-Socialist Machine Are Natural Allies

T he Left love to bash big business on behalf of the "little guy." Their rhetoric goes like this: *We'll use the power of government to protect consumers from the greedy robber barons of big business who constantly rip off customers and employees. Meanwhile, conservatives, at the behest of their corporate donors, cruelly block liberals from passing new laws protecting Americans from these evil corporations.*

There's just one problem with this narrative: it bears zero resemblance to reality.

Here is a more accurate narrative: big business knows the greatest threat to its survival is not government regulation, but competition with smaller, more innovative firms. So when the opportunity arises to cooperate with government in crafting new regulations for their industry, big business lobbyists don't oppose the reforms; instead, they help write the laws to their own advantage.

The sordid truth of the Left's push for ever-greater regulation of private industry is this: it is not meant to protect consumers against big business. It's meant to bring big business into their political machine.

The Left's message to business is simple: support our regulatory schemes or get crushed. In other words, either take a seat at the table, or risk being on the menu. And they know that big business— the only ones that can afford a seat at the table—will pay whatever it takes to join them.

In light of the Democrats' anti-big-business pose, many people are surprised to learn how much their supposed adversaries support them. As detailed in *Obamanomics*, a book by *Washington Examiner* lobbying editor Timothy Carney, during the 2008 election cycle, the securities, health insurance, and pharmaceutical industries, and even many of the biggest oil companies, gave more money to Democrats than Republicans.

This is nothing new. As the regulatory state has grown, big business has learned to use big government to protect itself from small business rivals. Meanwhile, the secular-socialist machine gladly accepts money and support from business interests. The Left can often easily pass new regulations when they get big business on board, and these laws help both parties: the Left create the illusion they're standing up for the little guy, and big business gets clauses put into the laws that damage their small competitors.

National Review editor Jonah Goldberg discusses the long history of big-government corporatism in his book *Liberal Fascism*, and Amity Shlaes explores the same phenomenon in her account of the Great Depression, *The Forgotten Man*. This history is incredibly instructive, though not well-known. For example, the regulatory reforms of the meat packing industry in the early 1900s, inspired by Upton Sinclair's muckraking book *The Jungle*, were enacted with the enthusiastic cooperation of America's largest meat packing corporations. That's because they knew only the largest corporations could afford to comply with the new regulations, which drove their smaller competitors out of business. Sinclair himself wrote in 1906, "The Federal inspection of meat was, historically, established at the packers' request. It is maintained and paid for by the people of the United States for the benefit of the packers."

There are countless similar examples. For instance, the railroad magnates of the late 1800s encouraged the government to protect them from smaller railroad lines, price wars, and the patchwork of inconsistent state laws. Although today's textbooks claim the government formed the Interstate Commerce Commission to stop the big railroad companies, in fact the Commission helped these companies to guarantee profits, squash competition, and ensure regulations worked in their favor. Then-Attorney General Richard Olney made this clear in an 1892 letter to Charles E. Pickering, President of the Chicago, Burlington, and Quincy Railroad:

> The Commission... can be made of great use to the railroads. It satisfies the popular clamor for a government supervision of the railroads, at the same time that the supervision is almost entirely nominal. Further, the older such a commission gets to be, the more it will be found to take the business and railroad view of things.... The part of wisdom is not to destroy the Commission, but to utilize it.

This pattern continued through the twentieth century as the regulatory state expanded. The famous lawyer Clarence Darrow, in his investigative report on the National Recovery Administration, part of President Roosevelt's New Deal, noted,

> [I]n virtually all the codes we have examined, one condition has been present.... In Industry after Industry, the larger units, sometimes through the agency of a [trade association],

sometimes by other means, have for their own advantage written the codes, and then, in effect and for their own advantage, assumed the administration of the code they have framed.

We heard a more callous view of this trend during the Clinton administration's attempt to take over healthcare. When the objection was raised that HillaryCare would drive many small insurers out of business, Hillary Clinton coldly responded, "I can't go out and save every undercapitalized entrepreneur in America."

And that's how much the Left really care about the little guy.

THE OBAMA-PELOSI-REID BIG BUSINESS AGENDA

The big business–big government alliance is alive and well today, despite the anti-business rhetoric of the Obama-Pelosi-Reid regime.

Timothy Carney has described the simple rule guiding the legislative process today: "No important bill passes unless a well connected special interest benefits from it." This, of course, reflects Saul Alinsky's rule that organizing should be based on self-interest.

Carney has written an astounding series of columns outlining how the miasma of new regulations and bureaucracies created by the Obama administration was authored by big business interests to benefit big business at the expense of their smaller competitors.

For instance, consider the food safety bill approved by the House of Representatives in July 2009, which will probably be debated in the Senate in 2010. Industry giants like the Kellogg food company and the Grocery Manufacturers of America heavily lobbied for the bill, which is also supported by President Obama. A collection of organic food advocates and small farms oppose the bill, and with good reason: the Farm to Consumer Legal Defense Fund says the bill will "break the backs of small farmers." Moreover, the Centers for Disease Control has noted that the bill, by further centralizing food production, could increase the risk of food contamination.

Consider Obama's healthcare reform. Although proponents often pitched the bill as a way to reign in big drug companies, the lobbying group for those very companies, PhRMA, pledged to spend $150 million to *support* the bill. Why? Because the new law offers drug companies lucrative benefits:

- It prohibits the use of funds from Health Savings Accounts for over-the-counter medications. This would encourage Americans to buy expensive prescription drugs made by big drug companies. It would also create inefficiencies by providing an incentive to go to the doctor for a prescription rather than simply buying medication over the counter.
- The bill's "individual mandate" requires every American to buy prescription drug insurance, which would further increase sales of prescription drugs.
- The bill creates special monopolies for complex drugs, called "biologics," that would get a special 12-year patent instead of the standard 5-year protection. Another provision extends the patent of one specific drug, Angiomax, through 2014.

We see the same big business–big government back scratching in the cap-and-trade bill. This is supposedly meant to punish big carbon polluters, yet many of America's biggest corporations joined together in the United States Climate Action Partnership to lobby *for* cap and trade. These firms, including PepsiCo, Dow Chemical, GE, Shell, and the Big Three automakers, aim to game the government's process for distributing carbon credits to gain an advantage over their smaller competitors. Since these credits will be traded on the open market, the government would essentially be giving the corporations free money.

You may also be surprised to learn that one of the biggest advocates of The Family Smoking Prevention and Tobacco Control Act, which gave the FDA the power to regulate tobacco, was Philip Morris, far and away America's largest cigarette manufacturer. The Philip Morris parent company, Altria, spent an average of $40,000 a day lobbying for the bill over five years. This, to say the least, casts doubt on President Obama's declaration that the bill passed "despite decades of lobbying and advertising by the tobacco industry." As Carney notes, the bill was opposed, as usual, by smaller manufacturers. After all, new marketing restrictions on cigarettes hurt lesser-known brands much more than famous ones.

Here's a final example: when the IRS recently proposed new regulations requiring all tax preparers to register with the IRS, pay fees, pass certification tests, and participate in continuing education programs, the rules earned the vociferous support of H&R Block, Jackson Hewitt, and Liberty Tax, three of America's biggest tax preparers. The reason was explained in a UBS analysis: the rules would make it more difficult for small tax preparers to enter the market. Additionally, the regulations would allow H&R Block to make money selling its own continuing education programs and certifications to other firms.

Thus, it's no surprise, really, that a former H&R Block executive, Deputy Commissioner Mark Ernst, is an Obama administration appointee at the IRS. Furthermore, H&R Block lobbying is done by the Podesta Group, a firm founded by John Podesta, the director of the Obama presidential transition.

So the next time a left-wing politician proposes new regulations to protect you from big business, look behind the scenes to see who will really profit. It probably isn't who you think.

CHAPTER EIGHT

The Corruption of Climate Science by the Secular-Socialist Machine

Conservatives, left-wingers argue, are "anti-science." President Obama implicitly made the accusation during his 2010 State of the Union speech, when he claimed opponents of cap-and-trade energy taxes "disagree with the overwhelming scientific evidence on climate change."

This sort of demagoguery is typical of the elitist Left; they explain the unpopularity of their values by suggesting they simply know better than the majority of ignorant Americans. Of course, the Left happily ignore and reject overwhelming scientific evidence when it's convenient for their agenda of expanding the regulatory state and enriching their allies.

For instance, trial lawyers, a key source of money for the secular-socialist machine, are incredibly "anti-science" in their willingness to rely on junk science to gin up lawsuits. This was borne out in a 2004 study by Dr. Joseph N. Gitlin. Six outside physician consultants were asked to review 492 chest X-rays that had previously been evaluated by physician experts (called B-readers) hired by plaintiffs in asbestos lawsuits. While the B-readers found evidence of asbestos-related damage in 95 percent of the X-rays, the outside group only found it in 4.5 percent.[1]

The origins of today's radical environmental movement provide a more disturbing example. That movement launched with a successful effort in the 1960s to effectively ban the insecticide DDT worldwide. This led to the reemergence of malaria in Africa, which has caused 1–2 million preventable deaths a year, according to the American Council on Science and Health. The crusade against DDT contradicts overwhelming evidence that the correct use of the chemical does not harm humans or the environment.

Likewise, the Luddite Left reject the use of all genetically modified crops despite their scientifically proven safety. Thus, for purely ideological reasons, these extremists oppose the cultivation of "golden rice," a modified strain of rice with beta-carotene (vitamin A). This crop represents an enormous potential health breakthrough for more than 100 million people in the third world who suffer from vitamin A deficiency, a condition that can cause blindness and other major problems, especially in children.

Similar examples abound: due to a left-wing demonization campaign, the process of food irradiation, which could have prevented America's 2006 e-coli outbreak, is barely used in the United States despite repeated tests verifying its safety.

But perhaps no anti-scientific argument is more dangerous today than the claim put forward by radical environmentalists, most notably Robert F. Kennedy Jr., that childhood vaccinations can cause autism. Numerous peer-reviewed studies have disproved this connection. Moreover, the *Lancet*, a prominent British journal that published a 1998 study confirming a vaccination-autism connection, recently retracted the study, whose findings had already been repudiated by ten of its thirteen co-authors.[2]

Yet some parents, worried by these rumors, have stopped vaccinating their children, endangering public health. Dr. Melinda Wharton of the U.S. Centers for Disease Control and Prevention told the AP that unvaccinated children contributed to measles outbreaks in 2008 in California, Illinois, Washington, Arizona, and New York. She added, "If we don't vaccinate, these diseases will come back."[3]

When their anti-scientific arguments are causing the return of deadly diseases once thought to have been eradicated in the United States, it's hard to see how the Left truly champion science.

CLIMATEGATE

Ironically, by using science as a weapon to further their political agenda, the Left are corrupting the very scientific process they claim to uphold.

This is shockingly evident in climate science. Indeed, recent revelations about the degree of groupthink, coercion, and financial corruption in this field make it seem more like a political machine than a community dedicated to pursuing scientific truth.

Reports by the United Nation's Intergovernmental Panel on Climate Change have been one of the major sources of information upon which international leaders have proposed action to curb greenhouse gas emissions. Known as the Fourth Assessment Report (AR4), the most recent report in 2007 won the IPCC, along with Al Gore, the Nobel Peace Prize. However, startling revelations have shown the report manipulated scientific research to further a political agenda.

The scandal emerged when an Internet hacker published emails from the Climate Research Unit (CRU) at Britain's University of

East Anglia, one of the IPCC's main sources of data. The emails showed a remarkably hostile and unscientific attitude among CRU scientists and their allies toward anyone who questioned their alarmist data on global warming.

In one exchange, scientists plotted to keep global warming skeptics from being published in peer-reviewed literature. The existence of this orchestrated campaign undermines a common argument from global warming alarmists—that skeptics should be ignored, because their findings are usually not peer reviewed.

Emails also suggested climate scientists were motivated more by money than scientific integrity. Here's a passage from one such email, in which a climate researcher asks how he should respond to an article by a global warming skeptic:

> How should I respond to the below? I'm in the process of trying to persuade Siemens Corp. (a company with half a million employees in 190 countries!) to donate me a little cash to do some CO2 measurements here in the UK—looking promising, so the last thing I need is news articles calling into question (again) observed temperature increases.[4]

These grants were no small potatoes: CRU director Phil Jones, who temporarily resigned that position after the emails were published, received an astounding $19 million in grants between 2000 and 2006[5]—including money from the U.S. Department of Energy, according to Britain's *Daily Telegraph*.[6] As Professor Ross McKitrick, a climate change skeptic who was mentioned in some of the CRU emails, noted, "Climate sceptics are always accused of taking money from industry but it is now clear the money is on the other side.... [Climate change scientists] are enjoying a funding gravy train."

The emails also suggested CRU scientists manipulated data to exaggerate warming trends. In the most famous email, Phil Jones discussed a "trick" to "hide the decline" in recent historical temperatures. When pressed, CRU admitted it had deleted the raw climate data from its servers. The lack of raw data justifying many of the CRU's findings has been a key complaint of skeptics, who rightfully argue that normal scientific practice requires scientists to make this information available for scrutiny by other scientists.

In a further blow to the CRU's credibility, the emails showed scientists discussing ways to avoid Freedom of Information Act requests, for example, by deleting correspondence and other information that might be sought. That seems to have been a particular concern for Phil Jones. In one email he writes, "Mike, can you delete any emails you may have had with Keith re AR4. . . . Can you also email Gene and get him to do the same. . . . We will be letting Caspar to do likewise." Another email from Jones is even more damning:

> The two MMs have been after the CRU station data for years. If they ever hear there is a Freedom of Information Act now in the UK, I think I'll delete the file rather than send to anyone. . . . We also have a data protection act, which I will hide behind. Tom Wigley has sent me a worried email when he heard about it—thought people could ask him for his model code. He has retired officially from UEA so he can hide behind that.[7]

The United Kingdom Information Commission found that the efforts to avoid Freedom of Information Act disclosures may have been illegal, but they could not be prosecuted because the statute of limitations had expired.

THE CORRUPTION OF THE IPCC REPORT

The Climategate scandal, as it became known, led to increasing scrutiny of the IPCC report. This resulted in new revelations undermining the report itself.

Several sources used in the report were not scientific or peer-reviewed studies, but talking points lifted from political organizations or recreational magazine articles. For instance, the report argued 40 percent of the Amazon's forests could be drastically affected by drier weather created by global warming—a claim taken from the World Wildlife Fund, an activist group that lobbies for big-government environmental policies like cap and trade.

One of the report's most controversial claims—that climate change was increasing the number and severity of natural disasters—also came from a non-peer reviewed source at the time. When the study was finally published in 2008, it included a key addendum: "We find insufficient evidence to claim a statistical relationship between global temperature increase and catastrophic losses."[8]

Equally embarrassing were the sources of the report's claims that ice is rapidly melting on the world's mountaintops, and that there is a "very high" possibility the Himalayan glaciers will disappear by 2035. The first claim was based on anecdotes from a *Climbing* magazine article and a student paper. The second claim once again came from the World Wildlife Fund.

The warning of disappearing Himalayan glaciers was particularly startling, since it could potentially affect hundreds of millions of Asians who depend on the glaciers as a source of water. The scientist who put the claim in the report, Dr. Murari Lal, later admitted it was included for purely political reasons: "We thought that if we can highlight it, it will impact policy-makers and politicians and encourage them to take some concrete action."

Unfortunately, the corruption of climate science goes beyond the IPCC and the CRU. A computer programmer named E. Michael

Smith recently discovered that NASA's Goddard Science and Space Institute and NOAA's Climate Data Center in North Carolina reduced the number of their temperature data stations from 6,000 in the 1970s to 1,500 in 1990. Most of the lost stations were in colder climates, creating a bias toward warmer readings.

If politics were poker, you could say the Left went "all in" on global warming, willing to use any means necessary to achieve their goals.

THE ENDGAME

The distressing corruption of climate science is intended to justify intrusive and coercive policies that the American people overwhelmingly oppose. Americans don't want to be banned from using our own natural resources, we don't want our companies bankrupted by suffocating regulations, and we don't want cap-and-trade energy taxes. But these are key goals of the secular socialists, because these policies centralize power in their machine.

Allowing American individuals and businesses to develop a vast, cheap supply of energy, as occurred throughout most of American history, doesn't further socialist goals. To the contrary, this kind of independent initiative threatens the machine. They say our energy development must be carefully planned, strictly regulated, and vigilantly overseen—and they just happen to be the planners, regulators, and overseers.

Secular socialists claim to champion science, yet they debase, distort, and deny the scientific process to further their political agenda. Science is supposed to be an open process of discovery and peer review, yet the most influential global warming alarmists worked furiously to hide their data and silence dissenting views. Meanwhile, the Left point to these scientists' corrupt, politicized research as "evidence" that the earth faces an imminent environmental apocalypse unless we adopt their extremist green policies.

In the end, secular socialists view science much like they view morality: it's just another tool to exploit for gaining and maintaining power.

CHAPTER NINE

Corruption at the United Nations

The United Nations was formed after World War II as a vehicle for world leaders to promote peace, human rights, and economic development. Tragically, from these noble origins, the UN has evolved into a corrupt, inept, bureaucratic machine that protects the world's worst dictatorships.

In some ways, the UN machine is even worse than the machine of the American Left; first, since even the most despotic governments are entitled to UN membership, the UN is not limited by elections or the need to keep up democratic appearances. And second, lacking America's legal framework for government transparency, the organization is even more prone to corruption than is the American Left.

Despite the fact that a handful of Western democracies pay the vast majority of the UN's annual budget (the United States alone pays 22 percent), the UN's most influential voting block is a group of 130 undeveloped countries called the G-77. Using the UN's one country–one vote system, the G-77 has hijacked the UN to turn it into a mechanism for redistributing wealth from developed to developing countries.

The most recent and dramatic example came out of the December 2009 UN Summit on Climate Change in Copenhagen. The agreement emerging from the conference called for transferring $100 billion a year from developed to undeveloped countries, a move ostensibly meant to repay the so-called "climate debt" that rich countries owe poor ones. One of the proposed methods for transferring this money is a 2 percent global tax on international monetary transactions among industrialized countries—in other words, taxation without representation.

Redistributing wealth is not some side project at the United Nations; it is the organization's main purpose today. In November 2009, a resolution sponsored by a number of oppressive and Marxist states, including China, Cuba, Iran, Nicaragua, Russia, Sudan, and Venezuela, and passed largely thanks to the G-77 block, called for, among other things, "the promotion of equitable access to benefits from international distribution of wealth."[1] It also reaffirms the need "to work urgently for the establishment of an international economic order . . . which shall correct inequalities and redress existing injustices, [and] make it possible to eliminate the widening gap between the developed world and the developing countries."[2]

Pursuing this agenda, it's unsurprising the G-77 uses its voting muscle to empower deeply anti-American, anti-Israel, and avowedly socialist activists within the UN bureaucracy.

For instance, a current member of the Human Rights Council Advisory Committee is Swiss national Jean Ziegler, who calls the United States an "imperialist dictatorship" whose trade embargo against Cuba constitutes "genocide." Another top UN diplomat is

Nicaraguan Miguel d'Escoto, President of the UN General Assembly for the 2008–2009 session. A former foreign minister in Daniel Ortega's far-left Sandinista government in the 1980s, he called Ronald Reagan a "butcher" and Israel an "apartheid" state. He also deemed Evo Morales, the staunchly socialist and anti-American Bolivian president, "World Hero of Mother Earth," and declared Fidel Castro "World Hero of Solidarity." D'Escoto claimed these human rights abusers "embody the virtues and values worth emulation by all of us."

These are the kinds of figures who run the UN bureaucracy. Attempts by Western democracies to elect responsible people with successful track records are routinely stymied, since we're outnumbered at the UN by the various interest blocs of the developing world. As a result, the UN has descended into an abyss of anti-Western extremism that will almost certainly grow even worse before it ever gets better.

INSTITUTIONALIZED CORRUPTION

Like all socialist machines, the UN is rife with corruption. It starts with the budgeting process. The UN website says the budget for 2008–2009 was $4.171 billion.[3] But this number does not include "extra-budgetary" items such as peacekeeping operations or UN organizations such as the UN Development Program and the World Food Program, which consume as much as $12 billion a year.

In fact, the UN's finances are so opaque that nobody knows what the annual budget really is. In 2009, when pressed by *Forbes* magazine about budget figures, the spokesperson for the Secretary General shockingly admitted that the budget is "not something that we keep track of in any systematic way."[4] Predictably, this lack of transparency facilitates massive corruption, the most infamous scandal being the Oil-for-Food program, from which Saddam Hussein's

Baath Party siphoned off an estimated $10 billion. A UN committee later found that the program's head, Benon Sevan, had received bribes and illicit kickbacks from the Iraqi government.

Since then, numerous reform efforts have been blocked or rendered toothless. The Procurement Task Force, an anti-fraud unit created in 2006 following the Oil-for-Food scandal, is a great example. After identifying fraud and waste in numerous UN programs, the program was shut down in 2009 due to pressure from Russia and Singapore, whose citizens had been cited by the task force for corruption.

Simply put, corruption is accepted and expected at the UN. And like the Left's political machine in the United States, reform efforts run up against systemic resistance. UN secretary general Ban Ki Moon has yet to approve a permanent director of investigation for the Office of Internal Oversight Services after more than two years. In fact, he has repeatedly blocked the person recommended by an independent panel, apparently because he's American.

Consequently, even after the Oil-for-Food scandal, corruption still runs rampant at the UN. For instance:

- One of the local UN Office for Project Service directors in Afghanistan spent $200,000 of UN funds to renovate his guesthouse.[5]
- The UN's auditors in the Sudan mission found UN personnel wasted $1.2 million in unused hotel rooms.[6]
- The UN's estimate for renovations to its New York City headquarters in 2003 was initially $953 million, then revised to $1.2 billion. By 2009, the estimate reached $1.9 billion.[7] The United States initially offered to finance the entire renovation with a low-interest loan, thus isolating the funding stream to create more accountability. But that method apparently didn't provide enough opportu-

nity for graft, so the funds were routed through the regular, unaccountable budgeting process. Even Donald Trump testified to Congress that his company could have taken over the project and completed the renovation for $700 million but was turned down.[8]

- Investigations into the UN Development Programme (UNDP), whose executive committee is chaired by Iran, showed that Kim Jong-Il's regime siphoned off aid sent for the North Korean people and also embezzled computers, software, and satellite receiving devices and spectrometers that can be used in military and nuclear weapons.[9]

- A 2007 audit by the Office of Internal Oversight Services of $1.4 billion in peacekeeping contracts showed that $619 million was subject to corruption—an astounding 44 percent corruption rate.[10]

The UN's culture of corruption begets more severe acts of lawlessness. UN personnel have been accused of sexual exploitation, including rape, in eleven countries. The worst cases were in the Congo, with thirty-eight allegations of sexual abuse and exploitation reported in 2008 alone. Additionally, the BBC[11] and Human Rights Watch[12] have both reported the UN has suppressed evidence of crimes committed by their peacekeepers in the Congo, including arms trafficking with the Congolese militia.

The UN tolerates corruption for a specific reason: it's viewed as another way to transfer wealth from developed to developing countries. But the beneficiaries of this graft are not poverty-stricken families suffering under dictatorships. To the contrary, the illicit funds go straight to their oppressors—the privileged, powerful bureaucrats that prop up despotic regimes.

BETRAYING HUMAN RIGHTS

Even though it was created in part to defend human rights, the UN has amassed an abysmal human rights record.

The UN Human Rights Council is a perverse, Orwellian institution that mainly acts to protect human rights abusers from international condemnation. With membership extended to oppressive nations like China, Saudi Arabia, and Cuba, the council focuses on condemning two countries: the United States and Israel.

In 2008, the council condemned Israel for human rights violations 120 times and the United States twenty-seven times, respectively. Meanwhile, dictatorships in China, Iran, and Cuba were condemned just nineteen, seventeen, and six times, respectively.

It's bad enough that human rights abusers use the council to protect each other. But in one unconscionable episode, the council has even abetted mass murder. In 2007, the UN recalled its human rights monitors from Sudan in the midst of the Darfur genocide due to pressure from China and Egypt. Just months later, in a stunning display of moral depravity, the G-77 selected the butchers of Sudan to chair its block for the 2009–2010 sessions.

Efforts to reform the UN human rights apparatus have failed. Ironically, the Human Rights Council itself stems from an attempt to reform its predecessor, the UN Commission on Human Rights, which also protected human rights abusers and condemned Western democracies.

Replacing the commission with a new, functioning human rights body was one of the recommendations of the Task Force on UN Reform, which I co-chaired with former Senate majority leader George Mitchell in 2005. Although this general idea was adopted, it couldn't survive the UN machine which, by refusing our recommendation to set strict standards for membership in the new council, insured the new body was just as much of a farce as its predecessor.

The Bush administration rightly withheld funding for the new council and boycotted its meetings in 2007 and 2008. But the Obama administration reversed course and joined the group, claiming the United States could reform the corrupt council by "engaging" it. The results have been appalling. While U.S. participation has not improved the council one iota, it *has* made the United States complicit in suppressing human rights throughout the globe.

For instance, at the behest of the Islamic bloc, the Human Rights Council has passed resolutions calling on governments to outlaw "defamation of religion." Typically, Islam is the only specific religion mentioned in these statutes, showing their true purpose is to ban criticism of Islam worldwide. This gives Islamic dictatorships the cover of international law to assault free speech, both at home and internationally, such as their efforts to censor the Danish Mohammad cartoons of 2005. While most Americans were horrified by the deadly rioting that broke out after the cartoons' publications, the UN's Islamic bloc insisted the problem was really that Western governments allowed newspapers to publish these "defamatory" cartoons in the first place.

Under Presidents Clinton and Bush, the United States rightly opposed UN anti-defamation measures. But that's changed under the Obama administration. Although it voted against some anti-defamation resolutions, it has not only supported but even co-sponsored one such measure. Condemning broad abstractions like "negative stereotyping of religions and racial groups," the resolution contradicts the spirit, if not the letter, of the First Amendment.

Furthermore, its overwhelming support for the Goldstone Report suggests the council is not being improved by United States membership. The report, assessing the 2008–2009 conflict between Israel and Hamas, accused both sides of war crimes. This was a textbook case of moral equivalence between a victim acting in self-defense—Israel— and an aggressor—the terrorist group Hamas, which provoked the conflict by targeting Israeli civilians with hundreds of rockets. The report even denied Hamas endangered Gaza civilians, a claim disproved when Israel released the 500-page Malam report, which published declassified photos, videos, interrogation records, and other evidence showing Hamas committed gross war crimes by operating out of mosques, schools, and hospitals.

THE LONG, HARD ROAD TO REFORM

It has now been almost five years since the Task Force on UN Reform, which I co-chaired, issued its recommendations. The task force was bipartisan, so its recommendations were not as aggressive as I would have preferred. Still, we agreed upon practical reforms that would turn the UN into a more effective champion of freedom and human rights around the globe.[*] Among them:

- Create an independent internal oversight board, functioning like a corporate independent audit committee, and create an official COO position.
- Develop a clear-cut definition of terrorism, emphasizing that violence against noncombatants or civilians is intolerable.
- Implement better targeted, better enforced sanctions against human rights abusers.
- Create a human rights body with strict membership standards.

The United States should champion a sustained anti-corruption drive to clean up the UN. Highlighting the cost of corruption to the world's poor, we must implement comprehensive, independent

---

[*] You can read the full report at www.usip.org/un/index.html.

audits and insist on transparency on UN staff salaries, expenses, and all other spending. The United States should place our UN funds in escrow until these provisions are implemented, and encourage other democracies to join us in fighting UN corruption and human rights abuse.

As we've seen with the Human Rights Council, the corrupt UN machine will twist reforms to its own advantage. Therefore, until the UN drops its resistance to anti-corruption measures, the United States should work to minimize the organization's importance. Wherever possible, we should operate through well-functioning bilateral and regional organizations outside the UN framework.

The UN could make an immense contribution to world peace, human rights, and the spread of democracy. But it is not doing that— and that's a tragedy. Having proven impervious to all attempts at reform, we need to sideline this dysfunctional, self-perpetuating, bureaucratic machine until it stops acting as a vehicle for the world's most oppressive states to exert their will over the world's free democracies.

CHAPTER TEN

The First Step in Defeating the Machine

As described in previous chapters, the secular-socialist machine gained power through dishonesty, deceit, and deception. But the American people have not been entirely innocent in this process. For years, we avoided hard choices by retreating into a fantasy world where difficult problems simply didn't exist. We thought our country could have wealth without working for it and security without defending it.

The inescapable truth is that we have not been honest with ourselves. We are emerging from a pattern of self-deception that transcends partisan and ideological lines. Repeatedly refusing to face the facts, we have been surprised by obvious events that we only missed due to our determination to deceive ourselves.

The most devastating example is the 9/11 attack—it should not have been a surprise.

In the 1990s, we witnessed the World Trade Center bombing, the bombing of U.S. forces at the Khobar Towers in Saudi Arabia, two U.S. embassies bombed in East Africa, and the bombing of the USS *Cole* in Yemen. Tom Clancy even wrote a novel in which an airliner deliberately crashed into the U.S. Capitol building. Yet most Americans, like our government, simply couldn't imagine a major terrorist attack on the American homeland. We thought we were safe and nothing could harm us, despite suffering terrorist attacks throughout the decade.

The economic crisis also should not have been a surprise. First, we assumed any information technology stock was guaranteed to rise in value—and created a bubble. Then we decided that houses were guaranteed to rise in value and that clever mortgages could allow people to live in houses they couldn't afford—and created another bubble. Then Wall Street's brilliant investors decided truly bizarre paper schemes were surefire winners—and created a third bubble.

The enormous budget deficits now paralyzing our state governments also should not have surprised us. Government spending is our fourth bubble in a decade. For years, we elected and re-elected self-serving politicians who made budgetary promises they knew they couldn't keep—and *we* knew they couldn't keep. Now the bill has come due and state governments must either cut spending or raise taxes. Guess which choice will win out in the more corrupt state capitols.

REPLACING DECEPTION WITH HONEST CONVERSATION AND TOUGH DECISIONS

Our long, bipartisan flight from reality has gotten us into an enormous mess. Fortunately, while Washington and many state capitols continue to live in a fantasy world where they can never run out of other people's money, more and more Americans are demanding honesty and accountability from our leaders. We are ending our habit of self-deception, and we are no longer so willing to let others deceive us.

Consider national security. Despite a terrorist massacre at Fort Hood and a potentially catastrophic near-miss terrorist attack in an airplane over Detroit, the Obama administration still refuses to be honest about the immediate threats we face. They hide behind euphemisms ("man-made disasters" instead of terrorist attacks) and political correctness, and insist on treating terrorists as criminals instead of wartime enemy combatants.

But the American people are not complacent anymore. The administration's blasé response to the attempted terror attack over Detroit, when Homeland Security chief Janet Napolitano declared "the system worked" after the terrorist was subdued by a civilian passenger, provoked widespread outrage and ridicule. That same response forced the administration to backpedal on their much-touted plans to try Khalid Sheikh Mohammad, the architect of the 9/11 attacks, in a New York City courtroom.

The Obama administration is perhaps even more deceptive in domestic policy. Even though the big-government stimulus bill failed to keep unemployment below 8 percent as the administration promised, Congress and the president have refused to rein in spending. Instead, they invented a brand new metric, "jobs saved or created," that allows them to conjure statistics out of thin air supposedly proving the stimulus worked, even as joblessness hovers around 10 percent.

The same deception is seen at the state level. Despite the destructive consequences of reckless spending promises to public employee unions that far outstrip what is offered to most private sector workers, state governments refuse to admit their budgets are unsustainable. Instead, they look to more Washington bailouts to keep the union gravy train running.

But once again, the American people are demanding to hear the truth. The tea party movement, born out of anger at the Wall Street bailouts and fueled by the runaway and brazen rush to socialism pursued by this administration and Congress, is a surefire sign Americans are emerging from our pattern of self-deception. When politicians of either party try to mislead their constituents, tea partiers call them out. They won't sit down, be quiet, and defer to the "experts." Insisting on straight talk, tea partiers won't be deceived, and they won't deceive themselves.

And they're not going away. Increasingly, Americans are pressing our leaders to be honest about how corrupt our state and federal governments have become, and how much of the current bureaucracy must be uprooted if our nation hopes to survive.

Why "2 + 2=4" Will Be the Most Important (and Most Controversial) Slogan of This Decade

Writing shortly after the defeat of Nazism, as the world faced the rapidly expanding threat of Soviet totalitarianism, Albert Camus wrote in his novel, *The Plague*, "Again and again there comes a time in history when the man who dares to say that two and two make four is punished with death."

Camus was describing more than the threat of dictatorship. He was describing the power of conformity that coerces people into denying the truth and saying things that are patently false but politically correct.

Similarly, the fraudulent party slogans the citizen must believe in George Orwell's classic dystopian novel, *1984*, are described by the book's protagonist, Winston Smith, as "2 + 2=5." Smith writes, "Freedom is the freedom to say that two plus two make four. If that is granted, all else follows."

The Polish people used the same 2 + 2=4 slogan in their fight against Poland's Communist dictatorship after Pope John Paul II's visit there in 1979. They were asserting that the truth would come out no matter what the dictatorship said or did. Ultimately, after a decade of struggle, the dictatorship collapsed and was replaced in free elections.

America is not a dictatorship, but we are facing a ruthless secular-socialist machine that repeats falsehood after falsehood and then intimidates—through cries of racism, hating the poor, or other spurious accusations—anyone who might challenge their lies. In order to defeat the machine once and for all, we must take inspiration from the brave Communist-era dissidents. We are already emerging from our pattern of self-deception, but we must accelerate this process; we must even more consistently, even more emphatically tell the truth in the face of enormous pressure to conform to the politically correct lies that now dominate our discourse.

Consider two examples where we are still reluctant to speak the common-sense truth in the face of the willful obfuscations of our leaders.

2 + 2=11: Why it has been impossible to accurately and honestly discuss immediate threats to American security

All the passion spent debating the proper U.S. troop strength in Afghanistan misses the larger reality about the war we are in and the threats we face.

Afghanistan is one theater in a larger war, much like Guadalcanal and Sicily were during World War II. They were important battles, but no one ever confused them with being the war itself.

It's a mistake to discuss our goals and strategies for Afghanistan without first having established our goals and strategies for the larger war—it's like trying to understand Guadalcanal without looking at Japan, or trying to understand Sicily while ignoring Fascist Italy and Nazi Germany.

Yet that's exactly what we're doing. Today, it is impossible to have a 2 + 2=4 conversation about the most pressing threats to U.S. security.

I have been illustrating this to audiences by relating a series of incidents: terrorist killings in Fort Hood; the arrest of five young American men in Pakistan who were trying to join al Qaeda to fight against America; and the arrests of would-be terrorists in Denver, Detroit, and New York.

I note that I will focus on a common characteristic of these stories that is politically acceptable to discuss. "Do you realize," I ask, "that not one of these people was a Rotarian?"

Audiences break up laughing as they understand the key point. The one common characteristic of these cases was that the terrorists were Islamists. Yet today we are so dominated by politically correct apologists, even for terrorists, that we cannot have an honest dialogue about the true scale of the threat to our survival.

We have to stop talking about Iraq, Afghanistan, and other theaters of the war on Islamism in isolation. Unless we honestly discuss the irreconcilable wing of Islam, we will never develop what Roosevelt and Churchill would have called a grand national strategy. And without that, we are unlikely to win the war.

Once we have the courage to insist that 2 + 2=4 in national security, we can rapidly develop a bold strategy to preserve our civilization against those who would destroy it. Until then we are likely to flounder and risk failure.

2 + 2=97: The housing bubble crash

Here's a quick 2 + 2 experiment: tell a friend you will give her the first half of a sentence and you want her to finish it.

The first half is, "If you can't afford to buy a house ... "

Most people will respond, "don't buy it" or "rent one."

Americans overwhelmingly understand that putting people into houses they can't afford is an invitation to disaster. Yet for a quarter century our governmental policy has repudiated this common-sense wisdom. Prodded by liberal guilt and a belief among many leaders in redistributionist, big-government policies, our government adopted ever-more aggressive and unsustainable housing policies. Prospective home owners were told:

If you do not have any credit, government will find a way.

If you cannot save for a down payment, government will waive the requirement.

If you cannot afford to pay the principal, government will give you an interest-only loan for the first three years.

If you cannot even afford full interest payments, government will give you a below market rate.

With one person, these policies might tragically lead to his or her bankruptcy. As national policy, they mired millions of families in debt, created a housing bubble, and sparked a financial collapse.

This was certainly a policy failure. But more significant, it was a cultural failure—too many Americans, against their better judgment, bought into the idea that they could get something for nothing.

Yet how often, if ever, have the leaders of either party admitted the housing market collapse and subsequent financial meltdown stemmed from destructive cultural values exacerbated by bad politics and bad government?

Ironically, the politicians whose policies contributed the most to the housing mess—left-wing Democrats like Barney Frank and Chris Dodd—ended up as chairs of the committees tasked with fixing the crisis. And of course, none of them will acknowledge the cultural roots of the problem, or the many ways their own demands for aggressive lending intensified the crisis.

They added 2 + 2 and got 97.

OUR MOST POWERFUL WEAPON
IS THE TRUTH

Despite the enormous challenge of defeating the secular-social-ist machine, I am an optimist for one simple reason: we have the truth on our side.

Free people insisting on telling the truth have changed history. Just a few years after Pope John Paul II visited Poland, President Reagan gave his famous speech in Berlin exclaiming, "Mr. Gor-bachev tear down this wall!" The end of the speech was little noticed, but in many ways it was even more profound than his chal-lenge to Gorbachev. Reagan said:

> Perhaps this gets to the root of the matter, to the most fundamental distinction of all between East and West. The totalitarian world produces backwardness because it does such violence to the spirit, thwarting the human impulse to create, to enjoy, to worship. The totalitarian world finds even symbols of love and of worship an affront.
>
> Years ago, before the East Germans began rebuilding their churches, they erected a secular structure: the televi-sion tower at Alexander Platz. Virtually ever since, the authorities have been working to correct what they view as the tower's one major flaw: treating the glass sphere at the top with paints and chemicals of every kind. Yet even today when the sun strikes that sphere, that sphere that towers over all Berlin, the light makes the sign of the cross. There in Berlin, like the city itself, symbols of love, symbols of wor-ship, cannot be suppressed.
>
> As I looked out a moment ago from the Reichstag, that embodiment of German unity, I noticed words crudely spray-painted upon the wall, perhaps by a young Berliner: "This wall will fall. Beliefs become reality."

Yes, across Europe, this wall will fall, for it cannot withstand faith; it cannot withstand truth. The wall cannot
withstand freedom.

Those who would reject the truth about the totalitarian nature of big
government, the truth that our rights come from our Creator, the
truth about the importance of the rule of law, the truth about the deep
cost of corruption—they should reread this speech and explain why
they think we Americans are less willing to stand up for the truth than
were Germans, Poles, or countless others during the dark days of
Communism.

The secular-socialist machine *can* be defeated. We *can* put an end
to self-serving, big-government corruption from Sacramento to
Washington, D.C.

The first step is to refuse to be silenced.

CHAPTER ELEVEN

Replace Not Reform

After we fully adopt the 2 + 2=4 rule and truthfully confront our problems head-on, we need to identify where to begin dismantling the secular-socialist machine. And that starting point is the bureaucracies where it hides.

Many of our state and federal bureaucracies are obsolete, having been founded on left-wing principles that simply do not work in the real world and that contradict traditional American values. Furthermore, the career bureaucrats who run them are often left-wing activists who aim to exploit their positions to reshape society—the Environmental Protection Agency (EPA) is a prime example.

A core element of the secular-socialist machine, these bureaucracies are impervious to reform, as demonstrated by twelve years of largely unsuccessful reform efforts by a Republican House and twenty years of futile attempts by Republican presidents. As previously described, the defeat of reform attempts by governors like California's Arnold Schwarzenegger shows these bureaucracies can be just as entrenched on the state level.

Simply put, bureaucracies have learned how to outlast elected officials and any reforms they may attempt. Some bureaucrats express this attitude with an arrogant term for political appointees to whom they nominally report: "the summer help." And any reform efforts that are actually attempted get stymied by the nearly impenetrable layers of process regulations, such as personnel selection, security clearance, public comment periods, and rules about what can and cannot be done.

To save America from the secular-socialist machine, it is not enough to expose and repudiate the Left in the next two elections. After all, once we win the elections, we still have to run the government effectively. If we fail, as Republicans did this past decade, the machine will simply bide its time until it regains power.

To succeed, it will not be enough simply to try to reform our failed bureaucracies. Instead, we must fundamentally replace them.

The difference between a reform and a replacement effort is not just rhetoric; it leads to drastically different conclusions about the scale of the effort. A system of replacement requires a new approach, new language, and a new majority coalition of citizens.

What's wrong with a reform strategy? Consider the White House czar system. It is an unconstitutional centralization of power in the hands of appointed, unaccountable bureaucrats. It is guaranteed to increase corruption, lead to political cronyism, and give the president unprecedented—and un-American—power to manipulate, coerce, and bribe people.

The solution is to eliminate the White House czar system, not to reform it.

The EPA has become an engine of undemocratic bureaucracy filled with people who seek to impose their fanatical views on an unwilling American population. The EPA and its entire regulation-litigation, Washington-centered, command-and-control bureaucracy needs to be replaced.

Fannie Mae and Freddie Mac, the multi-trillion dollar government-guaranteed housing agencies, are so thoroughly politicized and preside over such irresponsible lending policies that they need to be replaced with smaller, private companies operating without government guarantees, whose leaders focus on making a profit, not manipulating politicians.

Watching Bob Compton's movie *2 Million Minutes* about high schools in China, India, and America is a sobering warning of the risk to America's future competitiveness posed by the failures of our education system. Killing all attempts at meaningful reform, the union-dominated public education bureaucracy sacrifices our children's learning for its own financial interests. Despite the howls of outrage sure to ensue, that bureaucracy needs to be replaced, not reformed.

REPLACING POLICY

Along with the bureaucracies, we need to thoroughly replace failing policies with ones that work. This is not a new or impossible goal. I have been involved in numerous policy replacement efforts over the last thirty years.

Under President Reagan's leadership in 1981, we replaced the failed Keynesian tax-and-spend policies of the Carter years with a bold, three-year tax cut of 25 percent combined with dramatic deregulation, a strong-dollar federal reserve, and significant spending controls. The result was a 25-year period of continuous economic growth.

When President Reagan replaced the strategy of détente and accommodation toward the Soviet Union with a strategy of victory (or as he described the strategy, "We win, they lose"), his approach

was replacement, not reform. The result was the decline and collapse of the Soviet Union.

In 1996, the Republican Congress passed and President Clinton
signed a total replacement of the failed welfare system with a work-
study system that transformed the role of welfare offices from
increasing dependency to helping people become productive again.
With this bold change, 65 percent of welfare recipients went to work
or to school. It is the most successful conservative social change in
more than eighty years.

Although the number of irredeemably failed government policies
is too great to count here, we can consider just two major ones. First,
current energy regulatory policy cripples the development of American energy and keeps us dangerously dependent on foreign energy
sources. Second, our fiscal policies rely on over-spending and then
financing our deficit by selling bonds to regimes like China, which
now holds nearly $800 billion of our national debt.

You don't reform policies that fail that spectacularly. You replace
them.

THE CREAKING BUREAUCRATIC STRUCTURE

There is a structural gap between the emerging information-age
world of global markets and our current red-tape-ridden, rule-
bound, bureaucratic structures of government.

The emerging world is one of an explosion of science and technology (with 4–7 times more new scientific knowledge in the next
twenty-five years than in the last twenty-five) and a potentially huge
increase in productivity driven by new information technology capabilities, behavioral economics, and management systems.

Now, consider the origins of our bureaucracies today, as first
noted back in 1984 by Alvin and Heidi Toffler in *The Third Wave*:

- The public education bureaucracy is a holdover from a model first developed in the 1840s.
- The civil service model used in state and federal government, with its rigidity and job protections even for the incompetent, first arose in the 1880s.
- The concept of government by professional bureaucracies doing "the right thing" goes back to the Progressive movement of 1896–1916.
- Washington's large, paper-based bureaucracies were developed during the Great Depression and World War II (1933–1946).
- The system of Medicare and Medicaid as bureaucracies within the greater healthcare bureaucracy was developed in 1965.
- Washington-based environmental bureaucrats wielding power over private property through arbitrary decisions, punishments, red tape, and litigation date back to the creation of the Environmental Protection Agency in 1970.[1]

Imagine you were a private company using technology and practices from 1849 or 1880 or even 1970 to compete with China and India. How long would you survive?

Overall, our government bureaucracy has become a giant bubble. Like the bubbles we saw with information technology stocks, housing, and financial derivatives, government has become overvalued compared to its actual return on investment. It's subject to graft, it favors insiders, and it has become overleveraged to the tune of $11 trillion.

The sheer obsolescence of the culture, rules, and technology of the bulk of modern government means it has to be replaced—not reformed—if we want to remain competitive globally in the twenty-first century.

HOW THE LEFT WILL TRY TO DEFEAT REPLACEMENT: "REALISM"

The Left will bitterly oppose efforts to replace the failed policies and bureaucracies of government because these are all components in the machine the Left have created to stay in power.

One tactic they will use to outlast any replacement effort is a simple, seemingly commonsense demand for "realism." Whenever conservative candidates or elected officials propose sweeping changes, the media denounce them for being "unrealistic" or even "intellectually dishonest."

However, faced with the corruption and across-the-board failure of state and federal bureaucracies, the American people do not want "realism," as long as realism means being too cowardly to challenge the status quo.

When conservatives fall for the trap of being "realistic," they turn timid. This, in turn, dissipates the energy from the American people that generates voter turnout. And that turnout is what we need to replace the current generation of machine politicians and their outdated bureaucracies.

Ronald Reagan understood the importance of clear statements for real change. That is why, in February 1975, in the depths of the Republican collapse after the Watergate scandal, he told CPAC, the annual conservative convention, that conservatives had to nail their cause to banners of bold colors and avoid pale pastels.

Reagan used this strategy throughout his political career. He had defeated a popular incumbent California governor by more than a million votes because Reagan boldly and clearly declared his opposition to university student radicals, his rejection of more spending and higher taxes, and his commitment to bringing efficiency and eliminating waste in Sacramento.

He again contrasted his clear, profound beliefs with the temporizing "realism" of the Republican establishment in his 1976 presidential primary campaign against President Jerry Ford, when Reagan passionately advocated America's retention of the Panama Canal. His utter refusal to appease the Panamanian dictator was a stark divergence from Ford's "realistic" policy of negotiating the canal's surrender. And of course, in 1980 Reagan again offered Americans a clear choice between his vision of a resurgent America and President Carter's focus on adapting to American decline.

We can successfully apply Reagan's example across America, even in the bluest states. In California, 64 percent of voters opposed the 2009 ballot propositions to raise taxes. If a candidate in that state's 2010 gubernatorial election could galvanize those voters by staking out a convincing (albeit, according to the elites, unrealistic) strategy for fundamentally changing Sacramento, she will have a real opportunity to develop a massive majority to take on the machine.

Similarly, the New York machine has alienated a vast swath of the electorate with its heavy taxes, poor service, corrupt bureaucracy, and privileged unions. With the political class catering to interest groups rather than the general public, there is an opening for Rick Lazio or any other candidate with the courage to advocate replacement over reform. A candidate who vows to shrink Albany and return taxpayers' money to the rest of the state will enrage the union leadership and the big lobbyists, but he just might arouse enough enthusiasm among voters to overturn the machine.

THREE WINNING QUESTIONS

The 2010 and 2012 elections offer a historic opportunity for conservatives to channel Americans' widespread dissatisfaction with government into an energetic movement to finally replace the secular-socialist machine. We should boldly propose a replacement model, drawing clear distinctions between our policies and those of our opponents.

There are three questions in particular we can ask whose answers will point to the need for a replacement strategy. Those questions are:

1. Who are we?
2. What will it take to compete successfully with China and India and remain the most innovative, most productive, and most prosperous country in the world?
3. What threatens America, and what do we have to do to remain safe?

We discussed the first question in chapter one: we are an honest, entrepreneurial, democratic, and God-fearing people struggling against a corrupt, undemocratic, secular-socialist machine buried deep within the government bureaucracy. The solution is to replace that bureaucracy, not to reform it.

In the following chapters, I will discuss the other two questions, and why their solutions also require a replacement model. I will show why, on issue after issue, the Left's high-tax, big-bureaucracy, heavy-litigation system is incapable of keeping America globally competitive. And I will demonstrate why the Left's national security paradigm makes America substantially less safe.

All these policies are beyond hope of success. They cannot be tinkered with or renewed or reformed. They can only be abolished entirely and replaced with new ideas that work.

CHAPTER TWELVE

A New American Prosperity

With Peter Ferrara, Director of
Entitlement and Budget Policy at the
Institute for Policy Innovation

T he 1970s, when the Left last controlled Washington, was a
time of disastrous economic policy failure that should never
be repeated. Unfortunately, President Obama and the secular socialists now running Washington seem determined to bring
about an even bigger debacle.

Three ever-worsening recessions pounded the U.S. economy
from 1969 to 1982. Inflation soared to 11.6 percent in 1979 and 13.5
percent in 1980, a devastating 25 percent increase in prices in just
two years. The prime interest rate reached 21.5 percent in 1980,
with home mortgage interest rates soon rising to an absurd high of
14.7 percent. Unemployment began an upward climb during the
Carter years that eventually peaked at over 10 percent in 1982.

The poverty rate began increasing in 1978, eventually shooting
up an astounding 33 percent, from 11.4 percent to 15.2 percent. A

fall in real median family income that began in 1978 snowballed to a decline of almost 10 percent by 1982. Average real family income for the poorest 20 percent of Americans declined by 14.2 percent. Indeed, during the Carter years (1977 to 1981), real income declined for all Americans, from the lowest 20 percent to the highest 20 percent. Real average income of U.S. households was, in fact, in long-term decline from 1970 to 1980.

REAGANOMICS

In 1981, newly elected President Reagan abandoned long-fashionable Keynesian economic policies—the interventionist, big-government, "stimulus" approach that had produced these dismal results. Instead, he explicitly campaigned on, and then implemented, four specific economic policy components that became known as Reaganomics:

1. Tax cuts to restore incentives for economic growth. The top income tax rate of 70 percent was first cut to 50 percent, which probably produced a net increase in revenue by itself, and then there was a 25 percent across the board reduction in income tax rates. The 1986 tax reform reduced income tax rates further, leaving just two rates—28 percent and 15 percent. Thus, the top rate fell from 70 percent to 28 percent over five years.

2. Spending reductions, including a $31 billion cut in 1981. This was close to 5 percent of the federal budget then, or the equivalent of about $180 billion of spending cuts in a year nowadays. In constant dollars, non-defense discretionary spending declined by 14.4 percent from 1981 to 1982, and by 16.8 percent from 1981 to 1983. Moreover, in

constant dollars, this non-defense discretionary spending never returned to its 1981 level for the rest of Reagan's two terms. By 1988, this spending was still down 14.4 percent from its 1981 level in constant dollars.

Reagan's spending discipline led to several difficult struggles, including an illegal strike by air traffic controllers that forced him to choose between adopting inflationary spending increases and firing the controllers. So Reagan retained his policies and hired new controllers. The air transportation system survived, and the economy flourished. Even with Reagan's defense buildup, total federal spending declined from a high of 23.5 percent of GDP in 1983 to 21.3 percent in 1988 and 21.2 percent in 1989. That's a real 10 percent reduction in the size of government relative to the economy.

3. Anti-inflation monetary policy emphasizing the value of the dollar and restraining money supply growth, which led to much lower interest rates once inflation was tamed.

4. Deregulation, cutting red tape, and reducing bureaucracy saved consumers an estimated $100 billion per year in lower prices. Reagan's first executive order eliminated price controls on oil and natural gas. Production soared, and the price of oil declined by more than 50 percent. This was a remarkable contrast to President Carter's gasoline rationing, which limited us to buying gasoline every other day depending on the last number of our license plate. From scarcity of gasoline to abundance in six months—this was one of Reagan's first evident accomplishments.

Collectively, these were the most successful economic policies in U.S. history, turning a rapid economic decline into a raging economic boom. The Reagan recovery officially began in November 1982 and lasted ninety-two months without a recession until July 1990, when the tax increases of the 1990 budget deal ended the streak. This set a new record for the longest peacetime expansion ever, the previous high being fifty-eight months.

During these seven years, the economy grew by almost one-third, the equivalent of adding the entire economy of West Germany, the third largest in the world at the time, to the U.S. economy. In 1984 alone, real economic growth shot up 6.8 percent, the highest in fifty years, as nearly 20 million new jobs were created during the boom, increasing U.S. civilian employment by almost 20 percent. Unemployment fell to 5.3 percent by 1989 (almost half what it had been at the peak of the Carter recession). Labor force participation reached a record 66.5 percent that year, when a record 63 percent of the population was employed. Black labor force participation also hit a record 64.2 percent in 1989, with female labor force participation reaching an all-time record of 57.5 percent in 1990.

Real per capita disposable income increased 18 percent from 1982 to 1989, meaning the American standard of living grew almost 20 percent during the boom. The Carter decline in income for the bottom 20 percent of income earners was reversed, with average real household income for this group rising 12.2 percent from 1983 to 1989. The poverty rate, which had started increasing during the Carter years, declined every year from 1984 to 1989, dropping by one-sixth from its peak.

The shocking Carter-era rise in inflation was also reversed under Reagan. Spectacularly, inflation was reduced by more than half between 1980 and 1982, to 6.2 percent, and then was cut in half again for 1983, to 3.2 percent. The prime rate was cut by two-thirds by 1987 to 8.2 percent, going down to 6.25 percent by 1992. New home mortgage rates also declined steadily, reaching 9.19 percent by 1988, then 8 percent by 1992. This disproved a common argument made by opponents of Reagan's tax cuts—that they would increase interest rates.

The stock market more than tripled in value from 1980 to 1990, a larger increase than in any previous decade. Real personal assets rose 36 percent, from $15.5 trillion in 1980 to $21.1 trillion in 1990. Total real private net worth rose by $4.3 trillion from 1980 to 1989, totaling $17.1 trillion in constant dollars, an increase of one-third.

Even with the Reagan tax cuts, total federal revenues doubled from 1980 to 1990, growing from $517.1 billion to just over $1 trillion. In Reagan's last budget year, fiscal 1989, the federal deficit declined to $152.5 billion, about the same as a percentage of GDP as in 1980, 2.9 percent compared to 2.8 percent.

THE 25-YEAR REAGAN BOOM

In their incisive and prescient book *The End of Prosperity*, supply-side guru Art Laffer and *Wall Street Journal* chief financial writer Steve Moore note that Reagan's recovery grew into a 25-year boom, with just slight interruptions by short, shallow recessions in 1990 and 2001. They write:

> We call this period, 1982-2007, the twenty-five year boom—the greatest period of wealth creation in the history of the planet. In 1980, the net worth—assets minus liabilities—of all U.S. households and business . . . was $25 trillion in today's dollars. By 2007 . . . net worth was just shy of $57 trillion. Adjusting for inflation, more wealth was created in America in the twenty-five year boom than in the previous two hundred years.[1]

Similarly, Steve Forbes wrote in *Forbes* magazine,

Between the early 1980s and 2007 we lived in an economic Golden Age. Never before have so many people advanced so far economically in so short a period of time as they have during the last 25 years. Until the credit crisis, 70 million people a year [worldwide] were joining the middle class. The U.S. kicked off this long boom with the economic reforms of Ronald Reagan, particularly his enormous income tax cuts. We burst from the economic stagnation of the 1970s into a dynamic, innovative, high tech-oriented economy. Even in recent years the much maligned U.S. did well. Between year-end 2002 and year-end 2007 U.S. growth exceeded the entire size of China's economy.

In other words, just the *growth* in the U.S. economy from 2002 to 2007 was the equivalent of adding China's whole economy to the U.S. economy.

The 25-year boom was fueled by the tax cuts and other pro-growth policies adopted by the Republican congressional majorities in the 1990s, when I served as Speaker of the House. Indeed, the House passed a budget resolution in 1995 that would have cut federal spending by $1 trillion over ten years—and that was when $1 trillion was a lot of money. The full Congress did not implement all those cuts, but it did significantly reign in spending. This shows what can be accomplished by a change in political leadership.

Total federal discretionary spending, as well as the subcategory of non-defense discretionary spending, declined from 1995 to 1996 in actual nominal dollars. In constant dollars, adjusted for inflation, the decline was 5.4 percent. By 2000, total federal discretionary spending was still about the same as it was in 1995 in constant dollars. As a percentage of GDP, federal discretionary spending was slashed by 17.5 percent in just four years, from 1995 to 1999. Total federal spending relative to GDP declined from 1995 to 2000 by an astounding 12.5 percent, a reduction in the federal government relative to the economy of about one-eighth in just five years.

As a result, $200 billion annual federal deficits, which had prevailed for over fifteen years, became surpluses by 1998, peaking at a $236 billion surplus in 2000.

The much maligned Bush tax cuts of 2001 and 2003 also contributed to the 25-year boom. Restoring growth, they reversed the short, shallow 2001 recession and the economic damage of the 9/11 attacks. These cuts reduced the top income tax rate by 11 percent, the bottom income tax rate by 33 percent, the capital gains tax rate by 33 percent, and the dividends tax rate by 50 percent. After these rate cuts were fully implemented in 2003, the economy created 7.8 million new jobs, and the unemployment rate fell from over 6 percent to 4.4 percent. Real economic growth over the next three years doubled from the average for the prior three years, to 3.5 percent. Business investment spending, which had declined for nine straight quarters, reversed, increasing 6.7 percent per quarter. Manufacturing output soared to its highest level in twenty years. The stock market revived, creating almost $7 trillion in new shareholder wealth. From 2003 to 2007, the S&P 500 almost doubled.

By 2006, capital gains tax revenues had doubled, despite—or, as we argue, because of—the 25 percent rate cut. In fact, over the past forty years, capital gains tax revenues have increased every time the capital gains tax rate has been cut, and revenues have fallen every time the rate has increased.

As Laffer and Moore noted in 2008, "The economy in real terms is almost twice as large today as it was in the late 1970s." Moreover,

> In 1967 only one in 25 families earned an income of $100,000 or more in real income (in 2004 dollars), whereas now almost one in four families do. The percentage of families with an income of more than $75,000 a year has more

than tripled from 9 percent to almost 33 percent from 1967 to 2005.[2]

The authors also note, "A poor family in 1979 was more likely to be rich by the early 1990s than to still be poor." They cite a Congressional Budget Office (CBO) study, backed up by a later Treasury Department study, finding that "from 1994 to 2004 Americans in the bottom 20 percent of income actually had the highest increase in incomes." They continue,

> When you track real families—real people—over time, you find that people who are poor at the start . . . have the biggest subsequent gains in income. Amazingly, the richer a person is . . . the smaller the subsequent income gains. Those in the top 1% actually lose income over time.

Or, as Nobel Prize winning economic historian Robert Fogel wrote in 2004, "In every measure that we have bearing on the standard of living . . . the gains of the lower classes have been far greater than those experienced by the population as a whole." Under Reaganomics, the rich got richer and the poor got richer too.

THE KENNEDY TAX CUTS

Reagan was not the first to jumpstart the economy through sweeping tax cuts. It has happened four or five times in the last century with virtually the same result every time. One of these instances occurred under President Kennedy, who cut the top tax rate from 91 percent to 70 percent, with across the board rate cuts of 15 to 30 percent for the other tax brackets. Compared to national income and the total budget, the Kennedy tax cut was three times larger than the Bush tax cut, which only reduced the top tax rate by a measly 4.6 percentage points, from 39.6 percent to 35 percent. As Kennedy declared,

> Our true choice...is between two kinds of deficits—a chronic deficit of inertia, as the unwanted result of inadequate revenues and a restricted economy—or a temporary deficit of transition, resulting from a tax cut designed to boost the economy, produce revenues, and achieve a future budget surplus. The first type of deficit is a sign of waste and weakness—the second reflects an investment in the future.

A true supply-side tax cutter, Kennedy insisted tax cuts actually increase tax revenues, an argument the Left deny with religious intensity. Kennedy stated,

> It is a paradoxical truth that tax rates are too high today, and tax revenues are too low and the soundest way to raise the revenues in the long run is to cut the tax rates.... [A]n economy constrained by high tax rates will never produce enough revenue to balance the budget, just as it will never create enough jobs or profits.

In response to the Kennedy tax cuts, the economy grew by 10 percent in just two years, with the annual economic growth rate increasing 50 percent. More than 1 million jobs were created in the following four years, and unemployment fell to its lowest peacetime level in more than thirty years. Federal income tax revenues grew by 41 percent during those four years, causing *U.S News & World Report* to observe, "The unusual budget spectacle of sharply rising revenues following the biggest tax cut in history is beginning to astonish even those who pushed hardest for tax cuts in the first place."

THE END OF PROSPERITY

The 25-year boom ended because over the last eight years we abandoned every one of the planks of Reaganomics. One of the most harmful changes was ending Reagan's strong dollar monetary policies, as the Fed pursued overly-expansive policies from 2001 to 2006, including two and a half years with a *negative* real federal funds rate, during a time when the economy was still growing.[3] This was the central cause of the housing bubble that burst in 2007–2008, sparking the financial crisis.

Even before that, the Clinton administration, supported by congressional liberals, had adopted damaging "affordable housing" policies, first by strengthening the Community Reinvestment Act, and then via discrimination lawsuits filed by HUD and the Justice Department against banks accused of denying loans to low-income borrowers. These policies, reinforced by banking regulators, produced lower mortgage lending standards that set the stage for the subprime mortgage market meltdown. The interventions of the politically connected Fannie Mae and Freddie Mac, both guaranteed by government, exacerbated the problem by spreading trillions in toxic mortgage-backed securities throughout the U.S. and world financial systems. These policies began the housing bubble even before the Fed's miscalculations early in the Bush administration.

Other regulations contributed to the crisis as well. For example, mark-to-market accounting regulations forced financial institutions to list many sound mortgages on their balance sheet as worthless purely due to panic selling by other institutions. As these firms' balance sheets began showing artificial insolvency or near insolvency, their creditors cut them off, they lost all liquidity, and their stock price plunged—all this even though the firms' underlying business was often perfectly viable. This is how, with more than 90 percent of mortgages still paying on time, financial giants like Merrill Lynch, Bear Stearns, AIG, and Lehman Brothers went bankrupt almost overnight. These companies may well have survived under the "historical cost accounting" rules followed for decades before the advent of mark-to-market.

Additionally, the Sarbanes-Oxley Act of 2002 crippled small firms, killed millions of jobs, lengthened by years the time it took to bring a new company to market, and drove competent people off boards by increasing the risk of serving. The act's destructive regulations created an anti-business environment that degraded what had been the world's greatest system for creative, entrepreneurial start-ups. As Home Depot co-founder Bernie Marcus asserts, Home Depot could not have been created in today's regulatory environment.

President Bush and Congress also lost control of federal spending. When the financial crisis set in at the end of 2007, Bush and congressional Democrats rejected Reaganite supply-side tax rate cuts, instead opting for outdated, Keynesian-style tax rebates or cash grants. Speaker Pelosi, Majority Leader Reid, and their socialist allies stopped all attempts at pro-growth, pro-entrepreneur tax rate changes and regulatory reform. Many Republicans were complicit as the government sought to boost the economy by increasing government spending—a tried and true recipe for failure.

THE CIRCUS OF OBAMANOMICS

In 2008, the American people thought they were electing a young, forward-looking president to lead us into the future. He has proven instead to be a backward-looking ideologue wedded to failed ideas from the last century and even earlier.

A believer in Keynesian economics, then-Senator Obama vociferously supported the February 2008 Pelosi–Bush stimulus bill, which wasted $168 billion with no apparent economic benefits. Refusing to learn from his mistakes, President Obama advocated another stimulus bill in February 2009 that failed just like the previous stimulus did, but wasted more than four times as much money in the process.

The Left like these stimulus bills because they get to use big government to allocate massive sums of money to their favorite projects and interest groups. But this approach never improves the economy, because the underlying Keynesian economics are wrong. Runaway government spending, record deficits, unsustainable federal debt, and hundreds of billions in increased welfare spending will not renew the economic boom. Trickle-down bureaucracy does not create wealth. Obama's stimulus simply borrowed close to $1 trillion from the private economy to pour a trillion back in through increased government spending, producing no net economic gain.

This policy has failed time and again. The economy grows not through ever-greater spending, but through policies that increase incentives for savings, investment, work, creating new jobs, starting and expanding businesses, and entrepreneurship.

Pro-growth, pro-jobs policies, however, do not fit the Left's secular-socialist ideology. Obama touts the "tax cuts" in his stimulus bill, but those were tax credits that do not cut tax rates and, therefore, do not change the fundamental incentives that govern the economy. Indeed, Obama's own budget documents showed 35 percent of his supposed income tax cuts went to people who do not pay income taxes, meaning they were not tax cuts but welfare checks. This is why Obama's own budget accounted for this portion of his "tax cuts" as outlays rather than revenue reductions. Moreover, the centerpiece of that "tax cut" plan was a $400-per-worker tax credit that was supposed to fulfill his campaign promise to cut taxes for 95 percent of Americans. That credit, however, is slated to expire next year.

Obama's policies significantly delayed the incipient economic rebound we finally see today. The recession officially began in December 2007, according to the National Bureau of Economic Research. The average recession since World War II has lasted ten months, with the longest spanning sixteen months. But the Bush–Obama recession lasted almost *two years* thanks to the outdated Keynesian policies adopted by both presidents. As it turns out, contrary to President Bush's declaration, abandoning free-market principles doesn't help save the free market.

Moreover, the weak rebound violates a historical rule: the deeper the recession the stronger the recovery. Based on the severity of the past recession, real growth over 2010 should be 6–8 percent. Indeed, the major tax increases slated for 2011 should be causing even more rapid growth this year, as income is moved forward to avoid the coming tax hikes.

Instead, unemployment stands near 10 percent, with more than 15 million Americans now out of work and Depression-level rates for African-Americans, Hispanics, and younger Americans. Accounting for more than 9 million Americans who were involuntarily working part-time, and an additional 2 million who wanted and were available for work, we get a figure of nearly 27 million unemployed or underemployed, which amounts to a total effective unemployment rate of 17.5 percent. When the final data on wages and family income come out, they will show economic devastation for working people across the board.

The media insist America would be mired in another Great Depression but for the grace of President Obama. The tentative recovery, however, is really attributable to the economy's natural resiliency. Most Americans don't even remember the business cycle anymore because Reaganomics virtually eliminated it. But as the term *cycle* suggests, the economy naturally expands and contracts.

In the end, not only have President Obama's policies failed to spark a robust recovery, they are also undermining our entire economic future. Under Obama's budget policies, CBO projects the national debt will triple over the next ten years to $17.3 trillion, with the debt as a percentage of GDP soaring from 40 percent today to a shocking 82.4 percent, twice what it was when Reagan left office. By 2011, we will carry the burden of the seventh highest government debt-to-GDP ratio in the world, in the company of such economic powerhouses as Zimbabwe, Jamaica, and Lebanon.

The Government Accountability Office (GAO) projects that under current policies, federal debt will climb to almost 300 percent of GDP by 2040. Even during World War II, the national debt peaked at 113 percent of GDP. At least in return for that debt we vanquished Nazi Germany, Fascist Italy, and Imperial Japan.

The federal deficit last year clocked in at a record $1.4 trillion. That was an astounding 13 percent of GDP, one-eighth of the entire economy, and this year the deficit is expected to be even higher. In comparison, the deficit in the last budget adopted when Congress had Republican majorities was $162 billion, about one-tenth as high as today. Even the deficit for the big-spending final year of Bush's presidency, pumped up by two years of Democrat congressional majorities, was a third of Obama's 2009 deficit, or $458.6 billion.

The core problem, of course, is President Obama's runaway federal spending, which exploded from $3 trillion in 2008 to $4 trillion in 2009, a shocking increase of 33 percent in one year. Obama's budget busters include increasing federal welfare spending by one-third in just his first two years, with total welfare spending soaring to $1 trillion by 2014 and $10.3 trillion over the next ten years.

Along with that increased spending come higher taxes. Counting the tax hikes for 2011 in the Obama budget, the tax increases in the healthcare takeover, and state income taxes, the average top income tax rate in America will climb to about 52 percent. Our top rate would then be higher than in France, Germany, and Canada. In five Democratic-dominated states—California, New York, New Jersey, Hawaii, and Oregon—the total top tax rate would be higher than in *socialist Sweden!*

And this has not yet accounted for further tax hikes proposed by either Obama or his Democratic congressional allies. These range from crippling energy taxes (which advocates call "cap and trade") to a European-style value-added tax (VAT). Both these measures would violate Obama's campaign pledge not to raise any taxes on anyone making less than $250,000 a year. Then again, Obama already broke that promise when he raised cigarette taxes.

Obama's high-tax, high-spending approach along with the Fed's easy money, cheap-dollar policies have weakened the dollar so severely that foreign powers are now openly discussing replacing the dollar as the world's currency. If that happens, Americans will endure the expense of having to buy another currency in order to buy foreign oil or anything else from overseas. Under those conditions, any further weakness in the dollar will impose even higher costs on us.

These are policies for long-term economic stagnation, and perhaps another, even deeper, recession. If they are not completely replaced with pro-growth alternatives, we will suffer less opportunity, less upward mobility, and a long-term decline in America's standard of living—in other words, the end of the American Dream.

TOWARD A NEW AMERICAN PROSPERITY

We need a new economic policy to promote a robust economic recovery and a new, long-term economic boom. This requires sweeping change.

First, we should cut corporate taxes. America suffers from the second highest business tax rate in the industrialized world, with a federal rate of 35 percent, and states pushing it close to 40 percent. Much of the rest of the world, ironically, has learned the lessons of Reaganomics. The average corporate tax rate in the European Union has been slashed from 38 percent in 1996 to 24 percent today. Ireland has a corporate tax rate of 12.5 percent, which has caused per capita income to soar from the second lowest in the EU twenty years ago to the second highest today. Our own Treasury Department has said Ireland raises more corporate tax revenue as a percentage of GDP than we do with our much higher rates. Corporate tax rates in India and China, our emerging competitors, are lower as well. We should restore America's competitiveness in the world by reducing the federal business tax rate to match Ireland's rate of 12.5 percent.

Second, rather than increase capital gains tax rates by 66 percent as Democrats propose, we should match China's pro-jobs policies and abolish capital gains taxes altogether, both for individuals and corporations. By effectively double-taxing capital income, the capital gains levy discourages the venture capital that feeds start-ups and creates jobs. That is why fourteen out of thirty OECD countries, plus China, Taiwan, Hong Kong, Singapore, and others, already enjoy zero capital gains taxes.

With these two measures alone, America would become the most desirable country in the world in which to invest and start a business. That means new jobs and new prosperity.

Third, to alleviate the unemployment crisis, we should cut federal payroll taxes by 50 percent for two years, providing powerful, immediate relief to small businesses that create the most jobs. Follow this with a permanent personal account option for that portion of payroll taxes for younger workers, with the personal accounts substituting for an equivalent portion of future retirement benefits. Given historical capital market returns, workers would get much higher benefits than Social Security promises, let alone what it will actually be able to pay in the future. Workers holding these personal accounts should get a guarantee to get at least as much as Social Security promises today. This would provide a continuing gusher of new savings for capital investment, resulting in more jobs and higher wages.

Fourth, instead of reinstating the death tax with a 45 percent rate, as Obama and the Democrats want, we can create hundreds of thousands of new jobs by abolishing the death tax altogether. Taxpayers have already paid considerable taxes on any money saved over their lifetime. Taxing it again at death is abusive and unfair. No one should be required to go to the undertaker and the IRS in the same week. And no one should see their lifetime of hard work, prudent spending, and careful saving confiscated by the government and given to others.

Fifth, we should provide for immediate expensing for 100 percent of new equipment purchases by businesses, stimulating investment in new, productive technologies. Allowing businesses to write off their productive investments in one year will lead to massive investment in new machinery and new technology. It will ensure that American workers have the most modern and productive equipment in the world. It will also lead to a new birth of American manufacturing for machine tools and other expensable items.

Sixth, repudiating the regressive energy tax policies of Obama and the Democrats, we should implement the American Energy Plan discussed in chapter eighteen, which would unleash the private sector to produce low-cost, reliable energy supplies from American sources. This would create millions of new jobs and generate billions in new revenues for federal and state governments.

Seventh, we should repeal the disastrous mark-to-market accounting regulations and replace Sarbanes-Oxley with reasonable accounting requirements. We should also repeal the Community Reinvestment Act that contributed to the financial crisis. While we're at it, let's break up Fannie Mae and Freddie Mac and move their smaller successors off government guarantees and into the free market.

Eighth, we need to adopt Reagan-style strong-dollar monetary policies, guaranteeing the dollar remains the world's reserve currency, ensuring lower interest rates and more long-term capital investment, and averting any resurgence of inflation.

Ninth, analogous to the Reagan budget cuts of 1981, we should immediately cut federal spending by $180 billion. We should then adopt a budget that cuts future federal spending by $1 trillion, as we did in the House in 1995. Terminating TARP and all bailouts and repealing all unspent stimulus funding would be a good start. With these measures and a resultant booming economy, we can and should balance the budget within seven years. We should then make that policy permanent with a balanced budget amendment to the Constitution.

This comprehensive plan would cut unemployment to 3–4 percent and restore long-term economic growth. But we can do more. To generate another lasting economic boom, we need fundamental tax reform, similar to that proposed by Steve Forbes. We should adopt the optional 15 percent flat tax with generous personal exemptions of $12,000 per person. For a family of four, the first $48,000 in income would be tax free. Workers could stick with the current tax code if they prefer, but the new system would allow them to file with just a post-card. We could begin this transformation by cutting the current 25 percent income tax rate paid by the middle class to 15 percent, leaving 90 percent of workers effectively with a flat tax of 15 percent or less.

Finally, we should adopt the entitlement overhaul discussed in chapter fourteen. Personal accounts would be expanded over time to pay for all the benefits now financed by the payroll tax, allowing us to abolish that tax completely. Fundamental welfare reform based on work would be the single most effective contribution to eliminating poverty in America.

These reforms are not particularly complex, and they won't require thousand-plus page bills to be rammed through Congress. They are common-sense solutions that replicate policies that have worked, both in America and abroad, and that reject those that have failed.

Just as Reagan ushered in a 25-year economic boom, with the right policies we could launch a new boom lasting till 2035 and beyond.

CHAPTER THIRTEEN

A Small Business Plan *by* Small Businesses *for* Small Businesses

With Dan Varroney, COO of American Solutions

S mall business is the engine of job growth, creating three out of every four new jobs. And many of the remaining jobs are created by companies that began as small start-ups. So if you want to expand the economy and create jobs, you have to focus on small business.

American prosperity is the cumulative result of the creativity, courage, and leadership of individual men and women. In business, science, and the military, the relentless pursuit of innovative achievement has been the driving force of our success. This is the value of entrepreneurship. It is the spark of energy and purpose that leads individuals to create and manufacture something new and productive. It breaks through barriers, challenges the status quo, and draws upon the strengths of others to achieve results. It is the will to work hard, coupled with the intelligence to work smart. Fundamentally, entrepreneurship is the audacity, perseverance, and competence that turn an individual into a creator, whether of wealth, science, technology, or military success.

Throughout our history, Americans have found innovative and even revolutionary methods to accomplish what people thought was impossible. Benjamin Franklin harnessed the power of lightning. Samuel Morse's telegraph and Alexander Graham Bell's telephone allowed us to communicate across great distances. Henry Ford developed uniform car parts and from that created the assembly line, ushering in the system of mass production that would define twentieth-century America. Defying gravity, the Wright Brothers introduced manned flight. Charles Lindbergh extended this know-how to fly across the Atlantic Ocean, and NASA's Mercury and Apollo programs later took man into space. J. Robert Oppenheimer and the Manhattan Project unlocked nuclear power, a source of energy several orders of magnitude beyond any that had ever been conceived.

Government at every level can encourage thriving new businesses and job growth with low government costs, minimal regulation, low tax rates, solid education systems, and fair, predictable laws.

But government itself cannot create sustainable jobs.

The 2008 recession brought double digit unemployment, shut down businesses and factories, and put millions of Americans out of work. To overcome this adversity and spark long-term job creation, we need to focus on entrepreneurship, small jobs, innovation, and removing government obstacles to growth.

The floundering command and control approach of the Obama administration and Congress is proving once again that government doesn't create jobs. Introducing new taxes and regulations destroys jobs and restricts innovation. With unemployment hovering near 10 percent, we must change direction and position the United States to be the industrial powerhouse it can and should be.

WHAT WORKS FOR SMALL BUSINESS

When it comes to job creation, we know what works and what doesn't. As the Small Business & Entrepreneurship Council's "Small Business Survival Index 2009" puts it,

> In the end, government does not drive economic growth. Quite the contrary, growth comes from the private sector. The ultimate source of growth is economic risk taking in the private sector, that is, investing and entrepreneurship.... While consumers ultimately decide what works and what does not, the entrepreneurs, innovators and investors will invest the capital—including sweat equity—and offer the ideas that launch and build businesses, create new jobs, and grow the economy.
>
> Without a doubt, the biggest obstacle to entrepreneurship and investment is public policy gone awry. While most politicians talk a good game about entrepreneurs and small businesses, public policy too frequently raises costs, creates uncertainty and diminishes incentives for starting up, investing in and building a business.

State-by-state economic records of the past decade show us conclusively that low taxes create jobs and high taxes kill them.

For example, in 2003 North Dakota governor John Hoeven III encouraged the state legislature to overhaul the state's corporate income tax, reducing the top rate from 10.5 percent to 7 percent and providing a two-year tax exemption to encourage natural gas drilling. Now the state's economy is booming, boasting the lowest jobless rate in America—around 4 percent.

Consequently, S&P Rating Services upgraded the state's credit rating from AA to AA 1 in 2009. That lowered the interest rate on

North Dakota's state debt, which in turn lowered the tax burden on the state's residents. With the economy growing quickly and government spending remaining frugal, the state began considering a big tax cut that would boost the economy even more. As Reuters reported in March 2009,

> For the next biennium, the legislature is contemplating $400 million in property and income tax relief as they craft the next $7.5 billion all-funds, two-year budget.
>
> As for general obligation debt, the state has none, opting to pay cash for most capital expenditures.

Enacted the following month, the tax cuts sent a welcoming message to entrepreneurs looking to start or expand businesses. Note that the government has not created jobs in North Dakota, but its pro-growth policies have created a virtuous cycle that stimulates the private sector.

Now, for another example, let's compare Texas to Michigan and California.

Texas is ranked as the third friendliest state for entrepreneurship and small business. The top five states on the list—South Dakota, Nevada, Texas, Wyoming, and Washington—have no state personal income tax, no state individual capital gains tax, and no state corporate income tax. In contrast, California and Michigan are both textbook cases of union-dominated, high-tax, high-regulation states. Here's how these states have fared recently:

- From 2006 to 2008, Texas gained 550,000 jobs, while California lost more than 66,000 jobs and Michigan lost almost 170,000 jobs.
- Over a longer timeframe, from November 2004 to November 2009, Texas saw a net increase of more than 800,000 jobs, while California lost 444,500 jobs and Michigan lost more than 550,000 jobs.

It's clear which model works and which doesn't, yet left-wing Democrats are trying to expand the California and Michigan model on both the state and federal levels. It's almost as if they're motivated by ideology and cynical machine politics instead of real efforts at job creation.

SMALL BUSINESS OWNERS ARE AMERICA'S JOB CREATORS

Jobs are created on Main Street, not Wall Street. Small business, manufacturers, and entrepreneurs are the job growth engines of the American economy. From 2003 through 2006, firms that employed fewer than 100 people created more jobs than companies with 500 or more employees. In fact, while larger firms lost 214,233 jobs, smaller firms provided 109 percent of total job growth for the year on a net basis. In effect, small business was creating more jobs than big business was eliminating.

Total small business employment represented nearly 40 percent of total U.S. employment from 1996 to 2006. During that period, the number of people employed by small businesses increased by 4.2 million, or roughly 11 percent.

During the present job crisis, leaders at all levels of government must understand the needs of our small-business job creators. With that goal, American Solutions, a citizens action network for which I serve as general chairman and Dan Varroney serves as chief operating officer, conducted an online poll in December 2009 of more than 1,500 small business owners. Here is what they told us:[*]

- Forty-seven percent of small business owners cite high taxes as the toughest challenge facing their business.

---

[*] For more details on the survey, go to http://www.americansolutions.com/jobsfirst/2009/12/small-business-owners-respond-to-president-obamas-jobs-plan.php.

- A cut in payroll taxes is preferred 2 to 1 over President Obama's proposed targeted cut to capital gains for small businesses.
- Government regulation is a concern for one out of every four small businesses.
- Two out of three small businesses plan to lay off a worker in the next six months.
- Only 20 percent of respondents plan to purchase new equipment.
- Most small business owners want permanent tax reforms.
- Stimulus money funneled through big-government programs has not reached small business owners.
- Small business owners have little confidence in President Obama's claim that the healthcare reform will create jobs.
- Small businesses believe they will be hurt if the new energy tax (so-called "cap-and-trade") approved by the House of Representatives passes the Senate and becomes law.

A December 2009 survey of small business conducted by the National Federation of Independent Business found similar results—that a major reason for declining earnings at small businesses is increased costs, including taxes and regulation. Of the top three concerns for small business, two of them constitute government restrictions on small business growth—taxes and regulations.

AN AMERICAN SOLUTIONS JOBS PLAN FOR SMALL BUSINESS DESIGNED BY SMALL BUSINESS

At American Solutions, we know the job-creating potential of small businesses is being undermined by Washington's irresponsible tax-and-spend policies. And most Americans agree. In February 2009, a CBS News poll reported that, by a 59–22 margin, the American people favor business tax cuts over more government spending as the most effective way to create jobs.

Based on input from our small business members, American Solutions developed the following three-step job-creation plan:*

1. Reduce spending and replace inefficient and often corrupt government programs with limited, effective government in order to balance the budget.

From 1995 to 1998, while I was Speaker of the House, we had four straight balanced budgets while we paid off $405 billion in federal debt. During that time, all federal spending rose by an average of 2.9 percent per year (including entitlements), the lowest increase since the 1920s. We need to apply those same principles to create jobs today: smaller government, less spending, lower interest rates, and less debt. We also need, where necessary, to replace bad government with limited, effective government, as we did in the 1990s when we replaced a destructive welfare system with a new model of work and training.

2. Enact five key tax reforms to reward job creation, entrepreneurship, savings, and investment.

- **Immediate payroll tax relief.** Enact an immediate, two-year, 50 percent reduction of the payroll tax, which would boost the take-home pay of every worker and dramatically free up cash for every employer to hire and invest.

---

* For more details on the jobs plan, go to http://www.americansolutions.com/jobsfirst/.

- **Incentives for investing in new equipment.** Allow small businesses to expense 100 percent of new equipment purchases each year to help them invest in new, more productive technologies.
- **Zero taxes on capital gains.** Match the Chinese capital gains rate of zero. Former Fed Chairman Alan Greenspan testified in the 1990s that this was the best rate for economic growth.
- **Reduced tax rate for business.** America has the second highest business tax rate in the world. We should match the Irish business tax rate of 12.5 percent. Combined with a zero capital gains tax rate, America would become the most desirable country in the world in which to invest and start a business.
- **Eliminate the death tax.** Inheritance is the most powerful accumulator of capital. Studies show that eliminating the death tax would create hundreds of thousands of new jobs.

3. Implement an American energy plan to create American jobs and keep American money at home.

Developing more domestic energy while protecting the environment would mean millions of new American jobs and billions in new federal tax dollars, largely without the need for any new federal spending. Unfortunately, the federal government effectively embargoes new domestic oil, natural gas, and oil shale development, and has done little to expand our nuclear power generation. Our economic recovery largely depends on affordable domestic energy supplies.

AMERICAN SOLUTIONS ENTREPRENEURS REACT TO OUR JOBS PROGRAM

Eugene Sukup, Chairman of the Board
(Sukup Manufacturing, est. 1963, Sheffield, Iowa)

- The payroll tax cut "would be a real benefit to our employees.... If we can add $2,000 to their take home pay through the year, think what that does to 350 employees.... It's a real boost to this town and to them."
- "Reducing the corporate tax will give us close to half a million dollars to add to our machinery" and would contribute to "adding jobs."
- "This is what we need to create jobs in the United States...more money to offer better machinery and better jobs to our people."

D. L. Wright, CEO and Chairman of the Board
(Wirco Inc., est. 1978, Avilla, Indiana)

- "About $2,000 per employee per year would go back into their hands [with the payroll tax cut]. That's a lot of money for my employees."
- "[Global competitors] have state of the art equipment; we have a 60-year-old foundry. [The expensing of new equipment purchases] would mean for me somewhere around a half a million dollars over a period of two years that I could reinvest in our company to buy new equipment to better compete."

- "The death tax is of concern to me as I've been in this business 40 years now and my son now is the president."
- "The corporate income tax cut would be very meaningful to many of our customers. It would also be very meaningful to us. And I'd like to see it expanded in some fashion to incorporate S-CORPS, LLCs, and LLPs."
- "This is the right direction. It's a direction for growth."

Small business plays a vital role in nearly every American community. As Mr. Wright explained, "We impact about 800 lives. It's not just the people that work for us that count, it's their families. We pay their mortgages, we buy their food, we buy their clothes, we send them to school."

The backbone of America, small businesses deserve a smart, new government policy to help them lead our economy back to prosperity. So let's give it to them.

CHAPTER FOURTEEN

Replacing the Entitlement State with the Empowerment Society

With Peter Ferrara, Director of Entitlement and Budget Policy at the Institute for Policy Innovation

Even before Barack Obama took office, politicians had already promised far more entitlement benefits than Americans could possibly afford. The massive increase in government responsibility (and corresponding decrease in citizen responsibility) since 1932 had built a mountain of entitlements that threatened to crush the economy, impoverish taxpayers, and leave future generations mired in debt.

Federal projections showed that without reform, our big three entitlement programs—Social Security, Medicare, and Medicaid—would explode total federal spending in the coming decades from about 20 percent of GDP today, where it has remained stable for more than fifty years, to close to 40 percent.

Including state and local spending, government would consume more than 50 percent of GDP. That would fundamentally change our economy from a high-growth, market-oriented, free-enterprise system to a no-growth, European, socialist system. It would make our system similar to Greece, now on the verge of economic collapse, where 52 percent of the economy is run by government.

But that wasn't enough for the secular-socialist machine that took over Washington in 2008. Ignoring any pretense at budget discipline, President Obama, Speaker Pelosi, and Majority Leader Reid sought to *increase* the already unsustainable entitlement burden through their healthcare overhaul. That legislation will expand Medicaid to at least 15 million more people and will adopt a new entitlement program providing federal subsidies for the purchase of health insurance by families earning up to $88,000 per year.

The problem, of course, is that Medicaid, like Medicare and Social Security, is fiscally unsustainable. These programs can limp along in the short-term, but they will eventually cause an existential budget crisis. At that point, we'll have two stark choices: either radically slash these programs or enact unprecedented tax increases. The Left will never take the first course, so if they remain in charge, we can look forward to the second.

Do you want an economic system in which you pay most of the money you earn to the government, and the government gives you back benefits on terms and conditions decided by politicians and bureaucrats? That is not the America of freedom and prosperity we have known for more than 300 years. That is the vision of Karl Marx. Yet, this is what Washington's secular-socialist machine is giving us.

Americans firmly support a safety net for those in need. We are a compassionate people, and we don't want to see anyone suffer from want, especially when we live in a land of plenty. But what began as a safety net has transformed into a deluge of untenable spending that is jeopardizing our entire economy. So we need to replace our unsustainable entitlement programs, and do so with a clear goal: protect the vulnerable at a cost our country can afford, while offering everyone maximum economic opportunity and personal freedom.

Some want to empanel a commission of Washington experts to report to Congress on how to close long-term entitlement deficits and the resulting federal deficit. But Americans have learned over the past year we can't trust our future to unelected Washington insiders. Besides, any such commission would inevitably propose both major tax increases and large entitlement benefit cuts. And we know how that story will end: the benefit cuts will gradually be reversed, but the tax increases will be here to stay.

Instead of hiding behind opaque panels, our political leaders should present their specific solutions for entitlement reform directly to the people. That is what we elect these leaders to do, and if they can't do it they should step aside and let others lead.

Reformers must recognize we cannot avert the looming entitlement crisis by trying to cut promised benefits. The gap is too big, and the American people will oppose massive cuts that shred the safety net and leave vulnerable people suffering. Only a genuine replacement approach based on traditional American principles can solve the problem—and can solve it without cutting benefits.

The key is fundamental structural replacement to create the right incentives to promote productive activity and discourage dependency, while ensuring that efficient capital and labor markets serve the social goals of our current entitlements. Through such a replacement system, we can create new safety net programs that would be far more effective and cost much less than our current system.

THE 1996 WELFARE REFORM: BUILDING ON WHAT HAS WORKED

While I was Speaker of the House, we replaced the failing Aid to Families with Dependent Children (AFDC) program, which was originally adopted in the 1930s as a central component of the New Deal. Our replacement transformed the program's federal spending into "block grants" given to states to use in new programs they designed based on mandatory work or education for the able-bodied. The lynchpin was that the block grant is finite, not matching, so it does not vary with the amount a state spends. If a state spends more, it must pay the extra costs itself. If a state spends less, it keeps the savings.

Previously, the program's federal funding was based on a matching formula, with the federal government giving more to states the more they spent on the program. This was like paying the states to spend more, and they did, signing up more welfare recipients and thereby bringing more federal funds to their states while creating more dependency. To reflect the new emphasis on work, we changed the name of the program to Temporary Assistance to Needy Families (TANF).

The reform reduced the old AFDC rolls by close to 60 percent nationwide and by close to 80 percent in states that pushed work the most aggressively. Millions of poor people climbed the ladder of opportunity by going back to work and making their own living.

As Ron Haskins of the Brookings Institution (and a senior legislative staff writer for the reforms in 1996) reports in his book *Work over Welfare,* "The number of families receiving cash welfare is now the lowest . . . since 1969, and the percentage of children on welfare is lower than it has been since 1966."

As Haskins details, welfare reform dramatically increased employment among single mothers and never-married mothers. The total income of low-income families formerly on welfare increased by about 25 percent.

Perhaps most important, poverty rates fell steeply across virtually all age and demographic sectors. Between 1993 and 2000, child poverty rates fell every year, with African-American child poverty rates reaching historic lows. The Child and Youth Well-Being Index, published each year by Ken Land of Duke University and based on twenty-eight key indicators of child well-being, increased by 30 percentage points from 1995 to 2005.

Haskins cites a study by Isabel Sawhill and Paul Jargowsky that found,

> So great was the decline in poverty that the number of neighborhoods with concentrated poverty fell precipitously, as did the number of neighborhoods classified as underclass because of the concentration of poverty and the high frequency of problems such as school dropout, female headed families, welfare dependency, and labor force dropout by adult males.[1]

Haskins concludes,

> The pattern is clear: earnings up, welfare down. This is the very definition of reducing welfare dependency. Most low income mothers heading families appear to be financially better off because the mothers earn more money than they received from welfare. Taxpayers continue making a contribution to these families through the EITC and other work support programs, but the families earn a majority of their income. This explosion of employment and earnings constitutes an enormous achievement for the mothers themselves and for the nation's social policy.[2]

As suggested above, replacing the old welfare reform system with a new model of work and education actually *helped* the poor by drawing them into work and out of poverty. Moreover, federal spending on the program remained flat for a dozen years, saving huge sums of taxpayer dollars. Indeed, with the big decline in the number of wel-fare dependents, spending on the program could have been reduced by more than half. The Democrats prevented this, however, through a provision that blocked any reduction in overall spending, even if it resulted from increased effectiveness.

These same principles should now be extended to other federal welfare programs, including Food Stamps, Medicaid, SCHIP, hous-ing assistance programs, and other, smaller welfare programs. Indeed, the federal government operates eighty-five means tested programs providing assistance to low-income families, all of which should be turned into block grants for the states to modernize in a coordinated manner with minimum red tape.

ELIMINATING POVERTY IN AMERICA

In a new study published by the Heartland Institute, Peter Fer-rara, formerly of the White House Office of Policy Development under President Reagan, demonstrates the exciting possibilities that states could achieve with their new, sweeping authority under such reform. This would take welfare reform to the next level, effectively replacing the entire system with a better-functioning, more humane, and more affordable alternative.

Ferrara proposes that states use the funds from all the block grant programs primarily to aid the able-bodied through a guaranteed offer of work. (Those unable to work would receive benefits through a sep-arate program to help them move from disabilities to capabilities.) Those who report to their local welfare office before 9:00 a.m. would be guaranteed a day's work assignment, in the private sector when-ever possible, paying the minimum wage in cash. The welfare office would provide free daycare for participants' small children, who would receive medical examinations and treatment when necessary.

Those who work a minimum number of hours each month would get a Medicaid voucher to purchase basic private health insurance. Those who establish a dependable work history would be eligible for new housing assistance focused on help in purchasing a home.

Earning the federal minimum wage, these workers will receive $7.25 an hour, or roughly $15,000 for a full year's work. They would also continue to be eligible for the earned income tax credit, which is now worth $457 with no children, $3,000 for one child, and $5,000 for two children, as well as the child tax credit, worth an additional $1,000 per child. These tax credits are refundable, meaning the recipient gets these amounts regardless of his tax liability. Then there is the value of the child care and the health insurance.

More than adequate as a safety net, this system would save federal and state taxpayers enormous sums. First, private sector jobs would substitute earned wages for former welfare benefits from all the block grant programs. Thus, modern labor markets, rather than the government's transfer of taxes, will play the primary role in providing for the poor through productively earned income.

Second, this replacement eliminates all work disincentives from welfare. Nearly the only way for the able-bodied to get assistance is to work in the private sector, whether through this program or not. This would all but eliminate long-term welfare dependency and move millions still too dependent on the government into private sector self-support and self-reliance. The government safety net would be used only for short-term emergencies.

This system would also end all incentives for having children outside marriage. Someone, either the father or the mother, will have to work to support a child, so free benefits just for having children are all but eliminated. Furthermore, there is nothing to be gained by avoiding marriage or by couples splitting up, so marriage is not discouraged—a government welfare check does not become a substitute for a working husband. The result would be substantially fewer single parent households that cannot support themselves, and far more self-supporting, married families.

By eliminating the need to maintain and investigate eligibility requirements, this system would also minimize administrative costs. If Warren Buffett wants to show up for a work assignment before 9:00 a.m., he's free to do so like anyone else.

The ultimate payoff is this: the system would effectively eliminate real poverty in America. Everyone would have an assured job and an assured income worth roughly $25,000 to $30,000 per year or more, while the disabled would be assisted in maximzing their capabilities in a fundamentally different program.

This new work and opportunity system would be a historic breakthrough in raising up lower-income individuals and families, finally beating poverty through the tried and true principle of work.

PERSONAL ACCOUNTS INSTEAD OF THE PAYROLL TAX

Another key concept for positive, structural entitlement replacement is personal accounts for Social Security, which would let workers substitute savings and investment accounts for at least part of the current system.

Beginning at any size, the accounts could be expanded over time until workers can choose to substitute them for all their Social Security retirement benefits. This could be accomplished using just the 6.2 percent employee share of the Social Security payroll tax, still leaving workers with close to twice the benefits Social Security promises under current law (but which in the future it will not be able to pay).

The accounts could be expanded further, eventually substituting private life insurance for Social Security survivor's benefits, and private disability insurance for Social Security disability benefits. This could be accomplished with another 2.8 percent of the payroll tax, or a total of 9 percent, leaving workers even further ahead of Social Security's promised benefits.

Eventually, the accounts could be expanded to cover the payroll taxes for Medicare, another 2.9 percent of wages, with the saved funds financing monthly annuity benefits used to purchase private health insurance in retirement. The personal accounts would then total 11.9 percent of wages, a direct savings of about one-fourth from the current 15.3 percent total payroll tax. With the accounts paying for all the benefits currently financed by this tax, it could eventually be phased out completely.

Contributing these amounts to the account over a lifetime, couples with average incomes would likely reach retirement with a million dollars or more in today's dollars after adjusting for inflation. Such accounts would pay substantially more than Social Security currently promises, while still leaving enough to buy health insurance in retirement, taking over for the projected bankruptcy of Medicare. The major cost savings available through Health Savings Accounts would make this even more manageable for retirees. The general revenues that now finance over half of Medicare spending could be used to provide supplements to help lower income retirees buy adequate health insurance.

Retired workers will also be able to use a small fraction of their accumulated funds to buy long-term care nursing home insurance, protecting the rest of the funds in their account from such expenses. This would effectively privatize the major portion of Medicaid that now finances such long-term care for lower income workers. It would nicely complement the Medicaid block grants discussed above.

These accounts wouldn't just trim the growth of government spending, they would shift huge chunks of it from the public to the private sector, ultimately reducing federal spending by about 10 percent of GDP as the personal accounts replace this spending with market financed benefits. Such spending reductions would involve an unprecedented expansion of personal freedom and personal choice.

In the process, the payroll tax would ultimately be phased out completely and replaced by an engine of personal family wealth in the personal accounts. Workers would get much better benefits through these accounts because market investment returns over time are so much higher than the returns the non-invested, redistributive Social Security system can promise, let alone what it will be able to pay in future years. Workers across the board would accumulate $1 million or more in real terms by retirement, directly owned by each worker, which could be left to the family at death. That contrasts with zero estate accumulation under the current system—a situation that especially harms African-American males who have the shortest average life spans and under the current system accumulate nothing for their family despite a lifetime of paying Social Security taxes. This would do far more to reduce economic inequality than any other single reform.

What an exciting long-term vision for America. Indeed, such a program would be another historic breakthrough in the personal prosperity of working people. Retirees would be better off for all the reasons stated above, and taxpayers would be better off because the payroll tax would ultimately be phased out. Perhaps most important, the transition to personal accounts would eliminate the long-term Social Security financing crisis.

The bill introduced in Congress by Republican Paul Ryan, which benefited from substantial input from the Social Security Administration and from experienced Wall Street fund administrators, serves as a comprehensive model of how to structure such accounts.

That bill maintains the current social safety net in full by including a federal guarantee that if any retiree's account cannot pay at least what Social Security would under current law, the federal government would pay the difference. Because capital market returns are so much higher than what Social Security promises, however, it's unlikely the government would ever have to pay off this guarantee, especially when workers are investing in their personal accounts through a structured framework where they are choosing among highly diversified, professionally managed investment funds approved and regulated by the government for safety and soundness. These features follow the amazingly successful personal account program adopted in Chile over twenty-five years ago. Those accounts produced higher incomes for returns and higher economic growth for the country.

The transition to personal accounts can be financed by reducing the growth of other government spending and by the increased revenues stemming from the higher savings and investment in the accounts and the resulting higher economic growth. Indeed, the other structural entitlement changes discussed in this chapter can help greatly in financing this transition. Brian Riedl and the Heritage Foundation have advocated a limit on the growth of total federal spending that would be more than sufficient to finance the transition. He has also published for Heritage lists of wasteful federal spending that should be cut, as has the Cato Institute and others, which could help finance the transition as well. The popularity of personal accounts and the need to finance the transition would draw in the public to more actively support reducing such wasteful and even counterproductive spending.

A BETTER SYSTEM IS POSSIBLE

Entitlement replacement should involve fundamentally rethinking the structure of Medicaid and Medicare. That's also a key component of chapter fifteen on transforming the health system.

These structural entitlement replacements would solve the long-term entitlement crisis without tax increases or benefit cuts. The new, transformed safety net would serve the poor and senior citizens far better while reducing the size of government.

Now *that* would be change you can believe in.

Creating Better Health at Lower Cost

With Nancy Desmond
CEO, Center for Health Transformation

ObamaCare, like HillaryCare, is a dead end of higher taxes, bigger government, more bureaucracy, and a decaying health system.

However, the American people know we need health reform. So just saying no to ObamaCare won't do. We need to offer a better solution.

Our task is both to expose the disingenuous and destructive heath proposals of the secular-socialist Left and to promote and communicate a better system that will improve health outcomes, strengthen individual rights, and boost the economy.

It is impossible to save America without fundamentally improving our healthcare system. Morally, we cannot accept the needless death and suffering of millions of Americans each year from avoidable medical errors, preventable chronic diseases, and the lack of integrated information in our current system.

Nor can we as Americans accept a future where, according to analysts, we will be the first generation where our children and grandchildren are likely to live shorter and less healthy lives than the generations that preceded them.

Furthermore, we cannot save America without solving the economic challenges related to the costs of our current inefficient healthcare system. We cannot balance the budget or rein in the deficit without fixing what ails our healthcare system. Similarly, we can't create jobs competing in the world market if our healthcare system is dramatically more expensive than those of our competitors.

PRINCIPLES OF A TWENTY-FIRST CENTURY PERSONALIZED MODEL OF HEALTH

The current debate over covering the uninsured is a prime example of our unfortunate tendency to focus on only one part of the healthcare system. By concentrating on who we should tax in order to expand government coverage to more Americans, politicians are missing the real opportunity to rethink and transform the health system. The fact is, it is possible to have 300 million Americans living longer and living healthier in a twenty-first century intelligent health system with 100 percent coverage, but it requires changing much more than just financing.

At the Center for Health Transformation, we know the potential for positive transformation is enormous because we have spent years developing effective approaches and studying successful health innovators around America.[*]

---

* Go to www.healthtransformation.net for more details.

THE GOAL OF A TWENTY-FIRST CENTURY HEALTHCARE SYSTEM: ASSURING ALL AMERICANS ACCESS TO QUALITY HEALTH-CARE THAT IS AVAILABLE, AFFORDABLE, AND APPROPRIATE.

When everyday Americans consider healthcare reform, they do not focus on the nuances of insurance collectives and industry jargon. Rather, they ask the simple questions:

- Will healthcare be AVAILABLE for me and my family when we need it?
- Will we be able to AFFORD what we need?
- Will what is offered be APPROPRIATE for us?

As we consider the best way to transform our healthcare system, we must assure access includes these three elements.

Availability

There are regions of our country that don't have a single doctor, and there are others with plenty of hospitals and clinics, but where ill people cannot physically get to that care.

A twenty-first century healthcare system must use creative initiatives like medical education debt forgiveness to train more physicians and incentivize careers in primary care, especially in rural communities.

We must also transition from a physician-centric model to a physician-led team model of care that empowers and utilizes other medical professionals such as clinical nurse practitioners, physician assistants, pharmacists, and social workers who can provide distributed models of care that reach people where they live including in their homes and not just in hospitals or doctors' offices.

Most important, we must ensure that the pipeline of discovery and development of innovative medical products is nurtured by public and private investment so that cures become available for advanced cancer, Alzheimer's, diabetes, pandemics, and other ills.

Affordability

Many Americans wonder why the cost of their healthcare rises while the cost of flat screen TVs and cell phones decline even as their quality improves. The simple answer is that there is waste and inefficiency across the entire spectrum of discovery, development, and delivery of healthcare.

Creating a twenty-first century healthcare system that is affordable to both our nation and to every American requires a systematic effort at process improvement that is quality-focused and cost-conscious.

Expenditures for healthcare at the macro or national level as a percentage of GDP can be viewed as having two components: the purchase of goods and investment in research. This is no different from any other business model predicated upon continuous product improvement. When you purchase your computer, you are paying for the computer itself and all its features, but you are also providing the manufacturer with funds to do R&D to produce a better version tomorrow. Successful businesses have turned this model into an art form—they had to, because their survival depends on it. The healthcare system has created chaos in this process, and that must change; our personal survival depends on it.

Investment in Research and Development

The current system of medical research is broken. It's too slow (approximately ten years for the development of a drug and seventeen years for a discovery in the lab to be translated into a life-saving treatment in the clinic); it's too expensive (approximately $1.5 billion to develop one drug); it's too risky (only one out of a thousand compounds ever makes it into the clinic as a drug); and it's too fragmented (there is a lack of seamless integration between basic, translational, and clinical research essential for product development). The federal government, working through agencies such as the National Institutes of Health, the Food and Drug Administration, and the Center for Medicare and Medicaid, in conjunction with academia and industry, can radically improve this process of turning new knowledge into new cures.

Delivery

The system of product delivery today is plagued by fraud and abuse, contributing to a dramatic waste of money, time, talent, and expertise. Crucially, healthcare providers lack an adequate modern information technology system. Not only does our current paper-based system kill patients through unnecessary errors and inefficiencies, but it is killing the fundamental system of care delivery.

Visitors should be appalled by the number of forms they must fill out at most health facilities, and at the way the same process is repeated at every place within a facility. We can do better. Modern medical facilities like the Mayo Clinic, Intermountain Healthcare, Gundersen Lutheran, Sutter Health, and the Cleveland Clinic have found a better system of electronic medicine that makes a person's healthcare portable. It also improves access to data among different facilities in order to avoid unnecessary duplication of medical tests and procedures, a problem that costs significant money and time to both patients and doctors.

Whether apparent or not, fraud and abuse affect every person's healthcare. Stopping the thieves will save the system hundreds of billions of dollars per year. That's why eliminating fraud is essential, as described in the next chapter.

A twenty-first century health system can assure every American access to continuously improving, affordable, state-of-the-art care, just as we always expect to see better TVs or cell phones. It requires a new business model in which each producer or provider strives to produce the finest quality product or service in the most efficient manner, and the government creates a regulatory framework that assures these products and services are integrated into an efficient system that offers real choice to consumers.

Appropriateness

Perhaps Americans' most important healthcare concern is to receive the right care for the right reason that achieves the right outcome. In fact, there is no other reason than this to seek professional care. People trust and depend on the medical profession to consider their unique needs and to have the expertise and tools necessary to assure personalized care.

In the past, physicians made a diagnosis according to patient history, physical exam, lab tests, and X-rays. Then, based on treatments approved by the Food and Drug Administration (FDA) that had been tested on others, they prescribed a treatment plan, and both patient and physician hoped for the best. This hit or miss process should be a thing of the past.

Thanks to breakthroughs in science and technology, we will soon be able to radically transform healthcare so that treatment is no longer based on *population* medicine, but on *personalized* medicine.

This can begin with modernizing the FDA, which should create a science-based regulatory framework to approve medical products based on the scientific knowledge of their mechanism of action in individuals, not just on the observation of outcomes in large populations. By implementing this framework within large and diverse healthcare delivery systems, modern information management systems can monitor performance of medical products after regulatory approval. This can allow us to continuously define and communicate to patients and physicians the safety and effectiveness of those products.

We must also create a strategy for individual wellness that enables healthcare providers to use emerging tools of science and technology to identify risk or susceptibility to disease, and to personalize prevention strategies relating to lifestyle, nutrition, access to early detection, and continuous health management. Numerous creative interventions are now being developed that empower individuals to continuously engage in managing their own health using wireless at-home systems. Those systems can monitor health parameters and provide guidance for prevention interventions to Internet-based and employer worksite programs that promote wellness.

Appropriate care is the key to optimal quality at the lowest possible cost. For example, the FDA recently commissioned a study to use genomic data to help define the optimal dose of Coumadin, a blood thinner widely used to prevent blood clots. By using this new technology to better provide the right dose for patients, the right outcome was achieved. Fewer patients were under-dosed, which could cause continued clots resulting in strokes and other serious problems, and fewer patients were over-dosed, which could necessitate emergency treatment for bleeding. In spite of the cost of doing the genomic test in all patients, the projected cost savings for one year due to reduced complications requiring additional medical care reached hundreds of millions of dollars. The real story is not just saving money, but saving people the horrendous burden of an unnecessary stroke or hemorrhage.

HOW CAN WE ASSURE THAT CARE IS AVAILABLE, AFFORDABLE, AND APPROPRIATE? THE FOUR BOXES OF HEALTH AND HEALTHCARE THAT MUST BE CHANGED

To create a system of better healthcare at lower cost, we have to stop fighting over how much it would cost to expand the current system and talk instead about real change in the four distinct but interrelated boxes of health and healthcare:

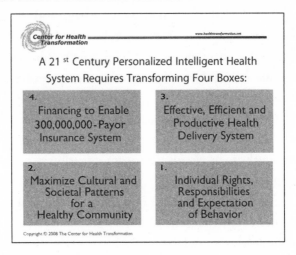

The Individual. A personalized health system will only work if the individual is empowered and engaged. This requires people to be equipped with the knowledge and access they need; they also have to understand, accept, and be incentivized to make responsible choices.

In this system, you will have more individual rights but also more responsibilities. You will have access to more information and choices but will be expected to become partners in your own health and healthcare. Even the best doctor, of course, can't help a patient who is unwilling to comply with medical and preventive recommendations.

The Culture and Society. We need to maximize positive cultural and societal patterns for a healthy community. This includes changing the policies, institutions, and environment that impact the choices made by individuals.

For example, given the current epidemic of childhood obesity, we should insist that schools serve healthy lunches, offer healthy snacks, and include physical education as part of the daily curriculum. Likewise, if we encourage healthy diets but high-risk neighborhoods have no access in their local stores to fresh fruit and vegetables—or if healthy food is prohibitively expensive—we will probably not have much impact.

The Delivery System. We have to create an effective, efficient, and productive health delivery system. This means we must adopt new technologies, new models, and a new culture. A future where the healthcare system focuses on the individual, where learning is constant and in real-time, and where innovations are much more rapidly driven through the system will require a different type of delivery system. There will be more partnering, increased reliance on IT-assisted knowledge and expert systems, and an emphasis on health professionals acting as consultants to one another.

The System of Financing. Finally, we need a financing method that enables not a single-payer system, but a 300 million-payer insurance system. There is no one-size-fits-all solution to expand insurance coverage, particularly because there are so many reasons why some Americans lack insurance. Some of the uninsured can afford insurance but have chosen not to buy it; some are temporarily uninsured because they have moved, lost a job, or their employer stopped offering coverage; and some are chronically uninsured and are essentially locked out of the system. The savings from better health and better quality care can be used to insure every American through a robust, competitive private market that leads to more choices at lower costs.

A PRO-JOBS, PRO-GROWTH PLAN FOR HEALTH REFORM:

The Center for Health Transformation's Plan for Better Health and Healthcare

The solution is to build a system that gives every American more choices of greater quality at lower costs. This will not be found in the giant healthcare bill passed by Congress. This encompassed the secular-socialist model of more spending, more regulations, and more bureaucracy.

At the Center for Health Transformation, we have been working for the past seven years to develop transformative solutions. If Americans want to build a system that is available, affordable, and appropriate for every American, we should take the following innovative, practical steps:

Reward health and wellness. The Centers for Disease Control and Prevention reports that 64 percent of adults are either overweight or obese. The CDC also states that diabetes is a major factor in killing more than 220,000 Americans every year. These two conditions, which cost our system hundreds of billions of dollars annually, mostly stem from poor individual choices. We must focus on health—then healthcare—and individuals must take an active role in becoming healthier. Tools like the Gallup-Healthways Well-Being Index can help identify and focus on communities most in need. Leadership like that shown by First Lady Michelle Obama with her "Let's Move" initiative is also essential.

We should give health plans, employers, and Medicare and Medicaid more latitude to design benefits to encourage, incentivize, and reward healthy behaviors. We should incentivize individuals to participate in worksite wellness programs, focus on prevention, and adopt healthy lifestyles. We should create broader incentives to purchase healthier foods in the food stamp and WIC programs. We should also increase federal funding to public schools that 1) have physical education five days a week for every K–12 student, and 2) provide breakfasts, lunches, and vending machines that promote healthy foods.

Meet the needs of the chronically ill. Most individuals with chronic diseases want to control their own care. The mother of an asthmatic child, for example, should have a device at home that measures the child's peak airflow and should be taught when to change her medication, rather than having to go to a doctor each time.

Being able to obtain and manage more health dollars in Health Savings Accounts is a start. A good model for self-management is the Cash and Counseling program for the homebound disabled under Medicaid. Program participants can manage their own budgets and hire and fire the people who provide them with custodial services and medical care. Satisfaction rates approach 100 percent, according to the Robert Wood Johnson Foundation.[1]

We should also encourage health plans to specialize in managing chronic diseases instead of demanding that every plan be all things to all people. For example, special-needs plans in Medicare Advantage actively compete to enroll and cover the sickest Medicare beneficiaries and stay in business by meeting their needs. This is the alternative to forcing insurers to take high-cost patients for cut-rate premiums, which guarantees these patients will be unwanted and ultimately untreated.

Speed medical breakthroughs to patients. Breakthrough drugs, innovative devices, and new therapies to treat rare, complex diseases and chronic conditions should be sped to the market. As discussed above, we can do this by cutting red tape before and during review by the FDA, and by deploying information technology to monitor the quality of drugs and devices once they reach the marketplace. Faster time to market will save lives and money.

Make insurance affordable. The current taxation of health insurance is arbitrary and unfair, giving lavish subsidies to some, like those who get "Cadillac" coverage from their employers, and almost no relief to people who have to buy their own policy. More equitable tax treatment, in addition to other market improvements, would lower costs for individuals and families. Many health economists argue tax relief for health insurance should be a fixed-dollar amount, independent of the amount of insurance purchased. We should give Americans the choice of a generous tax credit or the ability to deduct the value of their health insurance up to a certain amount.

Make health insurance more secure. The first step toward genuine security is portability, which is also the best way to solve the problems of pre-existing conditions. Employers should be encouraged to provide employees with insurance that travels with them from job to job and in and out of the labor market. Moreover, individuals should be allowed to buy health insurance across state lines. When insurers compete for consumers, prices will fall and quality will improve.

Help small businesses. The self-employed, small businesses, and certain organizations are legally prohibited from banding together to purchase health insurance. This limits not only the freedom of private citizens to collectively organize, but it creates an enormous barrier to obtaining health insurance. We should allow individuals and small businesses to pool together, giving these associations greater bargaining power for more affordable coverage.

Inform consumers. Patients and consumers need to have clear, reliable data on cost and quality before they make decisions about their care. In fact, they have a right to know this information. But finding such information is virtually impossible. Sources like Medicare claims data (stripped of patient information) can help consumers answer important questions about their care. Government data—paid for by the taxpayers—can answer these questions and should be made public. Websites like those created by former Governor Jeb Bush in Florida, Governor Sonny Perdue in Georgia, and insurers like WellPoint, as well as dozens of other resources, effectively inform consumers about the quality of the doctors and providers they see and the products and services they need. Genuine public access to valuable information data will push providers, health plans, public programs, and all other stakeholders to improve.

Allow doctors and patients to control costs. Doctors and patients are currently trapped by government-imposed payment rates. Under Medicare, doctors are not paid if they communicate with their patients by phone or e-mail. Medicare pays by tasks—there is a list of about 7,500 of them—but doctors do not get paid to advise patients on how to lower their drug costs or how to comparison shop online. In short, they get paid when people are sick, not to keep them healthy.

So long as total cost to the government does not rise and quality of care does not suffer, doctors should have the freedom to repackage and re-price their services. And payment should take into account the quality of the care delivered. A number of private insurers are experimenting with more effective and more pro-health payment systems, but the sheer size of Medicare gives it the potential to make a decisive difference.

Migrate every doctor to best practices. In order to ensure that health is the driving focus of our renewal efforts, we should determine what methods are actually saving lives and money, then design public policy to encourage their widespread adoption. For example, according to the *Dartmouth Health Atlas*, the definitive authority on healthcare quality and variation, if America's 5,500 hospitals provided care at the level of Intermountain Healthcare in Utah or the Mayo Clinic in Minnesota, Medicare alone would save 32 percent of total spending ever year—with better health outcomes.[2] We need to make best practice minimum practice.

We should create a private-sector-led best-practice initiative that educates the industry on documented, evidence-based best practices that work. This initiative should support the development and diffusion of knowledge in order to expand care, improve outcomes, and lower costs—and explicitly should not be used by government to ration care.

Paying for quality care. Our current payment system pays doctors and providers for simply delivering care regardless of the outcome. Doctors, hospitals, and other providers that deliver better care are mostly paid at the same rate as those who provide poorer care. Like any other rational market, we need a reimbursement model that takes into account the quality of the care delivered, not simply that it *was* delivered.

We must incentivize the use of best practices, chronic care management tools, and information technology. We need to eliminate the vast geographical differences in reimbursement, and to promote the development and use of primary care and its providers. The delivery reform proposal released in November 2008 by Kaiser, Intermountain Healthcare, and the Mayo Clinic provides a range of options that would be vast improvements over the status quo, including bundled or episode-based payments, Accountable Care Organizations, and chronic care coordination payments.[3]

Don't cut Medicare. Obama's health reform bill cut Medicare by around $500 billion. This is wrong. Medicare is undoubtedly unsustainable, as the government has promised far more than it can deliver. But this problem will not be solved by cutting the program in order to create new unfunded liabilities for young people.

A sound roadmap to shore up Medicare was released in 2000 by the National Bipartisan Commission on the Future of Medicare. Central pieces of that report have been implemented, most notably the prescription drug benefit, but others, particularly those that address the program's long-term solvency, have been ignored. Reviving many of these recommendations, along with new proposals, can save Medicare for future generations. Solutions include:

- Introducing premium support to stimulate competition among providers and private insurers.
- Increasing beneficiary choice.
- Introducing the same competitive features of the prescription drug benefit and the Medicare Advantage program to other areas, such as durable medical equipment and Part B drug pricing.
- Targeting assistance to lower- and moderate-income seniors.
- Incentivizing beneficiaries to seek out Centers of Excellence that deliver the highest-quality, lowest-cost care. Consumer demand will help address the egregious geographic variance in cost and quality.

Protect early retirees. More than 80 percent of the 78 million baby boomers will likely retire before they become eligible for Medicare. This is often the most difficult time for individuals and families to find affordable insurance. We can build a viable bridge to Medicare by allowing employers to obtain individually owned insurance for their retirees at group rates; allowing them to deposit some or all the premium amount for post-retirement insurance into a retiree's Health Savings Account; and allowing employers and younger employees to save tax-free for post-retirement health.

Transform Medicaid and drive innovation in the states. Governors and legislators know their constituents and understand the special needs of their local communities far better than anyone in Washington. They should have much more freedom to improve their Medicaid programs in their own communities. Key priorities should be to mainstream Medicaid beneficiaries into private insurance coverage, be it with an employer or an individual policy; to utilize modern information technology systems; and to identify and adopt the best practices in Medicaid across the country so that other states may duplicate and improve upon them. These kinds of changes will turn Medicaid from the disaster that it currently is into an effective, efficient program.

Stop healthcare fraud. Criminal fraud accounts for as much as 10 percent of all healthcare spending, according to the National Health Care Anti-Fraud Association. That is more than $200 billion every year. Medicare fraud alone could account for as much as $40 billion a year. This crime, enabled by our current paper-based system, can be detected, eliminated, and prevented with the right kind of electronic resources, such as enhanced coordination of benefits, third-party liability verification, and electronic payment.

Cut waste. If our healthcare system moved from manual paper and phone processes to electronic administration, we could save an estimated $30 billion a year. For example, today 90 percent of all medical claims are paid by printing a paper check and mailing it through the U.S. Postal Service. Electronic payment through direct deposit—think PayPal for health—could alone save an estimated $11 billion every year.

We should migrate all payers and providers to fully electronic processes for administration, including claims submission, insurance eligibility verification, claims status inquiry, claims remittance, and electronic payment. All payers—CMS, state Medicaid programs, and private plans—must lead by making a real investment in their own electronic processes building on claims submission, followed by rewarding and then requiring their use.

Eliminate junk lawsuits to reform civil justice and eliminate defensive medicine. Last year President Obama pledged to consider civil justice reform. We do not need to study or test medical malpractice any longer: the current system is unarguably broken. States across the country—Texas in particular—have already implemented key reforms including liability protection for using health information technology or following clinical standards of care; caps on non-economic damages; loser pays laws; and new alternative dispute resolutions where patients get compensated for unexpected, adverse medical outcomes without lawyers, courtrooms, judges, or juries.

Move from paper-based care to modern, electronic tools. The 2009 stimulus allocated tens of billions of dollars toward encouraging physicians and providers to adopt twenty-first century tools such as electronic prescribing and electronic health records. While I opposed the inclusion of this investment in the stimulus bill, these are valuable tools nonetheless. We have a new book at the Center for Health Transformation entitled *Paper Kills 2.0*, edited by David Merritt, that proves conclusively that technology saves lives and money. Updated, accurate, and comprehensive patient information at the point of care will prevent medical errors and will allow physicians, nurses, and providers to make better, more informed decisions. Electronic access to information will reduce duplicative and unnecessary tests and treatments. Automating cumbersome, manual processes will streamline workflow, eliminate inefficiencies, and lower costs. We must continue striving to get these technologies into the hands of doctors and nurses and to ensure that information is portable, accurate, secure, and protected.

The solutions presented here can be the foundation for an individual-centered system. We must insist that our elected leaders have the courage to embrace them.

A TIME TO CHOOSE

President Obama's healthcare reform will raise taxes, destroy jobs, and allow Washington bureaucrats to make decisions that ought to be made by individual Americans together with their families and doctors. At a time when we are already suffering from over-taxation, high unemployment, and excessive regulation, it's the last thing America needs.

We can create a better system, one that prioritizes individual health and wellness, delivers personalized, best practice care, and insures every American. The changes and solutions outlined in this plan are the right reforms to build such a future. By addressing health, quality, costs, and coverage:

- **We will not need to raise taxes.** We can bring down healthcare costs and save hundreds of billions of dollars by focusing on the right priorities.
- **We will not need to introduce a government-run plan into the private insurance market.** Choice is more powerful than a single government plan. Tax fairness, open markets, and access to insurance for all will deliver many more choices at lower cost.

- **We will not need nor should we ever resort to government rationing of healthcare.** More choices and higher quality will lower costs and empower consumers.
- **We will not need to cut Medicare.** We can save future generations from crushing debt by focusing on health, quality care, and efficiency.
- **We will not need to mandate that employers, including small businesses, provide health insurance.** The right reforms that balance a robust private sector with effective public programs will give all Americans the financial means and choices to get the coverage that is best for them and their families—without saddling small businesses with debt.

The choice is clear. We can implement transformative programs—for better health, more efficient delivery, sound public programs, and a competitive marketplace—that will assure that all Americans have access to quality healthcare that is available, affordable, and appropriate. Or we can accept the left-wing approach of ushering in a government-run system that will destroy our economy along with our health.

The choice is ours—and the time for choosing is now.

We should repeal the 2010 big-government act passed on a narrow partisan basis with extraordinary corruption and bribery, and start over in the right direction with the right policies.

CHAPTER SIXTEEN

Solutions for Stopping Healthcare Fraud

With Jim Frogue, Vice President of the Center for Health Transformation and Editor of *Stop Paying the Crooks*

Every year we taxpayers pay $70–120 billion to crooks through Medicare and Medicaid alone. This ought to be the first source of new money to pay for health reform.

Why raise taxes on honest people or cut health benefits for honest senior citizens or penalize honest doctors and hospitals when the system is run so incompetently that it currently gives billions to criminals every month?

This problem is so great that at the Center for Health Transformation, we have initiated an entire antitheft and antifraud project led by Jim Frogue, the coauthor of this chapter.

Fraud, waste, and abuse in our healthcare sector are more pervasive than people think—they constituted a third or more of the $2.5 trillion spent on healthcare services in 2009. To his credit, President

Obama noted in his September 9, 2009 address to Congress there are "hundreds of billions of dollars in waste and fraud" in the system.

Other top officials and representatives have drawn attention to the problem as well. Health and Human Services secretary Kathleen Sebelius said at the January 28, 2010 National Summit on Health Care Fraud, "We believe the problem of healthcare fraud is bigger than government, law enforcement, or private industry can handle alone."

At the White House Health Summit on February 25, 2010, Senator Tom Coburn suggested, "20 percent of the cost of government healthcare is fraud." Senator Chuck Schumer of New York later responded, "I was glad to hear my friend Tom Coburn's remarks. I think we agree with most of them, and particularly the point that about a third of all the spending that's done in Medicare and Medicaid... doesn't go to really good health care, goes to other things."

Unfortunately, while clearly aware of this debilitating problem, Congress and the administration have not developed meaningful proposals to solve it. But this is an urgent issue requiring fast, effective action.

According to an October 2009 white paper by Thomson Reuters, the overall American healthcare system wastes $600–850 billion *every year*. Here's the breakdown: [1]

- **Unnecessary care** (40 percent of healthcare waste): This includes defensive medical treatments whose primary purpose is to double cross every "t" and double dot every "i," lest the trial lawyers come calling.
- **Fraud** (19 percent of healthcare waste): This is willful theft, such as billing Medicare, Medicaid, and private insurers for products and services not rendered.
- **Administrative inefficiency** (17 percent of healthcare waste): Duplicative paperwork limits the ability of

healthcare professionals to spend the appropriate amount of time with sick and injured patients. One study found some nurses must spend one hour on paperwork for every hour of patient care.

- **Healthcare provider errors** (12 percent of healthcare waste): Mistakes by physicians and support staff are tremendously costly both in terms of dollars and human suffering. Too many errors happen as a result of illegible handwriting and exhaustion with paperwork.

- **Preventable conditions** (6 percent of healthcare waste): The personal choices made around prevention and treatment of diseases account for at least 50 percent of one's health status. For example, Type 2 diabetes is often preventable with the proper diet and exercise. Nevertheless, Type 2 diabetes now constitutes 90 percent of diabetes cases, accounting for tens of billions of dollars every year spent unnecessarily.

- **Lack of care coordination** (6 percent of healthcare waste): Better access to more accurate patient records via electronic health records and e-prescribing, with strong safeguards to ensure patient privacy, will improve health outcomes and eliminate unnecessary tests and contraindicated prescriptions.

Additional confirmation of the scale of fraud and waste comes from the Government Accountability Office (GAO), widely regarded as the gold standard for investigating government-run programs. In a January 2009 report on "high risk" programs, GAO experts found in 2007, the Medicaid improper payment rate was 10 percent, or $32.7 billion (FN).[2] This contrasts with the average improper payment rate of 3.9 percent across all government programs, according to the Congressional Research Service.[3]

So Medicaid has nearly three times the improper payment rate of all government. That is one reason the Left can tout low administrative costs for Medicare and Medicaid: they simply write checks without effective oversight. They pay more in fraud than they gain in lean administration.

In the Senate Finance Committee, Republican John Cornyn submitted an amendment to the Senate healthcare bill that made expansion of the Medicaid program contingent on GAO certifying that Medicaid's improper payment rate was at or below the government average. The amendment was defeated on a party-line vote.

Consider this: the federal department that oversees Medicaid *cannot even accurately measure* the extent of the problem. A letter dated August 26, 2009, from Stuart Wright with the U.S. Department of Health and Human Services Office of Inspector General to Cindy Mann, Director of State Operations at the Center for Medicare and Medicaid Services (CMS), outlined how current data collection methods fail to generate accurate and timely data about the program. As the old saying goes, "You can't manage what you can't measure." The conclusion to the 25-page letter reads:

> MSIS [Medicaid Statistical Information Statistics] is the only source of nationwide Medicaid claims and beneficiary eligibility information. CMS collects MSIS data directly from States to, among other things, assist in detecting fraud, waste, and abuse in the Medicaid program. Timely, accurate, and comprehensive MSIS data can contribute to more effective health care fraud, waste, and abuse identification and prevention.
>
> We determined that during FYs 2004–2006, MSIS data were an average of 1 ½ years old when it was released to all users. In addition, CMS did not fully disclose or document information about the accuracy of MSIS data. Furthermore,

MSIS did not capture many of the data elements that can assist in fraud, waste, and abuse detection.[4]

Medicare's improper payment rate is equally bad. A November 2009 report admitted to $47 billion in improper payments, which is, like Medicaid, roughly 10 percent of that program. Examples included payments to dead doctors and people using Medicare ID numbers with or without the beneficiary's knowledge to run up fake billing.[5]

An excellent segment on *60 Minutes* in October 2009 estimates $60 billion of Medicare spending annually is fraudulent. Steve Kroft warns in the opening that the show will "make your blood boil." The highlight of the piece is an interview with a convicted Medicare fraudster who explains how easy and lucrative it is to steal from Medicare. He made $20,000 to $30,000 a day, and he assures Kroft that, though he is behind bars, there are thousands of people like him stealing from the program.[6]

Consider this sampling of recent fraud in our healthcare system:[*]

- Healthcare fraud is luring criminals with easy money and short prison sentences. These gangsters are forgoing violent crime for white-collar scams—bilking U.S. taxpayers out of millions of dollars with little risk. According to a recent Associated Press article, "A Medicare scammer could easily net at least $25,000 a day while risking a relatively modest 10 years in prison if convicted on a single count. A cocaine dealer could take weeks to make that amount while risking up to life in prison."[7]

---

[*] We gather additional stories on a near-daily basis under the "Fraud in the News" section at our website, www.healthtransformation.net.

- So-called fraud "trouble spots" exist across the country. Federal agents recently arrested twenty-six people in three different states—Florida, New York, and Michigan—for Medicare fraud totaling more than $61 million. Accusations included faking medical certifications and bribing clinics to join the scams.[8]
- In 2005, South Florida clinics submitted $2.2 billion in HIV-drug infusion claims to Medicare, which is 22 *times* more than the rest of the country combined.[9]
- A Miami doctor falsely listed some of his patients as both blind and diabetic in order to bill Medicare for expensive twice-daily nurse visits. The doctor was arrested within weeks of the release of a DHHS report showing that Miami-Dade country received more than half a billion dollars in funding from Medicare in home health payments—more than the rest of the country combined.[10] In 2008, the average cost for home healthcare patients in Miami-Dade ran $11,928 every two months, which is 32 *times* the national average cost of $378.[11]
- A La Quinta, California doctor was sentenced to fifteen months in jail and ordered to pay more than $600,000 in restitution for "subdosing" AIDS patients and billing insurance companies for the full dosages.[12]
- A Miami man was recently arrested on fraud charges, having submitted $55 million in false claims for bogus HIV and cancer services. He used the money he received to buy Lamborghinis, Bentleys, Mercedes Benzes, and horses. To pose as owners of the fake clinics, he recruited illegal Cuban immigrants who later fled to Cuba when the ruse was discovered.[13]
- A Philadelphia couple recently billed Medicare more than $1.2 million for power wheelchairs and other med-

ical equipment that patients did not need. A U.S. Attorney said the case "involves breaches of trust at every level—from the medical office employees who sold patients' identity information to the people charged ... who used the Medicare Trust as their personal ATMs."[14] Separately, a Michigan businessman fraudulently billed Medicare for $18.4 million by submitting claims for non-existent therapy services. He also paid kickbacks to people for use of their Medicare numbers, another all-too-common fraudulent practice.[15]

- Owners of an ambulance service in Tennessee billed both Medicare and Medicaid for unnecessary and non-compliant ambulance rides for patients, using the proceeds to buy a Corvette and a Harley Davidson. Examples of their "service" include a patient riding in an ambulance jumping out to get take-out at a restaurant, and ambulances being loaded with a patient in both the front and back—"in effect acting as a taxi, charging the government in excess of $300 per round trip."[16]

- The Senate Permanent Subcommittee on Investigations identified $60–92 million in Medicare payments for services ordered by more than 16,500 deceased doctors in 2000–2007. Some doctors had been dead for more than ten years.[17]

- Facilities in southern California allegedly churned thousands of indigents through their sites and billed Medicare and Medi-Cal for costly and unjustified medical procedures. These facilities ran street-level operations, where runners collected indigents for unnecessary hospital services, dropping them back off on skid row by ambulance.[18]

- In 2005, the *New York Times* estimated New York state
  Medicaid fraud reached into the tens of billions.[19] That
  much abuse in a single state implies a mind-blowing
  amount of Medicaid fraud is occurring across the coun-
  try. Some cases just in New York:
  - A Brooklyn dentist billed as many as 991 proce-
    dures supposedly performed in a single day.
  - School officials enrolled tens of thousands of low-
    income students in speech therapy without the
    required evaluation, garnering more than $1 billion
    in questionable Medicaid payments. One school
    official sent 4,434 students into speech therapy in a
    single day.
  - Several criminal rings duped Medicaid into paying
    for an expensive, AIDS-related muscle-building
    drug that was diverted to bodybuilders at the cost
    of tens of millions.
  - James Mehmet, former chief state investigator for
    Medicaid fraud, reported that "40 percent of all
    claims are questionable."

The staggering amount of fraud in healthcare simply does not exist in
any other industry. That's because the American healthcare system is
mostly third party payer—the entity paying the bill for healthcare
services is not the patient or doctor. That arrangement necessarily
makes the patient and the doctor less concerned with using dollars
efficiently for legitimate treatments and less interested in stopping
fraud and abuse that may even be occurring in their name.

Another major reason for the abundant fraud is that the healthcare system is paper based. The bureaucrat is relying on out of date
paper while the crook is using his Blackberry and iPhone.

HOW NOT TO PAY CROOKS

We at the Center for Health Transformation published a book in 2009 titled *Stop Paying the Crooks* featuring proposed solutions from a diverse group of experts to stop healthcare fraud, waste, and abuse. Here are some of their solutions:

1. Patients and taxpayers have the right to know the cost and quality produced by every facility that receives taxpayer money and how and where scarce taxpayer dollars are spent. Thus, all Medicare and Medicaid claims and patient encounter data should be made public on a depersonalized basis. That data is the mother lode of everything you would ever want to know about both programs. We would be able track all the dollars as well as the health outcomes produced by every provider in the country that accepts Medicare and Medicaid—which is nearly all of them.

Selected academics have access to Medicare data and have produced excellent reports such as the Dartmouth Health Atlas. Among their many key findings is that per capita Medicare spending by locality is *inversely* correlated with the likelihood of receiving recommended care.[20]

As good as the Dartmouth team is, it is not as comprehensive as the collective wisdom of the general public looking at the data and developing new studies, patterns, and solutions.

This data should only be released, however, after being vigorously patient de-identified, as is done in the academic world. Patient privacy must remain paramount.

2. The federally administered Medicare program and the mostly state-administered Medicaid program must improve their sharing of patient data. Their failure to do so results in significant lost opportunities to coordinate care and catch fraud. A 2009 report by the

Kaiser Commission found insufficient controls and duplicate claims processing agents that invite fraud and abuse.

More than 8.8 million of Medicaid's 58 million beneficiaries are low-income senior citizens who are eligible for both Medicaid and Medicare.[21] That is close to 15 percent of Medicaid enrollment, but 40 percent of outlays. They comprise 18 percent of Medicare's enrollment, but Medicare spent even more on their care than Medicaid did. These so-called "dual eligibles" account for roughly $300 billion in annual spending, yet the care they receive is often haphazard, uncoordinated, and reactive because Medicare and Medicaid don't communicate with each other. The result is sub-optimization of patient health outcomes to accompany the waste and fraud.[22]

3. Outsource the authentication of new Medicare and Medicaid suppliers to Visa, Mastercard, or American Express. After forty years of failure, it is clear the status quo in Washington, D.C., is incapable of managing these programs, so let's turn to experts with a track record of success.

The American credit card industry processes over $2 trillion in transactions every year, and there are 800 million credit cards accepted by millions of vendors to buy countless products. Yet fraud constitutes just one-tenth of one percent of the credit card industry. Conservatively speaking, fraud in Medicare and Medicaid is 10 percent, making it 100 times worse.

4. The CMS-855S form that prospective durable medical equipment providers must fill out lacks even a simple, "under penalty of perjury" line by the signature. That little tweak alone would help prosecutors and perhaps even have some deterrent effect. Likewise, we should make the submission of bogus claims a reason for immediately revoking a supplier's billing number.

5. Allow seniors on Medicare the option of traveling to another city to receive major non-emergency surgeries. If a particular set of procedures costs thousands of dollars less in the next state over and the quality outcomes are as good or better, we should allow people the choice of facilities, especially if the individual receiving care can split the savings with taxpayers.

The commercial insurer Wellpoint launched a demonstration project that allows customers to travel to *India* for non-emergency elective procedures like plastic surgery. Surely it's not too radical to take advantage of arbitrage opportunities here in America within the Medicare system.

6. Enhance discovery of third party liability in Medicaid. Simply maximizing *self-reported* third party coverage by patients could save state Medicaid programs 1–2 percent per year. That is $4–7 billion a year the insurers would legitimately be paying that the taxpayers currently cover due to bureaucratic incompetence. A GAO report shows up to 13 percent of people on Medicaid with other coverage.[23]

7. Medicare and Medicaid should use private-sector standards for establishing the number of suppliers for a product or service in a defined area. California's Medicaid program has been doing this for nearly a decade in durable medical equipment. While there was some pushback from frustrated potential providers, there were no reports of access to care issues from beneficiaries.

In a related experiment last year, the South Carolina Medicaid program told its forty-eight Medicaid beneficiaries with the most number of prescriptions they could thenceforth only get prescriptions from one pharmacy, which they could choose themselves. After eight months those individuals had 40 percent fewer prescriptions, saving Medicaid $320,000.

8. Reduce the administrative red tape and lengthy appeals that cancelled suppliers often exploit. Currently, suppliers can drag out the process for months and usually get reinstated. In 2007 and 2008 the OIG conducted 1,581 unannounced site visits to durable medical equipment providers in South Florida and found 491 either didn't have an actual facility or were not properly staffed. All 491 billing privileges were revoked, 243 of those appealed, and 222 (91 percent) were reinstated. Of the 222 reinstated, 111 later had their billing privileges revoked again.[24]

The Florida Medicaid program requires suppliers to sign contracts agreeing the state has the right to terminate them at any time "without cause." This has been effective without harming access to care. Any public or private buyer of a service should retain the right to stop buying that service whenever she sees fit.

9. Move to a system of 100 percent electronic remittances. Paper bills and the postage required to mail them cost billions unnecessarily. Furthermore, paper records guarantee the bureaucrats are always many steps and many months behind the crooks. We currently have paper clerks chasing crooks who use iPhones and Blackberries. It is a hopeless mismatch of technologies favoring the crooks over the cops.

10. Use unique ID numbers for Medicare beneficiaries instead of their social security numbers. A stolen Social Security number leaves a person much more vulnerable to theft and fraud.

11. Require more timely updates from states on Medicaid enrollment data. Even senior congressmen, as of April 2010, can only get state-by-state Medicaid enrollment data up to 2007. The latest data available for Maine is 2004.[25] Compare that to FedEx and UPS, which track 23 million packages a day in real time, or to McDonald's,

which collects data or sales from 37,000 stores worldwide every night. As shown above, the existing data collection system urgently needs to be fixed.

12. Experiment with moving to biometric ID for Medicare and Medicaid beneficiaries. Cards are easily lost, stolen, copied, and forged, which contributes to uncoordinated care and fraud.

13. Recognize the shortcomings of isolated fee-for-service arrangements and follow two of MedPAC's key recommendations: expand the use of risk-adjusted plans in Medicare, and expand the medical home model particularly for people with one or more chronic conditions. Enhanced use of medical homes would be particularly helpful in a Medicare system where specialists are overpaid relative to primary care. The standard fee-for-service model rewards volume first and foremost, with coordination of care, improvement of patient health, and fraud as secondary considerations at best. The same recommendations are appropriate for Medicaid.[26]

14. Encouraging better data analytics across programs and jurisdictions is a must. The entire healthcare system could benefit tremendously from the same level of inter-agency data sharing that is common in law enforcement, particularly in the tracking of sex offenders. When sex offenders move between states they are required to register immediately with local law enforcement. If they miss their deadline, they are flagged instantly by sophisticated systems pulling information from public sources. Doctors who have been sanctioned for fraud, hospital administrators who have engaged in fraud, DME salesmen with fraudulent convictions, criminal beneficiaries, and others are much freer to set up shop in a new state—or to send a new, unknown member of a fraud ring into the system—without being reported from their prior jurisdiction.

15. Require Medicare and Medicaid to pay closer attention to Medicare ID numbers that show outlier behavior. Individuals who are excessively billing at, say, emergency rooms are likely getting poor, uncoordinated, inefficient care, or their Medicare/Medicaid cards are being billed by fraudulent providers with or without the patient's knowledge. In either case, both the individual's health and the taxpayer's pocketbook would be better served by being instantly identified.

16. Data sharing across departmental jurisdictions and with state and local governments should be done with the same seriousness as in national security. Prior to September 11, the CIA and the FBI rarely communicated. Now they compare intelligence frequently. There are multiple databases of Medicare and Medicaid providers and suppliers along with their disciplinary records.[27] But these databases are not as universally comprehensive or as accessible as, say, the National Instant Criminal Background Check System (NICS) used to keep guns out of the hands of criminals. The National Crime Information Center is another law enforcement tool that allows a local officer to have instant, nationwide access to a suspect's criminal background. These systems are not perfect, but they are good examples showing how individuals with criminal records and/or disciplinary actions in the healthcare field can at least be flagged early. This concept was part of President Obama's revised health proposal unveiled on February 22, 2010, based on legislation introduced by Congressman Mark Kirk with bipartisan support. We should utilize data from the Social Security Administration and IRS for these efforts as well.

17. Require cost reports for Ambulatory Surgical Centers (ASC) similar to what is currently required for hospitals by the Centers for Medicare and Medicaid Services (CMS). It is understood there are

specific differences between an ASC and a hospital, and the report requirements should be modified to accommodate this.

18. Migrate Medicare and Medicaid beneficiaries into arrangements with personal health accounts in which individuals have direct and immediate financial incentives to engage in behaviors that improve their health. The current system includes nothing to deter patients with Medicare, Medicaid, and most private plans from scheduling as many physician visits as they can. Indeed, a classic 2003 *New York Times* article, entitled "Patients Line Up for All That Medicare Covers," accurately captures a culture where seniors on Medicare can get as many healthcare services as they can fit on their calendar, regardless of cost to taxpayers or the lack of medical benefit.[28]

There are myriad ways to structure personal accounts, the least controversial being zero-balance accounts where beneficiaries are paid small amounts of money for achieving improved health status. The vast majority of healthcare spending in the coming decades will be on people with chronic conditions. This means personal choices around care regimens will have a major, long-term impact on quality outcomes and cost. We must continue developing and deploying models of healthcare financing that maximize patient behavior change toward patterns of good health. Ultimately, that is the only way to save American healthcare. Account-based plans are the most effective way to create incentives to accomplish this goal.

The topic of healthcare fraud, waste, and abuse is too vast for one chapter, one book, or even a ten-volume series. But it is crucial for the American people to grasp just how large a problem this is, how much money is involved, and that there are solutions that would drastically reduce the problem without limiting access to medical care.

CHAPTER SEVENTEEN

Green Conservatism Versus Left-wing Environmentalism

With Terry L. Maple, President and CEO of the Palm Beach Zoo

More and more people around the world are discovering "green conservatism," a new pathway to environmental stewardship and a compelling conservative alternative to the high-tax, big-bureaucracy, job-killing, and government-centralizing environmentalism of the Left. Green conservatives understand people can vigorously protect biodiversity and deliver cleaner forms of energy in a fiscally responsible way without the heavy-handed intervention and expansion of government. People with green core values who feel abandoned by extreme, big-government environmental positions are vastly more comfortable with the market-based, entrepreneurial approach of green conservatives.

Green conservatives are politically active in Australia, Canada, and the United Kingdom among other nations, and the label is increasingly claimed by an emerging center-right coalition in the United States. When we first applied the term in U.S. politics, we defined green conservatism as: "an optimistic, positive, science and technology-based, entrepreneurial, market-oriented, incentive-led, conservative environmentalism that creates more solutions faster and that will result in more biodiversity with less pollution and a safer planet."

More simply, green conservatism describes conservatives who incorporate green concerns into their ideology.

From the business side, entrepreneurial environmentalists are the new agents of change on the frontlines of a creative environmental movement. Government's role, rather than to dictate, is to incentivize. In homes throughout America, energy efficiency has been facilitated by government rebates and matching funds to encourage investment in efficient appliances, insulation, and technology.

Green conservatives worldwide are broadening their political platforms by including environmental initiatives. In the UK, conservative leader David Cameron has proposed a "smart power grid," incentives for small-scale renewables, sustainable public transit, and technological innovation to cut carbon emissions. In France, a conservative president presides over a nation whose investment in nuclear energy is a model for other European countries.

And in Canada, Preston Manning, founder of the Canadian Reform Party, insists Western Canadian conservatism, with its rural and populist origins, must reconcile its support for strong growth with the necessity of environmental protection.

As documented in our book *A Contract with the Earth*, many U.S. businesses and industries have already adopted sustainable practices for their employees and their facilities. Deploying fleets of electric, hybrid, natural gas, or hydrogen-powered cars and trucks, they are also building new plants that comply with green building practices such as LEED (Leadership in Energy and Environmental Design) guidelines. Combining innovation with LEED-type guidelines is an inspiring public platform for our new movement.

A COMMITMENT TO ENVIRONMENTAL LEADERSHIP

We believe unwavering political and citizen leadership is the key to effective environmental policies. Quality of life and environmental sustainability with continued economic growth in jobs and incomes must become national priorities. In the 2008 paperback edition of *A Contract with the Earth,* we proposed that green conservatives could provide leadership for a polarized and stalemated environmental movement:

> The fact that green conservatism is attracting converts from every political faction renders the movement mainstream. Breaking out from the current stalemate means we must find a way to get things done. An inclusive, bipartisan movement can be built on green conservative principles.[1]

In contrast, a global, left-wing environmental movement organized around a doomsday theory of climate change is pushing for a massive wealth transfer from the West to developing nations, and an enormous increase in bureaucratic control by governments. Meanwhile, UN-designated experts and an alliance of global bureaucrats are lobbying for treaties to enforce international climate change regulations within a system of global taxation. This entire "solution" is a kind of class warfare applied to nation states.

With our historical emphasis on free enterprise and national sovereignty, Americans have resisted these extreme measures. But we believe genuine environmental problems, many of them ignored due to the global warming obsession, cannot be resolved without U.S. leadership. Therefore, green conservatives must offer rational alternatives to the extremist positions now dominating the discussion. Pursuing affordable programs of worldwide reforestation, for example, could help capture carbon dioxide while protecting biodiversity—the ultimate win/win conservation strategy.

To lead on this issue, conservatives must determine how a healthy environment is compatible with key conservative political ideas. We can begin by advocating sustainability. Defined as "meeting the needs of the present without compromising the ability of future generations to meet their own needs," this concept is consistent with a conservative political philosophy. "Conservative," after all, comes from the same root as "conservation." Adherence to this fundamental principle will conserve future opportunity for optimal quality of life, economic stability, and human happiness. Ronald Reagan campaigned on these kinds of universal human aspirations.

For the sake of our children and grandchildren, we must act cooperatively to ensure a sustainable world. However, green conservatives are uniquely committed to empowering people rather than government.

The government can play a modest role setting the general direction. An example is the 1969 U.S. National Environmental Policy Act, which aimed to "create and maintain conditions under which man and nature can exist in productive harmony, and fulfill the social, economic and other requirements of present and future generations of Americans." The key connection is the need to achieve and sustain environmental and economic harmony.

Green conservatives must do more than simply say no to the big-government, environmental Left; we need to provide a clear and robust political alternative for local and global environmental stewardship. We must articulate this vision in party platforms, newspaper op-ed columns, community and national blogs, and other electronic media in order to generate a menu of green conservative ideas in the environmental marketplace.* Affiliating with the tea party movement is also a good opportunity to spread green conservatism, since many tea party activists strongly favor a healthy environment but oppose using socialist policies to achieve it.

Big government is not necessary or even conducive to sustainability. As we argued in *A Contract with the Earth*, business and industry are already greener than government, and they are innovating at a faster pace as well. So we should work with business and industry, local governments, and nonprofit groups to develop stewardship that is fast, focused, and flexible. We should also favor public-private partnerships and grassroots solutions by local people who understand the issues on the ground. An example is the NEXT network of volunteer organizations and groups that monitor sea turtle nests during their breeding seasons on the Florida coastline.

The sincere commitment of green conservatives to better environmental standards and practices is one of the media's best kept secrets. Green conservatives have to insist on a place at the environmental table. Above all, we should advance rational, responsible, and innovative solutions to help protect the natural resources that support all life on this planet. Effective environmental problem-solving requires the elbow grease and acumen of every political party in America. There are conservatives in both the Democratic and Republican parties; likewise, both Republicans and Democrats can be green.

CLEAN AMERICAN ENERGY

All nations unarguably require reliable, affordable energy for economic growth. This growth, in turn is an essential requirement for

---

* Public forums for green conservatism are included in our website, www.contractwiththeearth.com, and that of American Solutions, www.AmericanSolutions. com.

a healthy environment. A broad and green energy menu needs entrepreneurs rather than bureaucrats, incentives rather than regulation, markets rather than command and control, tax relief rather than litigation, and scientists rather than trial lawyers.

Other nations energetically locate and diversify their energy sources, while America shows inefficiency and timidity. Innovative and sustainable, a green conservative energy plan will allow us to lead the world in producing a wide array of sustainable energy technology and clean, renewable products.

Some industries are already moving in this direction. Our automobile industry has strongly committed to hybrid, hydrogen, and electric vehicles. Taking no federal stimulus money, Ford successfully developed a line of fuel-efficient cars that are highly competitive with Honda and Toyota. Fuel efficiency and cleaner emissions have become a winning green business strategy for Detroit.

But industry can't act alone; the federal government must help— not by getting bigger, but by getting smaller. Namely, the government must remove its restrictions on access to our key energy sources. Perhaps the most inexplicable such restriction is the maze of regulations that effectively prevents the spread of nuclear power—a clean, cheap, zero-emission source of electricity.

Currently, only one nuclear plant is under construction in the United States, while forty-four are being built in other countries.[2] Our leadership as a nuclear innovator is fading fast, as other countries pursue ways to overcome historical obstacles such as the waste problem. For example, Norway's state-owned energy company Statkraft is investigating the use of thorium to fuel nuclear reactors. Thorium is considered a greener alternative to uranium and plutonium, as it produces only a tiny fraction of the hazardous waste created by uranium-fuelled reactors.

Aside from being cheap and carbon-free, nuclear power offers other benefits as well. For example, once a plant is operational, nuclear energy is a relatively inexpensive power source for producing hydrogen, which could hasten the development of hydrogen-fueled cars and, ultimately, a low-carbon economy based on hydrogen. Nuclear power stations could also power desalination plants at lower cost to mitigate future droughts.

With all this promise just from nuclear power, imagine the possibilities if we develop environmentally responsible ways to tap America's full energy potential: natural gas, cleaner coal, domestic sources of offshore oil, and a wide array of renewable energy sources such as geothermal, biofuels, solar, and wind power. Other nations are pursuing these technologies, including China, so American innovation must be encouraged by tax incentives and public-private partnerships.

Much of this can be accomplished by eliminating red tape and facilitating active investments in new technology. This could bring about new, clean energy sources most people aren't even aware of today. For example, a new high-temperature technology known as plasma gasification promises to provide a way to burn off landfill waste and provide energy for nearby industries and towns. New to the United States, this technology is already operating successfully in Japan. Gasification technology can also be utilized in the clean coal process by capturing carbon dioxide. Public-private partnerships in research and development will ultimately lead to other effective methods to turn environmental liabilities into community assets.

Local governments are already developing green conservative programs. An example is Grand Rapids, Michigan, which has rooftop gardens, rainwater cisterns, solar panels, and the highest per capita number of buildings that comply with the standards set by the U.S. Green Building Council. The city plans to draw 100 percent of its electricity from renewable sources, mostly wind power, by 2020. Its residents are predominantly conservative and religious, deriving their environmental values from a Biblically inspired sense of stewardship.

THE BLAME GAME

The extremist environmental movement asserts that we will soon face global warming-induced environmental catastrophes that can only be avoided by forcing Western capitalist nations, especially America, to adopt devastating energy taxes, ruinous new environmental regulations, and a massive wealth transfer to developing countries. This mantra has become so popular, both among the American Left and abroad, that even Osama bin Laden in a recent recording thought he could win support by blaming the West for global warming.

This narrative fails to recognize that capitalist democracies are among the most environmentally conscious nations in the world. As a rule, the more socialist a nation becomes, the more the environment suffers—just look at the environmental degradation that characterized nearly every Cold War-era Communist nation. As we noted in *A Contract with the Earth*, wealth and freedom generally lead to better environmental practices; forests are declining in poor nations but expanding in wealthy ones.

The international Left relentlessly condemn our alleged over-consumption of energy and services. Sometimes they invoke the spurious statistic of "per-capita use of energy," comparing us unfavorably with China and India. This is absurd. China and India are major industrial polluters and carbon emitters. But simply because their populations are so large, their per capita output is relatively small.

So, in formulating a comprehensive environmental policy, the first thing we should do is to ignore the unfair, anti-American critique of the Left. We must develop our own policy based on conservative principles. Under such a policy, America should be a leader in environmental philanthropy and foreign aid to countries facing environmental challenges. This aid would be given on a case-by-case basis to nations with pressing environmental problems and accountable plans for fixing them. Operating like a sound business, our international environmental aid will depend on prudent management and our national financial situation at any given time.

This system would be an alternative to the current demands for coercive international mandates. Our Constitution requires the people's consent in matters of war and finance; no foreign or world government has the mandate to tax U.S. citizens to combat global climate change or any other environmental danger. In particular, a proposed global carbon tax, calculated and regulated by the United Nations, would violate our sovereignty and must be resisted.

History has repeatedly demonstrated the incredible generosity of the American people, American private enterprise, and American institutions. The United States is already a global leader in environmental philanthropy, whether it be responding to the Asian tsunami or the Haitian earthquake. We should prioritize environmental sustainability, both in America and across the globe, but we must not allow the Left to exploit the global warming panic in order to degrade our liberties and entwine us in a new, corrupt, international climate change bureaucracy that would undoubtedly be dominated by dictatorships and kleptocratic governments.

MORE SCIENCE, BETTER SCIENCE, NONPARTISAN SCIENCE: CLIMATE SCIENCE AND THE LESSONS OF Y2K

We have to be more skeptical of climate scientists and the UN-appointed International Panel on Climate Change (IPCC) given the revelations of the "climategate" incident, discussed in chapter eight. As demonstrated in the hacked emails, some of the world's top climate scientists unprofessionally and unethically tried to silence critics and avoid disclosing their own data.

Sound science depends on constructive criticism and a rigorous system of peer review. That's why the argument that global warming trends are "settled science" is so disturbing. In the academy, debates in every field rage for decades as trends and theories are revised according to new data. With the hockey stick trend in global warming now discredited and scientific climate models yielding hypothetical data at best, we are still debating the meaning of the information we have now. Unshakable predictions of a looming, carbon-induced doomsday look more and more like the anti-climatic Y2K panic.

The rational antidote to global warming hysteria is continued investigation into global climate change. Green conservatives should advocate better climate research through the National Science Foundation and other professional sources. To augment federal funding, privately funded prizes can help incentivize scientific breakthroughs. We could also offer prizes for breakthroughs in climate modeling, metrics, and measurement technology. Furthermore, we need fiscally responsible green conservatives who understand the need for more and better climate science to carefully scrutinize UN proposals, such as a recent demand for more than $60 billion to measure climate variables.

The American people should also continue to rely on the National Academy of Sciences to monitor progress in global climate change research. This is an incredibly intricate, fluid topic, notwithstanding the Left's bogus claims that the science is settled. In fact, a 2010 article in the journal *Nature* by Olive Heffernan predicted that improving technology will cause scientists to admit to even *greater* uncertainty about the effects of climate change. The debate will really heat up when the next major IPCC report, due in 2013, moves beyond projected climate scenarios to consider explicit predictions.[3]

Although environmental radicals refuse to acknowledge it, we can prepare now to adapt to almost any future change in climate. Consider the argument made by Nigel Lawson in his book *An Appeal to Reason:*

The only rational, practical and cost-effective policy response to global warming is to adapt to it if and when it occurs—that is, to act to prevent, or mitigate, any adverse consequences, while taking full advantage of the many beneficial consequences. This is manifestly the case, not least because the projected adverse consequences are simply the relatively marginal exacerbation of problems that already exist.[4]

Green conservatives should be skeptical, prudent, and smart. We must demand complete objectivity from our scientists and our policymakers. Our country is blessed with the world's best graduate schools and a critical mass of brilliant scientists and engineers. If carbon overload should lead to major problems, our continuing investment in science and technology will give us the best chance of averting or adapting to the consequences.

A GREEN CONSERVATIVE PLATFORM

The next conservative U.S. government cannot ignore the environment. Conservative candidates must first convince centrists they can solve environmental problems, while the Left are only using the environment as an excuse for bigger government with higher taxes and more bureaucratic controls. Meanwhile, the conservative base should increase the visibility of its environmental positions.

For environmentalists of all persuasions, an optimal election is one in which both parties are equally committed to protecting the earth, while strenuously debating the right way to get it done. Conservatives must stop allowing the Left to own this issue. We must be prepared to offer an environmental agenda that breaks new ground and broadens the coalition of green conservatives. No one should be more committed to a healthy planet than green conservatives.

The green conservative platform should strive for a cleaner, greener world while protecting the freedom and dignity of all people and ensuring their right to a better economic future. Green conservatives seek a world where biodiversity is growing, not shrinking, and all ecosystems are vibrant and healthy. While some regulation will always be necessary, government intervention into our use of natural resources should not over-reach, nor should regulation violate citizens' property rights.

Commerce and conservation can co-exist in harmony, with private philanthropy as the most powerful tool for biodiversity and habitat protection. Green conservatives should actively campaign for clean air and water, a non-toxic food chain, and the steady improvement of our quality of life.

The vision of a conservative conservation movement should be achieved through grassroots community networking. Green conservative action derives from the people, not the government. Green conservatives embrace flexibility, innovation, and speed while avoiding bureaucracy and red tape. Our commitment to future generations requires that we leave to them healthy oceans, lakes, rivers, and streams. Indeed, conservative core values require us to deliver to our children a world at least as bountiful and pristine as the one we inherited from our parents. Not only is this a moral imperative, it's a winning political position.

CHAPTER EIGHTEEN

An American Energy Plan

With Steve Everley, Energy Policy
Manager for American Solutions

Amerca suffers.

America has plenty of energy, but we send hundreds of billions of dollars a year overseas to buy energy we could be producing domestically. This raises energy prices at home, forcing companies to shift jobs overseas. In one recent small business meeting American Solutions hosted in Akron, Ohio, manufacturers cited rising energy costs as a major reason for laying off workers, downsizing operations, and in some cases closing factories.

Washington elites have artificially restricted American energy resources, ranging from a 25-year ban on offshore drilling (which was recently overturned formally but remains active in practice) to an unofficial ban on the expansion of nuclear energy to the encouragement of frivolous environmental lawsuits. The result has been an energy crisis created by environmental extremists, politicians, and bureaucrats who, for ideological reasons, favor high energy prices and severely limited energy consumption. They are willing to pay for this policy with foreign imports, killed American jobs, and substantial American reliance on foreign dictatorships. The vast majority of Americans—79 percent in an American Solutions survey—oppose this policy.

Ironically, many left-wing politicians advocate energy independence even as their own policies sabotage that goal. In fact, every U.S. President since Richard Nixon has rhetorically championed American energy, yet in the past thirty years we have become increasingly dependent on foreign energy.

It doesn't have to be this way. Contrary to popular belief, America has more energy than any other nation on earth. All that's keeping us from becoming energy independent is a lack of political will to do so.

Rather than picking winners and losers or paying off some industries by taxing others, our elected leaders should craft an energy policy based on a clear set of choices:

- Do we value prosperity and happiness or punishment through taxes and regulation?
- Do we value national independence, or are we willing to remain vulnerable to blackmail from energy dictatorships like Saudi Arabia, Iran, and Venezuela?
- Do we prefer to keep our money here in America to create jobs and increase our standard of living, or are we comfortable sending hundreds of billions a year to foreigners for energy we could be producing here at home?

In an America that values both prosperity and happiness, both national security and the environment, we can have more energy and a stronger economy while protecting the environment. Indeed, a growing economy requires affordable and reliable energy, which means more energy consumption, not less.

In contrast, in an America that values punishment through taxes and regulations, you will find high energy prices, less energy, and less economic growth.

Blessed with enormous energy reserves, America also has the scientists and engineers who could create unprecedented technological breakthroughs in all our energy sources. We must begin encouraging energy innovation, not discouraging energy production. As this chapter will show, we have both the resources and the capability to rapidly become energy independent.

OIL AND NATURAL GAS

America has more oil and natural gas than most people can even imagine. Unfortunately, our own politicians won't let us use huge reserves of it.

Offshore we have an estimated 86 billion barrels of oil and over 400 trillion cubic feet of natural gas, all of which was illegal to develop until Congress and the president let their offshore drilling bans expire amidst spiraling gas prices in 2008.

Onshore we have billions more barrels of oil, including potentially more than a trillion barrels locked away in shale in the Rocky Mountains. The Green River Formation in Colorado, Utah, and Wyoming is considered the largest shale oil deposit in the world, with an estimated 800 billion barrels of oil, or three times the proven reserves of Saudi Arabia.[1] But nearly all those deposits are unused, since federal law bans most drilling for shale oil.

We also have so much natural gas that even many industry experts cannot develop a top-end estimate. In addition to the hundreds of trillions of cubic feet located offshore, we have exponentially more locked away in ice. Known as methane hydrates, this frozen form of natural gas could make an enormous contribution to our energy independence: we have over 300,000 trillion cubic feet. To put that in perspective, if we could harness just 1 percent of that energy, we could satisfy America's natural gas needs for more than 100 years.

And there is every reason to believe we have even more oil and natural gas. Methods of finding and developing these resources have become much more efficient even in the past ten years, resulting in the discovery of billions of additional barrels of oil and hundreds of trillions of additional cubic feet of natural gas. Consider:

- Geologists recently had to increase their estimate of oil in the Bakken Formation in North Dakota and Montana by an astounding 2,500 percent.
- BP's recent discoveries of up to 6 billion barrels of oil and natural gas in the Gulf of Mexico rank among the largest such discoveries in American history.[2]
- The U.S. Geological Survey reported in 2009 that the Arctic Circle and the Chukchi Sea near Alaska could hold as much as 13 percent of the world's undiscovered oil and 30 percent of the world's undiscovered natural gas.
- The Marcellus Formation, a shale deposit rich in natural gas stretching from New York to Ohio, was estimated by the U.S. Geological Survey in 2002 to have approximately 2 trillion cubic feet of natural gas. In 2008, professors at Penn State and the City University of New York, Fredonia, raised the estimate to an astounding 500 trillion cubic feet or more.[3]

The new estimate at Marcellus is a good example of the power of technology. About eight years ago, engineers applied deep sea drilling techniques to natural gas exploration—they had learned how to drill down 8,000 feet and then drill out horizontally four miles in every direction. Suddenly small pockets of shale gas became commercially viable, because you could find many pockets from one well. This new technology will revolutionize natural gas availability in the United States and possibly in Europe.

The potential for American jobs and American prosperity, however, is being delayed by regulations and litigation specifically designed to stop energy development.

Following the gasoline price spike of 2008 and American Solutions' "Drill Here, Drill Now, Pay Less" petition drive, public anger forced politicians to allow the bans on offshore drilling to expire. But last year, Secretary of the Interior Ken Salazar delayed leasing in the Outer Continental Shelf by extending a comment period for six additional months. That period ended in September 2009, but as of this writing the Department of Interior has still not released the tabulated results of the public comments, another stalling tactic used by the Obama administration to thwart the will of the American people.

Solutions for More American Oil and Natural Gas

- **Stop bureaucratic delays.** Congress should cut off all funding for the Department of Interior until that bureaucracy stops ignoring the American people and allows offshore energy development.
- **End the ban on oil shale development in the American west.** It is unacceptable that we have three times the amount of oil as Saudi Arabia but continue to send the Saudis billions of dollars for oil because we have banned responsible development in America.
- **Give coastal states federal royalty revenue sharing.** States such as Wyoming with land-based oil and gas

projects earn 48 percent of federal royalties from those operations, while most coastal states get zero federal royalties from offshore development. The prospect of earning billions in new revenue would provide coastal states with a strong incentive to accept new offshore drilling with appropriate environmental safeguards.

- **Finance cleaner energy with new oil and gas royalties.** Allowing offshore drilling would also generate billions in federal royalties, which could help finance renewable projects and other technologies like carbon sequestration for coal.

COAL

America has roughly 27 percent of the world's coal supply, the most of any nation. We have 1.5 times as much as Russia, which has the second largest reserves, and twice as much as China. Our reserves can last us for another 200-250 years, and that estimate assumes zero technological innovation over the next two centuries. Furthermore, Alaska may hold more coal than the entire lower forty-eight states combined.

America unquestionably has tremendous potential for a coal-based energy supply whose development would create thousands of new jobs and cut the cost of electricity. But in order to realize that opportunity, we must use coal in a smart, environmentally responsible way.

Encouraging coal power also means developing and expanding clean coal technologies, including carbon sequestration, gasification, and conversion to liquid fuels. These may sound like pie-in-the-sky concepts, but several of these technologies are already available. For example, carbon capture technology is taking root around the world, and America has several demonstration plants in West Virginia, Ohio, Alabama, Washington, and Kentucky.[4]

Even the U.S. Department of Energy had a carbon capture demonstration project in Mattoon, Illinois, known as FutureGen. Were it not for bureaucratic delays that effectively stopped the project, the United States would today have the finest clean coal demonstration project in the world. It's now being restarted, but only after we lost ground to the Chinese, who have an aggressive clean coal program.

For decades in west Texas, oil companies have been using carbon dioxide to extract more oil from older fields in a process known as enhanced oil recovery, or EOR. The carbon used in this process is then locked into air tight underground basins, taking carbon out of the air and giving us more American energy.

Gasification, which breaks down coal into its basic chemical elements while producing electricity, is used commercially in the United States and abroad. Allowing for easier capture of carbon dioxide, many gasifiers also can produce hydrogen, which in turn could be used to develop new fleets of hydrogen vehicles. Our own Department of Energy also has a coal gasification research and development program.

Converting coal to liquid fuels (CTL) would lessen our dependence on foreign oil for our vehicles. Rather than burning coal as in a traditional plant, CTL technology either gasifies or liquefies coal, and the product can then substitute for oil. South Africa has used this technology to fuel many of its vehicles for decades.

Although coal provides half of our electricity and is a big reason why so many Americans have reliable and affordable power, it is vilified by radical environmentalists. However, shutting down coal plants, as they often advocate, would not solve any substantial environmental problems, but it *would* literally turn off the lights on millions of Americans and drive millions of jobs abroad.

Nevertheless, the crusade against coal continues. Consider these examples:

- Dr. James Hansen, a top NASA scientist, is a leading anti-coal advocate who supports prosecuting oil companies for alleged crimes against humanity. He has also called for halting production of any more coal plants, and was even arrested while protesting coal operations.[5] Yet we pay his salary as a public servant as he advocates bankrupting millions of Americans.

- In 2008, Democratic congressman Henry Waxman, now chairman of the House Energy and Commerce Committee, endorsed a moratorium on all proposed coal plants.[6]

- Barack Obama, while campaigning for president, told the *San Francisco Chronicle* his energy plan would bankrupt the coal industry.

- The Environmental Protection Agency recently cancelled a permit it had issued for the Spruce coal mine in West Virginia, despite previous positive assessments by the state, the Army Corps of Engineers, and even the EPA itself.

Rather than attacking the coal industry through regulation and taxation, a more sensible approach would encourage coal operations through innovative technologies including carbon sequestration and even gasification. Rather than limiting the supply of American energy, we can expand it while also encouraging technological breakthroughs among our brightest scientists and engineers.

Solutions for More American Coal

- **Accelerate the FutureGen clean coal demonstration plant.** The fact that America was on pace to beat China on clean coal and then suddenly fell behind due to bureaucratic incompetence is shameful and unacceptable. Congress and the Department of Energy should work together with industry to fast-track FutureGen's completion.

- **Encourage retrofitting of existing plants with CCS.** Congress should develop a tax credit for any energy company that retrofits its coal plants with carbon capture and sequestration (CCS) technology.
- **Incentivize new technologies and innovations with coal.** Congress should approve a series of tax-free prizes for major new innovations that will allow us to use coal in cleaner and more efficient ways.

NUCLEAR

Today, America gets about 20 percent of its electricity from our 104 nuclear power plants, which provide massive amounts of around-the-clock, safe, pollution-free power. According to the Nuclear Energy Institute, we are going to need at least thirty-five more nuclear plants just to meet the projected increase in electricity demand by 2030.

This is a bold challenge, as the United States has not licensed and built a new nuclear plant since the 1970s. But, once again, the problem is not the energy companies. Instead, government regulation and frivolous lawsuits are stifling construction of new plants.

If we value affordable, clean, and reliable energy, then nuclear power must be part of the solution. Wind and solar are clean forms of energy, but they are not yet affordable solutions, nor are they reliable, as the sun is not always shining and the wind is not always blowing. To have reliable base load electricity, nuclear power, along with coal, must be a major supplier for the next generation or even longer.

Despite the horror stories, nuclear power is incredibly safe. The Nuclear Regulatory Commission closely monitors each plant to guarantee all operations meet the highest standards, including worker safety. From 2000 to 2007, the average accident rate for workers in nuclear plants was miniscule—less than 0.2 accidents per 200,000 workers.

As for radiation, the National Cancer Institute determined that nuclear plant workers do not face an elevated risk of dying from cancer. Ideological extremists who oppose nuclear power would have us believe that anyone living near a nuclear plant faces enormous health risks from plant radiation. But if the workers themselves do not face elevated risks, why would residents living miles away?

In fact, nuclear plants are so well-designed that, for people living near the plant, only about 1 percent of their radiation exposure comes from the plant. The rest comes from the sun and from naturally occurring radiation in the environment.

Countries worldwide rely on nuclear power because it's safe and it's more reliable than any other form of clean energy. Since the 1970s, Japan has built dozens of new plants, and France has built even more. In fact, the French get 75 percent of their energy from nuclear power. If the United States matched that percentage, we would pump 2.2 billion fewer tons of CO_2 into the atmosphere every year.

And the future of nuclear power will be even safer, more affordable, and more reliable. Companies such as Hyperion Power Generation, Babcock & Wilcox, and NuScale, Inc., are developing smaller reactors that could fit in a large meeting room. These advanced small modular reactors (or ASMRs) could power 25,000 homes each, while requiring a fraction of the initial capital costs of a big nuclear plant.

These reactors could also be exported to developing countries that struggle to find reliable sources of electricity. Countries across the globe, including Japan and South Africa, are developing this technology, and our own Department of Energy has recognized its potential.

Our American energy policy must encourage all forms of nuclear power. As with any other product, if the government stifles innovation of modular reactors, America will not produce them, which means fewer exports and fewer American jobs.

Solutions for More American Nuclear Energy

- **Create a streamlined regulatory and tax regime.** It's time government bureaucrats and anti-nuclear politicians recognize the safety of nuclear power with less burdensome regulations on this vital power source.
- **Incentivize safe disposal and reuse of waste.** Congress should pass prize legislation that would reward any company that develops safe storage or improved recycling technology.
- **Recognize small modular reactors.** The Nuclear Regulatory Commission should conduct more research into modular reactors and establish a consistent system for permitting this advanced technology with minimum paperwork and minimum regulatory costs.

RENEWABLES

Contrary to what proponents of new energy taxes would have us believe, those of us who favor more American energy are not opposed to renewables such as wind and solar power. In fact, these technologies must be part of any real American energy plan to achieve energy independence.

Although we currently get less than 1 percent of our electricity from wind power, it has enormous potential. One study from Stanford University found that North America has the greatest potential for wind power in the entire world, due primarily to the powerful breezes around the Great Lakes and on the coasts. This clean, renewable energy has no carbon emissions.

Solar power also has great potential. The American southwest already has numerous solar projects, as well as proposals for new ones. Meanwhile, advances in solar panel technology are allowing many homebuilders to generate their own electricity by placing panels on their roofs. In fact, the southwest has so much sunlight that if companies constructed a series of solar plants covering 100 square miles, those plants could generate as much electricity as all the fossil fuel-fired plants in America.[7]

Over the past decade, companies from around the world have begun investing in solar projects, many of them in the United States, as they recognize the possibility for a booming market in solar technology.

While solar and wind are intermittent technologies that cannot produce energy twenty-four hours per day like a coal plant or nuclear reactor, they will be an essential part of our energy future. But their development requires us to rethink many aspects of our current system, including litigation reform.

Here's an example why: a recently proposed wind project in West Virginia would have been another big step toward making wind power more affordable and the technology even more efficient. But environmental groups sued the developer, Beech Ridge Energy, claiming the project would harm bats. The judge, Roger W. Titus, sided with the environmental groups and ruled against responsible American energy development, killing the plan for more than 120 wind turbines.[8]

Similarly, in California, solar power company BrightSource Energy proposed building in the Mojave Desert three solar plants with enough energy to power 142,000 homes, a project that would generate billions of dollars in revenue. The site was perfect, as the Mojave has powerful sunlight every day, and the proposed site already has transmission lines. Predictably, radical environmental groups are trying to block the plan, citing the alleged impact on an estimated twenty-five desert tortoises.[9]

If we cannot develop a major solar power project in the middle of the desert, then where can we?

Many of these environmental groups are the same ones pushing for devastating new energy taxes like cap and trade, claiming economic punishment will spur investment in environmentally virtuous solar and wind technologies.

But their lawsuits against the very solutions they propose reveal their real motives. They are not interested in getting energy from alternative sources. Opposing nearly any form of economic development, they aim to use government regulation and litigation to punish Americans who use energy.

Solutions for More American Renewable Energy

- **Enact a loser-pays law.** This would force the loser in an environmental lawsuit to pay all the legal costs for the other side. Guaranteeing only the most serious lawsuits will be brought to court, it will reduce the numerous frivolous lawsuits every year that solely aim to stall development, including those blocking renewable energy.
- **Make permanent the wind and solar tax credits.** Having a consistent tax policy for renewable energy will provide certainty for future investment in these vital technologies.
- **Develop long-distance transmission lines.** Our potential in renewable energy is enormous, but technologies like wind and solar are limited geographically. With the proper connections, major urban centers in

America could utilize renewable energy produced hundreds of miles away.

BIOFUELS

Biofuels are best thought of as an organic use of solar power. Instead of man-made solar arrays, corn and other plants (and algae) provide a biological factory for converting solar power into usable energy.

Biofuels offer America an opportunity to use our unrivaled agricultural skills to create pure American energy. In 2007 we produced over 6 billion gallons of ethanol, a number we can expect to rise in the future as technology improves and the biofuels themselves become more efficient.

The projected explosion in corn yields per acre guarantee there will be enormous increases in potential biofuel production (especially ethanol) in the next two decades. In fact, without the growth in biofuel yields, the American grain farmer will drown in a glut of production, and farm incomes will collapse.

In 2008, the ethanol industry was responsible for creating more than 200,000 new American jobs and adding more than $60 billion to our economy. Ethanol fuels also eliminated the need to import over 300 million barrels of foreign oil.[10] Furthermore, we can expect the next generation of biofuels to create even more jobs, be dramatically less expensive, and provide greater efficiency.

Cellulosic ethanol has the potential to fundamentally change how we fuel our cars and trucks. Because they can be processed from agricultural byproducts (including corn stalks), cellulosic fuels could be made anywhere in the country, not just in the traditional Midwestern farming states.

Although cellulosic fuels are currently more expensive than gasoline, rapid advances in technology suggest this type of fuel could be commercially competitive in the near future.

But once again, we will not achieve the necessary advancements in biofuels by taxing other American energy producers.

In fact, one breakthrough has already occurred without any new taxes. Mark Holtzapple, a professor at Texas A&M University, has invented a system of converting garbage to bio-gasoline called the MixAlco process, which uses bacteria found commonly in soil as the catalyst for the initial chemical reaction. When fully developed, Holtzapple hopes to produce about 100 gallons of bio-gasoline per day from his experimental facility.[11] His company recently signed a contract with WasteManagement, the largest garbage collection company in the United States, emphasizing not only the viability of this technology, but also its potential for growth.

The MixAlco process was not mandated by the government, nor was it the result of penalizing other types of transportation fuels. Instead, it arose from the ingenuity that we must incentivize throughout America, an ingenuity that will solve our energy crisis faster and cheaper than any approach that relies on taxes and regulations.

Solutions for More American Biofuels

- **Create an open fuel standard.** An Open Fuel Standard would incentivize the creation of flex-fuel vehicles (FFVs), which can use different types of fuels. An FFV costs only about $100 more than a traditional, gasoline-only vehicle, and an Open Fuel Standard would provide Americans more choice and more price competition at the pump.
- **Provide refundable tax credits for alternative energy vehicles.** Since U.S. auto companies get billions in tax credits but still aren't seeing profits, the federal government could make these credits refundable, turning the incentives into useful money. This

would not only include biofuel vehicles such as FFVs, but also hydrogen vehicles and electric cars.

- **Incentivize new fuel distribution stations.** Any company that invests in ethanol or hydrogen supply stations should receive a substantial tax break, as should any company investing in new fuel pipelines.

HYDROGEN FUEL CELLS

Hydrogen fuel cells, especially in vehicles, offer obvious benefits: less air pollution, fewer tailpipe emissions, and increased fuel efficiency, all of which are goals shared by the current administration and most of the leadership in Congress.

Average consumers currently pay $600 per month to lease the hydrogen-powered Honda Clarity, even though the infrastructure to support hydrogen fuel cell vehicles (HFCVs) is not as friendly as it could be. GM's Equinox is also currently in the hands of consumers.

Initially, hydrogen power plants were seen as being prohibitively expensive. Recent technological advances, however, have brought the price down to less than $100 per kW, and the Department of Energy estimates the cost will approach $70 per kW.

Once the price reaches $40–50 per kW, which is entirely possible in full production mode, a hydrogen fuel cell engine will cost the same as a standard internal combustion engine. Note that a fuel cell has an efficiency of about 60 percent, whereas the typical automobile engine runs at just under 20 percent.

A recent study by the National Research Council of the National Academy of Sciences concluded hydrogen vehicles could be commercially available by 2015, and that HFCVs would be getting the equivalent of 80 miles per gallon. Within fifteen years HFCVs could be fully cost competitive with gasoline-burning vehicles.

But we cannot reach that point without a national commitment that emphasizes America's ingenuity. We must not begin by penalizing Americans for energy use through taxes and other command-and-control elements. In fact, the NAS study on hydrogen insists energy taxes "will do little on their own to encourage commercialization of transformative technologies, such as hydrogen, for the foreseeable future."

Shifting to a hydrogen economy will ultimately reduce pollution, increase available energy supplies, and help to stabilize energy costs. But trying to achieve those goals with hydrogen by regulating other industries into extinction will only weaken the economy and worsen the problem.

Solutions for More American Hydrogen Fuel Cells

- **Incentivize commercially viable Hydrogen Fuel Cell Vehicles.** Congress should approve a billion dollar tax-free prize to the first company that can offer hydrogen fuel cell vehicles (HFCVs) to consumers for $40,000 or less.
- **Provide tax breaks for investment in infrastructure.** Creating a tax break for the construction of hydrogen refueling stations would accelerate the adoption of HFCVs. Providing a uniform set of codes and standards for transporting and shipping hydrogen would also provide increased certainty to investors.
- **Increase public investment in fuel cell technology.** The National Academy of Sciences outlined the need for a $16 billion investment in HFCVs, of which $5 billion would come from the government, between now and 2023. While this sounds expensive, it is

dwarfed by the several hundred billion dollars we spend *each year* just to purchase oil from OPEC.

WE HAVE THE POWER, BUT DO WE HAVE THE WILL?

For years, bureaucrats and Washington elites have moved us further away from energy independence by mandating what kind of energy Americans use, how much we can use, and where we can use it. Many on the far Left regard energy usage as a moral failure or an environmental sin.

Unfortunately, many of these same people have been in charge of our energy policy for several decades, and we can see the result: an increasing reliance on foreign dictators for our energy, volatile energy prices, and persistent, avoidable energy crises. Ironically, these anti-energy zealots blame the energy producers for the energy crisis. Likewise, the big-government, anti-energy politicians blame Big Oil or Big Coal for high energy prices, ignoring the galaxy of taxes and regulations that have been foisted on these firms.

The extremists also blame the American people simply for using energy. But Americans are the victims, not the culprits. It's shameful that decades of anti-energy policies are ignored as career politicians blame the very taxpayers who put them into office.

But Americans know better, and they deserve better.

Polling consistently shows Americans favor expanding all forms of energy. Every new tax and every new regulation drives up the price of American energy and puts more money in the pockets of Hugo Chavez and Saudi sheikhs. As our energy policy becomes more restrictive, OPEC leaders laugh as they head straight to the bank with our money.

As we have shown, America could become energy independent. We have more energy resources than any other nation, and together with our top scientists and engineers, we have enormous possibilities in new technologies, many of which we cannot even predict today.

Imagine going back in time a hundred years and talking to Henry Ford about a hybrid electric engine. Odds are he never even thought about how to create such a thing.

Or explain to the Wright Brothers the U.S. military's stealth bombers. Or talk to Edison about three dimensional full color IMAX movies.

None of these inventions could have been built even if they could have been imagined that long ago. More important, none of them were developed based on taxing and regulating other industries into extinction. They were the product of American ingenuity, not government mandates.

So while America has enormous potential with hundreds of new technologies and every source of energy, we can only fully unleash the power of American innovation if we allow our brightest minds to succeed. And since no one can predict the next major energy technology, why would we try to pick winners and losers with taxes and regulations on energy producers, which in turn could prevent the next Ford, Edison, or Wright brothers from finding the next breakthrough technology?

Current proposals to tax certain forms of energy, such as a cap-and-trade system for carbon emissions, assume energy independence requires us to fundamentally change our economy. They suggest achieving energy *independence* means reducing our energy *dependence*.

As this chapter has shown, energy independence does not require a radical economic transformation, nor does it mean we have to believe energy usage is morally wrong.

But energy independence does require that we completely transform our national priorities, especially our energy policy. The truth is simple: if we tax American energy, we will get less American energy, which leads to more foreign energy. And if we encourage the development of American energy, we will get more American energy.

Until our elected leaders recognize the massive energy potential this country has, and as long as their solutions consist of taxing and regulating energy producers, we will only move further away from the very energy independence that all Americans want, all Americans deserve, and all Americans could have.

CHAPTER NINETEEN

There Is No Liberty without Religious Liberty

With Rick Tyler, Founding Director
of Renewing American Leadership
www.RenewingAmericanLeadership.com

"The God who gave us life gave us liberty."
THOMAS JEFFERSON, 1774,
A SUMMARY VIEW OF THE RIGHTS OF BRITISH AMERICA

The revolutionary idea contained in the Declaration of Independence is that certain fundamental human rights can neither be accorded nor taken away by government. They are gifts from God, which makes those rights "unalienable." Life, liberty, and the pursuit of happiness are listed in that order, for without life there can be no liberty, and without liberty there can be no pursuit of happiness. This central idea was the foundation upon which a free people determined to govern themselves.

The forerunner of the Declaration was signed over a century and a half earlier in 1620. The forty-one families who signed the Mayflower Compact knew their very survival would depend on their ability to rely upon each other and upon God. Plymouth, Massachusetts, being their "accidental" landing place, they were in unchartered territory. Beginning with the words, "In the name of God. Amen," the extraordinary Compact created the terms of self-government that bound one to another and each to God. Unlike the Magna Carta, the Compact was not a contract between a king and a servant or a superior and a subordinate. It reflected the radical notion that by binding themselves together as equals before God, they could govern themselves without a king. It was a covenant.

Covenantal language was found in dozens of organizing documents in seventeenth- and eighteenth-century colonial America. The fifty-six signers of the Declaration similarly pledged themselves to each other and each to God. They placed their pens to the parchment with full knowledge that a massive British armada was assembling on behalf of the most powerful empire in the world in order to crush the rebellion.

> *We, therefore, the Representatives of the united States of America, in General Congress, Assembled, appealing to the Supreme Judge of the world for the rectitude of our intentions, do, in the Name, and by Authority of the good People of these Colonies, solemnly publish and declare, That these United Colonies are, and of Right ought to be Free and Independent States; that they are Absolved from all Allegiance to the British Crown, and that all political connection between them and the State of Great Britain, is and ought to be totally dissolved; and that as Free and Independent States, they have full Power to levy War, conclude Peace, contract Alliances, establish Commerce, and to do all other Acts and Things which Independent States may of right do. And for the support of this Declaration, with a firm reliance on the protection of divine Providence, we mutually pledge to each other our Lives, our Fortunes and our sacred Honor.*

Later, in Philadelphia during the Constitutional Convention in 1787, some of the delegates worried that, as drafted, the Constitution would not adequately protect the rights of individuals. To address these concerns, James Madison drafted amendments that Congress sent to the states for ratification, eventually forming our Bill of Rights. These ten amendments offered the protections necessary to secure individual liberty. Together they guard the individual from infringements the Founders recognized would inevitably result from instituting a strong central government. These amendments reflect the Founders' understanding of the inherent dignity and value of each individual. Every person has certain rights because those rights ultimately come from God.

The First Amendment begins, "Congress shall make no law respecting an establishment of religion, or prohibiting the free exercise thereof."

With this right, the Founders prohibited the establishment of any church at the national level while protecting the individual's free exercise of religion. The First Amendment was not written because the Founders were anti-religious, but precisely because they *favored* religion.

Today, the foundations for religious freedom are being eroded. The secular-socialist Left have twisted the meaning of the First Amendment to fit a post-modern world they helped create.

People of faith have been systematically marginalized by a two-part secular campaign waged by the cultural elite. First, there has been a sustained effort to change the culture by spreading propaganda through the schools and through the media, where the values of the secular-socialist Left are advanced while historic American values of God-given rights are silenced and mocked. The second part of the campaign is to give secular values the authority of law through the courts, state houses, and the Congress, while removing the individual's right to, as Jefferson put it, "profess and by argument to maintain, their opinions in matters of religion."

As a result, public expressions of faith have gone from normal to unacceptable. The abuses are well documented. Year after year, the courts are filled with hundreds of cases based upon the anti-religious misconceptions of the First Amendment created by the secular-socialist Left and often reinforced by judges.

The reason secular socialists adhere to an agenda that includes tearing down crosses, arresting people for talking about their faith in shopping malls, redefining marriage, prohibiting crèches and menorahs on public property, preventing students from reading the Bible, and removing God from the public square, is really quite simple: the religious worldview is the single most serious threat to the secular Left's utopian vision. This vision relies upon a powerful, centralized, bureaucratic government that must be the highest authority in the land to ensure compliance. Dissent is not tolerated. Adherence is essential. Every aspect of the lives of citizens must be controlled by the authority of state law, including personal belief.

America, however, was founded on Judeo-Christian principles with a *limited* national government that upheld the individual's rights of conscience. Therefore, it is necessary for the secular Left to keep citizens ignorant about their history, their heritage, the Judeo-Christian roots of American culture, and even their Creator if they are to impose their secular-socialist agenda on this nation.

Protecting religious liberty is the foundation stone for protecting all liberty. The liberty of every American, whether religious or not, is at risk if even one American's religious liberty is abridged. There is a profound reason our religious liberties are delineated in the *first* sentence of the *First* Amendment.

In the twentieth century, hundreds of millions of people were killed by the totalitarian ideologies of Marxism, Nazism, and Fascism, each of which required the use of a powerful, centralized state authority to control every aspect of the citizens' lives. Those who resisted were eliminated, often by imprisonment or death. Religion was enemy number one and the first to go. The regimes tore down crosses, destroyed churches, hounded and coerced church officials, crushed free worship, and replaced religious texts with nationalist propaganda in schools. The enemy of dictatorship was God.

There are many parallels between the anti-religious governments of the twentieth century and the anti-religious elite of the United States in the twenty-first. But our country wasn't always ruled by secular absolutists. Before the United States entered World War II, President Roosevelt, the most successful liberal Democrat in the twentieth century, invoked the imagery of religious battle to describe who we were and who the enemy was: "Today the whole world is divided between human slavery and human freedom—between pagan brutality and the Christian ideal. We choose human freedom—which is the Christian ideal."

In less than a generation, the cultural elites have created a national amnesia about both our history and our Godly heritage. Today, the Founders' original intent is all but lost in a post-modern world patrolled by the totalitarian impulses of self-appointed enforcers of political correctness.

Eleven score and fourteen years from the signing of the Declaration of Independence, Lincoln's injunction at Gettysburg remains as relevant as when he uttered it: "That this nation, under God, shall have a new birth of freedom—and that government: of the people, by the people, for the people, shall not perish from the earth."

SOLUTIONS TO PROTECT RELIGIOUS LIBERTY

Ensuring religious liberty is a sacred tenet of America's foundational principles. Below is a list of immediate steps to protect people of faith from further government encroachment on their liberties.

Restoring Our Crucial System of Constitutional Checks and Balances

We must restore constitutional limited government by reviving our system of checks and balances. Failure to invoke constitutional checks and balances has allowed the Judicial Branch to legislate from the bench, imposing its judgments on the elected branches of government. This is the main reason why religious liberty is under such sustained assault today. Here's what we need to do:

- Congress must exercise its constitutional responsibilities to check the abuses of the Judicial Branch by restricting the jurisdiction of the courts where necessary and even by following President Jefferson's precedent of abolishing or threatening to abolish defiant courts, as per the Judicial Reform Act of 1802.
- The president and his attorney general must exercise their constitutional responsibilities by only nominating judicial candidates who are committed to upholding the original intent of the Founders of our nation and to overturning the malignant decisions of previous judges that have violated those principles.
- The Senate must exercise its responsibility to assure that the only judges or justices that it confirms are committed to upholding the Founders' original intent.
- Citizens must ensure that candidates for the U.S. Senate commit to carrying out these policies once they are elected. And they must hold those who violate their pledge accountable and defeat them.

- Citizens must also ensure they elect candidates at the state and local level who are committed to resisting the preemption of their proper, constitutional roles and functions by the federal government.

Freedom of Speech and the Right to Assemble

The liberties of both religious expression and speech in general are guaranteed by the First Amendment. We must preserve these foundations of our republic by educating Americans about their true meaning and relevance so they can defend their own rights. Therefore, the following measures should be pursued:

- *Repeal so-called "hate speech" legislation.* Allowing the courts to broadly determine what they consider "hate speech" is profoundly dangerous to a free people. Congress has no constitutional authority to regulate thought. Speech is already protected, and criminal activities are already legally defined, as are their punishments. Religious leaders who speak either from the pulpits and or by electronic medium are particularly vulnerable to state punishment for alleged violations of hate speech, even if that speech reflects their religious teachings. While religious leaders are most at risk, we cannot seek a free speech dispensation for one class of people. Therefore, all Americans must be protected from this arbitrary abridgement of their rights.
- *Protect personal religious expression.* The individual has an inherent right to express her faith either in speech, religious displays, or on her person. The Founders clearly believed in freedom of religion, not freedom against religion. Congress and the state legislatures

should ensure that an individual's rights to take a Bible to work, have a religious bumper sticker on her vehicle, talk about her faith, or wear clothing or jewelry that contains religious symbols or expressions are not infringed.

- *Bar public universities that enforce campus speech codes from using taxpayer funding.* The forerunner to recently passed "hate speech" legislation can be found in many of today's publicly funded universities. College campuses historically have been the incubator of ideas and the strongholds of free expression. Today, those same schools that once promoted freedom have instituted intolerant rules and reporting systems designed to silence speech deemed politically incorrect.

- *Ensure equal access to public facilities.* People of faith and their organizations have as much right to assemble as any other group. Therefore, religious organizations should have equal access to public facilities. Invoking the First Amendment's establishment clause as an excuse for denying access should not be tolerated. The use of a public facility by a religious group no more constitutes an establishment of religion than the same use by the local garden club or any other non-religious organization.

- *Keep the so-called Employment Non-Discrimination Act (ENDA) from becoming law.* People of faith have the right to organize and seek like-minded people to fulfill their ministries. Religious organizations must be able to freely choose their members, employees, and leadership while remaining immune from state-imposed membership or employment quotas. It violates the Constitution's guarantee of free exercise of religion to require that a person who does not hold the beliefs of the religious group be considered for membership, leadership, or employment. Faith organizations must not be forced to either abandon or dilute their mission to meet a government ideological quota.

- Congress and the state legislatures must protect the right of citizens and clergy in civil settings to pray according to their own religious traditions.

Limited Government

Because government power expands at the direct expense of individual freedom, the best way to protect liberty, particularly religious liberty, is to limit the size and scope of governments at all levels. To do that, we should:

- *Pass a balanced budget amendment.* Passing on our massive federal debt to the next generation is immoral. The best way to stop the politicians from bankrupting our country and limiting freedom is to pass a balanced budget amendment to the Constitution.
- *Help the poor by expanding opportunity.* Americans, who are far and away the most generous people in the world, have always been committed to helping those in need, but we must recognize that the government is not the best vehicle to render this assistance. Historically, the churches and other organizations Tocqueville called "intermediating institutions" most effectively helped the poor because they ministered to more than their earthly needs. We need to relearn that model for helping those in need and unlearn our dependence on the welfare state. The Founders were clear on the right to pursue happiness, which speaks to self-reliance. Therefore, the government should foster the condition

where the self-reliant have the best opportunity to prosper.

Healthcare

President Obama and Congress have put us on the road to nationalized healthcare. State-run healthcare services are typically intolerant of religious objections by medical workers to certain procedures. If national healthcare can't be undone, we must ensure the system maintains freedom of religious conscience. To protect the doctor-patient relationship and put personal or religious conscience over the policies of the state, we should:

- *Protect healthcare workers' right to conscience.* People of faith have as much right to pursue careers in the healing arts as anyone. If conscience dictates, healthcare workers should not be required to either participate in or refer procedures such as abortion.
- *Put individuals ahead of "society."* "First do no harm" is the physician's covenant to his patients. We must oppose the state's inclination to put the physician's obligation to "society" before his obligation to individual patients.

Education

The myth that the establishment clause requires government to purge religion from public life is omnipresent in our public schools, contrary to the express intention of the Founders. To protect religious liberty in education we should adhere to the following:

- Since it is the prerogative and the responsibility of parents to choose the instruction that is best for their child, we must preserve the homeschooling option.

- Homeschooled children and their families should not be denied participation in extra-curricular, school-related activities that their tax dollars help fund.

- No individual should be denied equal access to government employment or education based on the accreditation status of his credits, diploma, or degree. This is a situation often faced by homeschool and Christian-school students.

- School districts should be allowed to offer optional religious instruction including Bible study. Providing this option in no way constitutes an establishment of religion.

- Parents should be free to choose the school of their choice, including religious schools. They should be given an education credit coupon (a Pell Grant for K–12) allowing them more options to choose a school that best fits their own values, not those imposed by the state.

- Parents must have the right to choose which value instruction their child receives and therefore must be able to opt out without qualification.

- Teachers should not be discouraged from or punished for using historical examples that involve religion in their classroom. Nor should they be discouraged from answering questions about religion or discussing it objectively in the classroom.

- Teachers and education workers should have the same protections of religious expression as any other citizen in a free society.

- Students should be allowed to study, on their own time, religious texts or engage in religious expression at school without fear of punishment or ridicule from school officials.

- Art, drama, and music classes should not exclude religious themes.
- U.S. history classes should study the influences of religion on the Founders and other historical figures. They should specifically study and explain the religious themes and foundations contained in our historical documents, including the Mayflower Compact, the Declaration of Independence, and the Northwest Ordinance.
- Religious texts, including Bibles and scriptures, should not be banned in public schools.
- Federal regulation of local faith-based residential child-care facilities should be repealed and these responsibilities returned to the states where the Founders intentionally left them.

GOD IN THE PUBLIC SQUARE

In a single generation, religious expression in the public square has become abnormal. This cultural shift is no accident. The secular Left, first through the media and the schools, then through the courts and now the legislative bodies, have effectively denied people the right of corporate and individual religious expression in public. The following measures will help counter the secular assault on public expression of faith:

- Remove the financial incentive for secular groups like the ACLU to sue towns, counties, and states over establishment clause issues by eliminating the financial damages that can be rewarded in these cases.
- Congress should remove the jurisdiction of any court review of our nation's motto "In God We Trust" and the phrase "under God" in the Pledge of Allegiance.

- Congress and the state legislatures should pass laws stating that the display of crosses, crèches, and menorahs do not constitute the establishment of a religion by the state.
- Congress and the states should clarify that government employees have the same rights to express religious opinions as people who are expressing secular opinions. Moreover, they should be protected from harassment for wearing jewelry or other clothing that displays symbols of their faith.

RIGHT TO LIFE

Few areas of public policy stir passion like the life issue does. Listed first of the three unalienable rights of the Declaration, the Founders clearly intended the federal government's chief priority to be protecting life. People of faith have brought the issue of life—not limited to abortion—to the forefront time and again. At a minimum, we must acknowledge that life is a precious gift from God.

Americans, more than most other nations, place life in high cultural regard. Anytime a child is lost, a hiker is stuck on a mountain, or people are in harm's way, we move mountain and earth to save life. Valuing life from beginning to end is central to a healthy culture. To uphold life we should:

- Ensure that taxpayer dollars are never used for funding elective abortions, which are cases that don't involve rape or incest or where it is necessary to save the life of the mother.
- Defund the United Nations Population Fund (UNFPA), which is using U.S. taxpayer dollars to help enforce China's mandatory one-child policy that compels,

sometimes through force, millions of women to undergo abortions.

- Reinstate the "Mexico City Policy," which banned funding to organizations that promote and/or perform abortion overseas. President Obama rescinded it shortly after his inauguration.
- Protect the frail, the infirm, and the elderly from the state's arbitrary decision to terminate life.

WHAT YOU CAN DO

- Pray—for our nation and its leaders, that God will continue to pour out his blessings on America.
- Register to vote.
- Learn about the issues, especially those that threaten religious liberty.
- Learn the religious liberty positions and records of elected officials and candidates for office.
- Vote in every election. No candidate will agree with you on every issue, every time, but vote for the candidates who most closely represent your views.
- Use your influence to educate and persuade others about the importance of being informed and voting.
- If you know someone who has leadership ability and understands the importance of protecting religious liberty, encourage them to run for office.
- If you have leadership ability and want to fight to protect freedom, consider running for office yourself.
- If you are concerned that a measure in Congress, your state house, or county or town board will adversely

impact religious freedom, tell your elected representatives how you want them to vote.

- When you see or experience an encroachment on religious freedom, write a letter to the editor or an opinion article for your local paper, or call talk radio. If you don't speak up, maybe no one will. But if you do, you can frame the debate and help get good legislation passed and bad legislation defeated.
- Organize a voter registration drive at your church.

WHAT CHURCHES CAN DO

In 1954, when then-Senator Lyndon Johnson wanted to silence opposition from some non-profit groups, he attached an amendment to a bill that prohibited non-profits from engaging in political activities. The bill passed. Since then, the secularists have used that law to convince churches and their leaders that they cannot be involved in politics. So for over four decades, many churches have been silent and uninvolved.

Before 1954, Christian clergy and other religious leaders were a dominant influence upon the culture, the issues, and political campaigns. It was the pastors in colonial times who were speaking about rights coming from God, long before Jefferson used that concept in the Declaration of Independence. It was the sermons preached by George Whitefield, an English evangelist who made seven tours in the colonies during the first Great Awakening, that helped spark a rebellion that led to the American Revolution. It was pastors that founded the great learning institutions of Harvard, Yale, Princeton, Columbia, William and Mary, and others for one specific reason: they understood the importance of an educated and moral citizenry to the survival of a free society. And after America became a country, abolitionism was a religiously inspired movement led from the pulpit.

Pastors for most of America's history were the thought and opinion leaders of the nation. But today, too many have confined themselves and their cultural influence within the walls of their churches. That must end.

There are three centers of influence in America today—economic, political, and spiritual. Wall Street will not restore America's foundations. Politicians mostly reflect the culture that keeps them in office. That leaves pastors, priests, and rabbis as the last best hope for renewing freedom.

But where do churches start? What can they do? What should they do and not do?

All good questions. Here are some answers.

Churches are uniquely deemed non-profit by definition. Every election year, the secular advocacy group People United for the Separation of Church and State sends letters to pastors warning them their not-for-profit status could be revoked if they talk about political issues or get involved in elections. But that letter is pure intimidation that stands on thin legal precedent. No church in America has ever lost its non-profit status. Not one.

There are many ways churches and pastors can address the issues of our day. The idea is not to make churches and their leaders into political operations. That is not the purpose of a church. But if churches don't provide moral leadership to the citizens in their pews and apply their teachings to today's issues, they are doing a major disservice to their congregations and their communities. There is a lot of ground to make up if we are to reverse our cultural decay.

Here are some basic, fully legal forms of church engagement:

- Churches can conduct voter registration drives to make sure every congregant is registered to vote. Better yet, have all the members stand and ask those who are registered to sit down, leaving those unregistered standing. Have ushers pass out voter registration cards and pens and ask them to fill them out right then and there. The ushers should then collect them and get them to the registrar of voters.

- Talk about issues from the pulpit. Don't wait until election time, when your congregation may get uncomfortable hearing the pastor address contemporary issues for the first time. Get them used to hearing about how Biblical principals apply to today's issues. There are organizations that provide sermon resources on how to do this correctly, such as United in Purpose (www.unitedinpurpose.org) and the Pastors Rapid Response Team.
- At election time, talk about the importance of voting. American history is full of wonderful stories showing how people of faith created this great nation. You can use these stories to encourage your members to vote.
- Make voter guides available explaining issues that affect your church and where the candidates stand on those issues. Many faith organizations like Wallbuilders (www.wallbuilders.com) produce them.
- Invite guest speakers who have expertise in America's Godly heritage to address your congregation.

If every church and synagogue did these things, it would be very difficult for the secular Left to get their candidates elected. The secular socialists know this. That's why they work so hard to intimidate churches from getting involved. But does it really make sense for people of faith not to be involved when the secularists are working overtime?

There are nearly 65 million evangelical Christians in the United States who are eligible to vote. But in some areas, nearly half are not registered, and up to half of those who register don't bother to vote. That's almost 45 million Americans who sit out some elections. If only 10 percent of those voted in every election, the secular-socialist Left would be in dire straits. They're terrified people of faith will wake up one day and decide never to sit out the process again. But it is up to the faith leaders to mobilize them.

A couple precautions: under current law, churches cannot endorse candidates but pastors can, if done correctly. Politicians can speak to the congregation but they cannot ask people to vote for them. To find out what churches can and cannot do legally, contact either Liberty Council (www.lc.org) or the Alliance Defense Fund (www.alliancedefensefund.org). If a church is threatened, these groups can provide the legal defense, usually pro bono.

The Founders who declared our independence and created a government based upon their understanding of God's principles were committed to the idea of a federal government with limited power. Because of their success, our government today is now the oldest government on earth. The best way to ensure its continuation and to secure religious liberty is to further limit federal powers and maintain the right of redress articulated in the Declaration of Independence:

> *That to secure these rights, Governments are instituted among Men, deriving their just powers from the consent of the governed,—That whenever any Form of Government becomes destructive of these ends, it is the Right of the People to alter or to abolish it, and to institute new Government, laying its foun-*

dation on such principles and organizing its powers in such form, as to them shall seem most likely to effect their Safety and Happiness.

Remember Jefferson's great insight: "The God who gave us life gave us liberty." Religious liberty is much too precious to allow it to be further eroded. People of faith must educate themselves, get involved, and encourage others to do the same. For too long the secularist campaign against religious freedom has gone unanswered. But to change that we need only reflect on Psalm 11:3 (NIV): "When the foundations are being destroyed, what can the righteous do?"

There is a great deal we can do. And when we do it we will not be without God's help. Our national motto says it all: "In God we trust."

CHAPTER TWENTY

Solving the Education Crisis

With

Lisa Graham Keegan—Advisor, American Solutions Learning Project

Nancy Sinnott Dwight—Advisor, American Solutions Learning Project

Fred Asbell—American Solutions Education Policy Director

No American should underestimate the continuing crisis in our educational system or the threat that crisis poses to our nation.

This is not a new problem. More than a quarter century ago, in 1983, the Reagan administration released "A Nation at Risk." That devastating critique of our education bureaucracy declared that if a foreign power were doing as much damage to our children as our unionized, bureaucratic, government schools, we would consider it an act of war.

Nearly a decade ago, in March 2001, the Hart-Rudman Commission on National Security—the most comprehensive review of national security requirements since 1947—warned the second greatest threat to America was the failure of math and science education and the failure to sustain our scientific investments. It argued this failure was a greater threat than any conceivable conventional war.

Today, any American can go to 2mmillion.com and see Bob Compton's remarkable documentary film *2 Million Minutes*, which compares two Indian, two Chinese, and two American high school students. Even though the Americans are from a "high-performing" high school, they simply cannot compete with their Chinese and Indian peers. Compton has since filmed a movie on the Basis School in Tucson, Arizona, which he asserts is the best high school in the world. He upholds the school as proof Americans can perform and compete when the system is changed from bureaucratic mediocrity into a learning-oriented, high-standards model that both challenges and reinforces students.

THREE IMPORTANT LEARNING TRENDS IN TODAY'S AMERICA

The challenge we face involves three crucial trends:

1. The coming revolution in learning through technology and brain science.
2. The requirement that all Americans learn all their lives.
3. The failure of unionized bureaucratic education and the need to replace it with a student- and parent-centered competitive model.

First, we are on the edge of a revolution that will outstrip anything we have ever imagined possible in human learning and adaptation. The combination of breakthroughs in neuroscience and the emergence of inexpensive wireless technologies with massive computational powers (enabling expert systems and personalized learning feedback applications) will revolutionize how we think about learning in the next decade.

Therefore, we must design a system of learning that is available 24/7 every day for all Americans to learn with unprecedented speed and effectiveness at their convenience and in their homes or communities. The work of Apple on iPhone applications, of Amazon on Kindle applications, and of neuroscientists who have developed many startup companies studying how advances in brain science might improve our lives, are all encouraging indicators of a future learning system more personalized, more convenient, and more effective than anything we have in the unionized, 1840s-era bureaucratic model of education today.

Second, we have to think about learning policies for every American at every age. Every American will have to learn virtually his entire life. We cannot go into states like Michigan with massive structural unemployment and consign thousands of middle-aged Americans to unemployment or underemployment for the rest of their lives. With huge scientific advances (4 to 7 times as much new science in the next twenty-five years) combined with the pressures of competing in a world market, Americans will have to commit to lifetime learning if they want to be effective.

Furthermore, we will discover we need to learn different things at different times. Someone can be an expert in one area and a beginner in another. We must integrate learning at every age and on every topic so there is a seamless web of opportunity that Americans can access. This requires Congress and the state legislatures to rethink the artificial divisions they now have between primary learning, vocational education, adult education, and the like. We may need new committees that cover the entire spectrum of learning. We may also need to rethink how learning is organized in the state and federal government to bring together activities that today are spread across the Department of Education, the Labor Department, the Commerce Department, Health and Human Services, the National Science Foundation, and the National Institutes of Health.

Third, we have to recognize the greatest barrier to the coming revolution in effective, convenient learning for all ages is the unionized, bureaucratic systems that absorb vast amounts of money while protecting bad teachers and bad schools. This system cripples the future of young Americans, especially the poor and minorities. As long as our system is characterized by waste such as New York City's $65 million-per-year rubber rooms for failed teachers, it will never substantially improve learning outcomes.

Instead of wasting resources harboring incompetence, we should be investing in a new campaign to recruit the finest and the fittest to lead our classrooms and laboratories, an "Operation Teach" that spotlights the twenty-first century imperative of teacher recruitment. We should build on programs that pull highly qualified college graduates into teaching, such as Teach for America, KIPP schools, and others.

While attracting the very young into this vital profession, older generations could be mobilized to patiently teach the generations to come. We should recruit retired professionals eager to share their knowledge with the next wave of learners: museum and library workers to teach science and literature; retired military officers to lead classrooms in mathematics and geography; retired medical professionals to share their knowledge in biology sections; journalists to teach the texting generation how to write and read. This will require a whole new approach to part-time and specialized teachers that breaks all the molds of bureaucratic structure, useless credentials, and tenured unionization.

Twenty-first century teachers should be masters of their subject's content and methodology, earning salaries that reflect a community's real commitment to learning. Teacher certification should no longer be tied to the vagaries of union demands but to measured student advancement and performance.

This requirement for a fundamental improvement in learning is more than a national security issue or an economic issue. It is the issue that will determine our nation's future. Learning and its fraternal twin, education, are this century's battleground in a three-century quest for equality in America—this is the number one civil rights issue of the twenty-first century.

At American Solutions, we believe lifelong, limitless (but not effortless) learning is the key to a successful America, an America that embodies prosperity, safety, and freedom for every American of every background and every neighborhood.

We must be an intellectually hungry, morally strong, and urgently demanding nation with an education system capable of responding to a voracious American desire to learn. The following solutions can put American education on that path:

1. A model charter school law featuring freedom in personnel decisions, direct and full funding, and no limits on growth should be adopted in every state with these provisions:
    a. All the money allocated for student education goes directly to the school.
    b. The school manages its own staff, whereby it is exempt from laws regarding tenure and unionization.
    c. The school defines its own curriculum in line with state standards and assessments. Students in charters are not exempt from state assessments. The schools are not exempt from reporting requirements, nor should they be.

d.   State law allows the schools to "franchise" its model without limitation. That means they need not apply for a new school every time they want to build one. If they have the demand, they should be allowed to meet it.

e.   The state has no caps on the number of charter schools that can be approved, and the process for approving charter schools is smooth and efficient.

2.   All states should use student achievement and outside performance data as key components of teacher evaluation. Exceptional teachers deserve greater leadership roles and higher pay, and this judgment must be made by reviewing the success of the students they teach.

3.   Parents whose children are currently trapped in failing schools must be given immediate, broad options for change.

4.   The president and all fifty state governors should make learning and education reform a top priority and pledge specific action.

5.   States should revise their teacher certification processes to provide preferential and expedited access to unquestionable excellence. Every state should open its systems up to part-time expert teachers so that retired physicists, neighborhood pharmacists, local accountants, and others can teach one or two hours a day, bringing knowledge to the classroom and business-like adult expectations to the students. Programs like Teach for America should be encouraged and expanded.

6.   States should adopt new technologies in teaching, including online schools and the use of web-based curricula within their legal frameworks.

7. Business leadership should engage directly in partnerships with schools to create job-ready graduates.

8. States and school districts should provide expansion incentives for any school with a breakthrough record of achievement.

9. Every state should adopt an early learner program so students can learn faster than the state curriculum. Students who can graduate early could be awarded the cost of the years they skip as scholarships toward college or vocational school.

These initial, practical steps can be adopted in the near future with bipartisan majorities. President Obama and his secretary of education, Arne Duncan, have advocated similar measures such as open-ended charter schools, real accountability for teachers and schools, and a much faster system of firing bad teachers and attracting better ones. We should act now on these issues.

Ultimately, I favor a "Pell Grant for kindergarten through twelfth grade" (as Senator Lamar Alexander describes it) so all parents can send their child to the school they believe is best for that child. The Netherlands and Israel have done well with this kind of open-ended public funding of non-bureaucratic learning, which sparks competition and encourages start-ups and creativity.

Liberals passionately support Pell Grants for colleges so poor children can continue their education, but they tend to oppose Pell Grants before college. As a result, they keep America's poorest and most disadvantaged children trapped in bureaucracies that cripple their future and leave them without enough education to ever use a college Pell Grant.

It's time we learned form the success of America's competitive, open-ended higher education system and applied the same principles of choice and competition to K–12 learning. We would immediately increase learning and dramatically reduce the ineffective, unionized bureaucracy. America would be stronger on both counts.

CHAPTER TWENTY-ONE

Why the Second Amendment Is Vital to Preserving Our Freedom

I n order to preserve liberty from encroachment by government and politicians, the Founding Fathers passed a Bill of Rights consisting of ten amendments to the Constitution. The Second Amendment says, "A well regulated Militia being necessary to the security of a free State, the right of the people to keep and bear arms, shall not be infringed."

The secular-socialist Left argue that militias no longer exist the way they did in the eighteenth century. Thus, they say, the Second Amendment is antiquated and the individual's right to arms is no longer relevant.

This is a willfully false reading of the amendment. The experiences and writings of the Founding Fathers indisputably demonstrate they intended for the Second Amendment to be understood as an individual right that exists outside the context of using weapons as part of service in a militia.

Nine provisions written in state constitutions during the eighteenth and early nineteenth centuries included language asserting the people's right to "bear arms in defense of themselves" as well as in defense of their state. So the right to bear arms was commonly understood at the time as applying to self-defense.

But more important, the Second Amendment not only guarantees the individual's right to defend one's self, family, and property, but to defend against the inherent danger of tyrannical government.

The men who wrote and enacted the Second Amendment had a keen sense of words and a thorough knowledge of history. In addition to their own experiences fighting against British tyranny, they were steeped in Greek, Roman, and English history. From this, they concluded that politicians could not be trusted, that power corrupts, and that governments were a permanent threat to liberty.

The lessons of the English Civil War taught the Founders that government had to be controlled by the people or it would drift into a tyranny over the people. And the experience of their own American Revolution, especially the battles of Lexington and Concord, convinced them that an armed citizenry was an essential requirement for preserving freedom.

David Hackett Fischer, in his brilliant history *Paul Revere's Ride*, captures the lesson. The British Army had had a long experience of crushing peasant rebellions in Ireland, Scotland, and rural England. Faced with rabble, the disciplined force of a relatively few men could dominate and impose the government's will.

That is why the colonists' victories at Lexington and Concord were such an enormous shock for the British Army. As Fischer recounts in vivid and compelling detail, more than a century of self-defense, self-organization, and self-government had created communities capable of governing themselves and defending themselves. When the British collided with this organized community, they were outnumbered and in many ways outgunned.

Civilian soldiers made a crucial contribution to victory during the agonizing eight years of the Revolutionary War. At Saratoga, one of the greatest victories of the entire war (and the key event in convincing France to enter the war on our side), the militia played a decisive role in isolating and surrounding an entire British Army.

The Founding Fathers knew full well the original march to Concord and Lexington aimed to seize the largest powder supply in New England. They knew the British believed disarming citizens was the key step toward controlling and subjugating them.

Throughout history, we have constantly seen regimes attempt to disarm and thereby control people—and with good reason. Armed, independent civilians are a threat to tyrants.

Thus, the right to bear arms became a key building block in the fabric of freedom.

Since the Founding Fathers deeply believed in the weakness of human nature and the tendency of power to corrupt those who wield it, they wanted to preserve the citizens' ability to defend themselves against tyranny, even against a tyrant of their own nationality.

In *The Federalist* No. 46, James Madison wrote that if the federal government were ever to act in a way that violated the rights of Americans, a federal army "would be opposed [by] a militia amounting to near half a million citizens with arms in their hands." Madison argued that if the people of Europe, where "the governments are afraid to trust people with arms," had a militia organized by local government, "the throne of every tyranny in Europe would be speedily overturned in spite of the legions which surround it."

Madison's point has held true in more modern times. Imagine a Nazi Germany in which the Nazis hadn't passed special laws to disarm Jews and other anti-Nazi groups. Under those conditions, the Holocaust would have been virtually impossible to implement.

Anyone who has studied Afghan history knows that the power of the Afghan people to resist every foreign invader—including the British, Russian, and Soviet empires—is based on the Afghans' widespread ownership of arms and skill in their use. Our own commanders in Afghanistan know if they were to alienate the Afghan population, the country would be ungovernable. We can be in Afghanistan as liberators and allies, but never as conquerors or dominators.

INTERNATIONAL GUN GRABBERS

Despite the clear link between freedom and the right to bear arms in self-defense, today we find intense opposition to Americans exercising their Second Amendment rights.

Secular socialists, with their mania for government power, deeply oppose the notion of armed Americans preserving their freedom by bearing their own firearms. And so they've decided to do something about it.

Because the National Rifle Association has so effectively organized grassroots Americans to protect their Second Amendment rights, the Left have opted for an international strategy to take away those rights. They know they cannot pass such legislation through the United States Congress because Republicans and even many Democrats would oppose it.

Thus, George Soros, Secretary of State Hillary Clinton, and others have been pushing for a United Nations agreement that could limit the right to keep and bear arms in the United States.

Proponents of this "UN Arms Trade Treaty" say it would not affect the individual's rights to bear arms, that it is solely aimed at regulating international gun trafficking.

As Bob Barr and John Bolton have pointed out, however, it's hard to imagine an effective set of laws to regulate international small arms sales that would not require some sort of new regulations and tracking on the national level.

Since all international treaties require two-thirds of the Senate to enact, it's vital that defenders of the Second Amendment oppose this treaty as vigorously as they have opposed all previous attempts to infringe on this unalienable right, whether originating at home or abroad.

Americans must understand that our opponents are well-organized and relentless. The international Left have already succeeded in ginning up support for laws radically restricting gun rights in Australia and elsewhere. America, though, is their prime target, for if they could disarm the citizenry in a country with such a strong tradition of gun rights, then they probably could do it just about anywhere.

Everyone who believes in protecting freedom and everyone who believes in the Second Amendment should prepare for an all-out fight against any effort by the secular-socialist Left to strip us of our constitutional rights.

CHAPTER TWENTY-TWO

Twenty-first Century Threats to National Security

I magine that someone said to you, "I've been driving for years, and I've never had a wreck, so I'm going to stop using my seat belt."

What would you say to convince him of the danger he's courting? How would you persuade him that the other driver might be at fault, or there might be a mechanical failure, or the weather might cause a crash?

The point is, long-term success can lead to overconfidence and a lack of imagination. This is a problem we face in national security after seventy years of nearly uninterrupted success. In just forty-four months after the attack at Pearl Harbor on December 7, 1941, we built up the forces that defeated Nazi Germany, Fascist Italy, and

Imperial Japan. By 1945 we had become the most powerful military force in history.

Then for forty-four years, from 1947 to 1991, we maintained a worldwide coalition and a powerful military to contain the Soviet Union and win the Cold War.

Because we never endured a nuclear attack, it's easy to forget how dangerous the Soviet Union really was. I remember walking to my part-time job at the Atlanta Public Library in October 1962 and wondering if the Cuban Missile Crisis would go nuclear and wipe out the whole city.

It actually could have gone that way. The threat we faced in the Cold War was real and ever-present. The Soviets could have launched a nuclear spasm attack (firing everything at once) to annihilate the United States. President Eisenhower captured some of the danger when he said he would not want to survive an all-out nuclear attack because he would not want to confront the horrors of a post-nuclear world.

Since the Soviets did not actually attack us, it's easy to shrug off the threat as an exaggeration. That's exactly like not using your seat belt because you have not yet crashed. And even after 9/11, many people assumed the enemy had pulled off a lucky attack that could never be repeated.

The unfortunate reality is that America now faces five national security threats, each as great as the Soviet Union was at its peak.

All these dangers are challenging our national security establishment in new ways. Because we invest so much in our current, highly effective capabilities, inertia prevents our leaders from considering wrenching changes or assuming additional burdens to respond to new threats.

In many ways, U.S. national security today is like the leading companies cited by Clayton Christiansen in *The Innovator's Dilemma*. He describes companies that dominated existing technologies and so satisfied their existing markets that they had trouble adapting to emerging, disruptive technologies.[1] Thus IBM dominated big computers but found it hard to invest in small, home computers. Similarly, the very strengths of U.S. national security make it hard to contemplate fundamental shifts in strategy, structure, and investments to meet emerging threats.

Yet these threats are potentially catastrophic.

We cannot merely shift resources from current activities. Instead, we must create a bigger national security system with a bigger budget and a more robust capacity to deal with multiple threats simultaneously.

We face this problem of parallel investment all the time in our daily lives. You don't get to choose between gasoline, oil, and tires for your car. You have to find a way to invest in all three, or your car eventually becomes useless.

Likewise, we do not get to pick and choose which threat we will meet and which we will ignore. Any threat we ignore could potentially destroy us, so we must develop a national and homeland security system that meets all the dangers.

The five potentially catastrophic threats to American national security are:

1. Terrorists with nuclear weapons
2. Electromagnetic pulse attack
3. Cyberwarfare
4. Biological warfare
5. The potential gap between Chinese and American capabilities over the next generation

Each of these threats could destroy our economy and our freedom.
Each could lead to the end of America as we know it.
Each has to be understood and met on its own terms.

THREAT NUMBER ONE: TERRORISTS WITH NUCLEAR WEAPONS

Those of us who advocate an aggressive campaign to defeat the irreconcilable wing of Islam know this danger will eventually evolve from a conventional threat to a nuclear threat. We also know we face a more urgent threat from nuclear weapons in the hands of suicidal Islamic fanatics than from nuclear weapons controlled by a Russian or Chinese bureaucracy.

The militant wing of Islam—comprising 3–6 percent of Islam, or around 36–100 million people worldwide—cannot be reconciled with the modern world. Its adherents do not accept women in public, or working, or driving, or voting, or shopping unaccompanied by their husbands. They want medieval sharia law that allows a husband to murder his wife or daughter in an honor killing. Contrary to politically correct pieties, we will never find an accommodation with these zealots.

Since they know their way of life is incompatible with ours and since they believe Allah wants them to die while killing infidels, they are prepared to commit unfathomable levels of violence against civilians.

The result is a mortal threat to our very existence as a free society.

Now ask yourself this: if someone is willing to kill himself in an attack using a body bomb or a car bomb, why would you think he would refuse to do the same with a nuclear weapon?

If Mahmoud Ahmadinejad and the Iranian ayatollahs are as religiously committed to their cause as are suicide bombers, what would constrain them from launching nukes if they succeed in developing them?

Aside from the Iranians' breakneck nuclear development program, there are other ways for Islamic terrorists to get hold of nuclear weapons. North Korea could sell one, or Islamist sympathizers in Pakistan might give one away. And these devices don't have to be a sleek, missile-deliverable, modern system. A large, clunky, truck-carried or boat-delivered device would be devastating if delivered effectively.

Facing such a dire threat, we need to get serious about the war we are fighting. But when our border is still porous and open to easy infiltration, we are not yet serious.

When a father—a well-known Nigerian banker—warns the U.S. embassy his son may be a terrorist, and we can't bring ourselves to block the son from getting on an airplane with an underwear bomb, we are not yet serious.

When a U.S. army major can make viciously anti-American statements, publicly advocate jihad, communicate with a radical imam in Yemen with links to the 9/11 attackers, and no one stops him until he massacres thirteen Americans at Fort Hood, we are not yet serious.

When we have an energy policy that enriches Saudi sheikhs who are the leading funders of worldwide Islamic extremism, we are not yet serious.

When we cannot even use honest language to describe our enemies, we are not yet serious.

Every time you read about a terrorist incident, remember, "That, but for the grace of God, could have been a nuclear event."

Every time you read about our pathetic inability to secure our border, remember that a nuclear weapon delivered by truck could be as devastating as one delivered by missile.

We have been under attack by the irreconcilable wing of Islam since the Iranians illegally seized our embassy in 1979. For thirty-one years our enemies have been plotting and maneuvering to kill us.

Time is not on our side.

We have to defeat them decisively before they acquire weapons that could destroy our very civilization.

THREAT NUMBER TWO:
ELECTROMAGNETIC PULSE ATTACK

We have known about electromagnetic pulse effects (EMP) for more than a generation. In the mid-twentieth century, it became apparent that with the right design and at the right altitude, a nuclear weapon could be shaped to give off the equivalent of an enormous lightning strike. The power of the energy wave would burn out lights, electric generators, car engines, and anything else that used electricity. Early tests of hydrogen weapons in the Pacific knocked out electric lights in Honolulu 1,200 miles away.[2]

Anyone who has had an electric surge knock out appliances can understand the effect of an EMP attack.

While our military has taken a few measures against this threat, for years we have not seriously considered the civilian implications of an EMP attack.

One of the few comprehensive studies of a potential EMP attack was done by a panel convened by Congressman Roscoe Bartlett in 2005 on behalf of the Armed Services Committee. The panel, comprising prominent nuclear physicists with deep experience in the Cold War, reported that EMP was a real threat, that one EMP weapon over Omaha would knock out half the economy, that China, Russia, and North Korea were all working on EMP weapons, and that we were much more vulnerable to a catastrophic EMP attack than anyone in the national security system was willing to consider.

Ironically, the very scale of the problem caused our military leaders to dismiss the threat as unsolvable.

My friend and coauthor Bill Forstchen wrote a horrifying novel about an EMP attacked titled *One Second After*. In that remarkable adventure story, he outlined a year in the life of a small North Carolina town after electricity had been knocked out by an EMP assault.[3] If you have any doubt how serious this threat is, you should read his novel. You'll never be complacent about EMP again.

The United States needs to develop and fund a national security and homeland security plan to migrate our entire society to a hardened, survivable system over the next decade. The need for such a plan should be a major issue during the next few elections. In light of this potentially catastrophic threat, we have no choice but to prepare for it as a matter of national survival.

THREAT NUMBER THREE: CYBERWARFARE

The United States is engaged in cyberwarfare every day.

There are constant skirmishes in cyberspace between attacking hackers and security systems. Companies are routinely penetrated and their secrets stolen. Even the Pentagon is under siege as thousands of hackers—most of them Chinese—try to penetrate its security walls.

There are three aspects of this emerging cyberwarfare: offensive, defensive, and strategic.

Offensively, we try to penetrate other systems, and they try to penetrate ours. This has been going on at least since America and Britain began stealing German and Japanese communication codes in the 1930s. (Back then it was called signals intelligence.) Many of the biggest advantages the Allies had in World War II came from their extraordinary success in breaking enemy codes. Indeed, the American victory at Midway would have been impossible without our codebreakers.

The entire Cold War was marked by massive, continuing efforts to "read each other's mail." In fact, the National Security Agency is the most sophisticated electronic systems developer, interceptor, and analyzer in the world.

And of course, while each of us is trying to penetrate and understand the other, we are simultaneously on defense trying to block others from penetrating and understanding us.

Despite our historic advantage in these efforts, today our competitors' capabilities are growing quickly. The Russians are technically the best. The Chinese are still learning, but they make up in sheer numbers what they lack in sophistication. By some estimates there may be as many as 150,000 or more Chinese nationals engaged in cyberintelligence.[4]

All of us understand the importance of virus protection on our computer. Imagine the depth of defense the Pentagon and other institutions now must build to block competitors from penetrating and learning our secrets. Cybersecurity is clearly a growth industry.

Cyberdefense will become a more expensive part of national security, increasingly pervading the entire system of both government and private sector communications. It will involve deep investments in math and science education to produce people who are good enough to stay ahead of the Russians, Chinese, and others.

Strategic cyberwarfare is a fundamentally different type of threat from anything we've previously seen. In strategic cyberwarfare your opponents use their capability to disrupt your society. For example, smartgrids are a current buzzword in electricity distribution. Yet, the very nature of a smartgrid makes them vulnerable to cyberpenetration. Imagine an opponent turning off all the electricity distribution in the United States.

The first strategic cyberattack occurred in 2007 in Estonia, after that government relocated a Soviet World War II memorial along with the graves of some Soviet soldiers.[5] The move incensed the Russian government and provoked retaliation from Russian computer hackers. Since Estonia had recently become a paperless government, its pride in its new Internet- and computer-based administrative system suddenly became a nightmare as the Russians systematically disrupted it, along with basic Internet service.

The Estonian incident provides a case study in cyberwar. Without killing or even injuring anyone, Russia put enormous pressure on a small neighbor and intimidated other countries.

How vulnerable is America to a cyberattack? It's hard to say, because no one really knows exactly how sophisticated Russian, Chinese, and other investments in strategic cyberwar have become.

This is not a threat of the future.

This is the reality of today.

Because cyberattacks are non-lethal, they don't receive much attention. But views would change if our economy and our government were wrecked in a cyberattack.

We must make as big an investment in cyber capabilities as we made over the last two generations in strategic nuclear systems. This goal will require an increase of about two orders of magnitude (100-fold) from our current cyber investments.

THREAT NUMBER FOUR: BIOLOGICAL WARFARE

Biological warfare is probably less of a threat than nuclear, EMP, or cyber attacks. Nonetheless it has to be taken seriously both because of the explosion of new knowledge in biology and because of the level of mass fear that even a small biological attack would generate.

Sadly, the breakthroughs in biological knowledge that will extend our lives create the potential for someone to use the same science to develop mutations and adaptations to create new biological threats.

However, the routine work done by the Centers for Disease Control and the National Institutes of Health, combined with the specialized work of national security labs, creates a reasonably strong capability to respond to a biological threat.

Our greatest vulnerability is in having a public health system and a health information system that react and share information too slowly. We should invest in an electronic health system to ensure that any attack would be detected early and analyzed quickly, and that countermeasures would be rapidly implemented.

Such a real-time electronic health system will save thousands and possibly even millions of lives if we are hit with a biological attack. It would also save lives in the event of a pandemic.

Investing in these health systems is less expensive than preparing for cyberattacks or EMP attacks, but it's a vital national and home-land security measure to enable us to outlast our enemies and protect the American people.

THREAT NUMBER FIVE: THE GROWING GAP BETWEEN CHINESE AND AMERICAN CAPABILITIES

As this book details, the United States has become mired in many policies and institutions whose development is increasingly being outpaced by China.

While we remain a bigger economic power than China and our mil-itary is vastly stronger, all the trend lines are in the wrong direction.

Our schools are inadequate.

Our litigation system is destructive.

Our regulatory system ties us up and inhibits effective development.

Our tax policy is anti-investment, anti-saving, and anti-jobs.

Our aging infrastructure is becoming uncompetitive in the world market.

The cost of our government is robbing the economy of vital resources and is piling up debt that will burden the next generation.

We are sending billions a year to China to pay for interest on the U.S. debt, money that the Chinese invest in more modern and more competitive systems.

If these trends continue, we will face two grave national security threats, one quantitative and one qualitative.

Quantitatively, we could face a Chinese competitor a generation from now that can out-manufacture and out-produce the U.S. economy. This would be the first time since 1840 that we would not be the world's most productive economy. All our great victories for 170 years have relied on our ability to drown our opponents with resources they could not match. America has truly been the arsenal of democracy. Losing this quantitative edge would jeopardize our national security.

Qualitatively, the Chinese insistence on good education and investment in science and technology could begin to produce capabilities we literally will not understand. The rate of evolution in scientific knowledge is rapidly accelerating, and there is no reason to believe competition with China can be won by a redistributionist, bureaucratic, anti-growth America that protects incompetent schools and favors becoming a lawyer over becoming a scientist or engineer.

If we allow ourselves to drift into a world in which China is both quantitatively and qualitatively superior to us, we should expect to lose our independence and be forced to exist within the framework of Chinese demands. That would be the end of America as we know it.

Note that everything we need to do to compete with China is within our own power. If we replace our policies and our institutions with ones that emphasize free markets, individual rights, and rapid economic and energy development, we will mitigate the Chinese threat for the next fifty years.

The burden is on us, and the challenge is here in America.

CHAPTER TWENTY-THREE

Why the Tea Party Movement Is Good for America

The rise of the tea party movement in 2009 is a great example of the American people's courageous tradition of rejecting elitism and insisting on freedom.

The American colonists who rebelled against the British government felt their rights as "free Englishmen"—which they claimed regardless of their ethnic background—were being abused by a tyrannical government whose judges, bureaucrats, and politicians showed no respect for Americans.

The revolutionary flag depicting a snake with the motto "Don't tread on me" was another visceral expression of this proud sense of independence. Likewise, the original Boston Tea Party of 1773 was an act of defiance meant to show the British government that it could not impose its will on Americans.

Having long admired the tea party as a model of political activism, in 1994 I encouraged a friend of mine, Sharon Cooper (now a state representative in Georgia), to write a book called *Taxpayer's Tea Party*. Rush Limbaugh wrote the foreword. I led a group to Boston on April 15 that year to protest the Clinton tax increases, an event that helped set the stage for the Contract with America campaign that would result in Republicans winning control of Congress that fall.

We see a similar energy among grassroots Americans today, propelled by the Left's arrogant, big-tax, big-spending, big-deficit, politician-centered policies. But the anger actually began simmering earlier, with the bailouts and failed stimulus plans of the late Bush administration. The Obama campaign promised something different—"change you can believe in"—but once in power simply increased federal spending dramatically with even more bailouts and an even bigger stimulus bill.

The spark that transformed widespread outrage into a political movement was lit on February 19, 2009, with the now-famous rant by CNBC correspondent Rick Santelli. Appalled at President Obama's bailout of people with delinquent mortgages, Santelli exclaimed on live TV, "How many of you want to pay for your neighbor's mortgage?" He continued, "President Obama, are you listening? People are of the notion that you can't buy your way into prosperity.... If you read our Founding Fathers, people like Benjamin Franklin and Jefferson...what we're doing in this country now is making them roll over in their graves!"[1]

The original American rebels had committees of correspondence; the 2009 rebels had the Internet. Clips of Santelli's rant went viral as Americans, just as in 1773, began thinking and talking about their rights, responsibilities, and what it means to be an American. Inspired by this discussion, an estimated 30,000 people attended tea parties in fifty cities on February 27, 2009.

Despite the efforts of the elite media to either ignore or downplay the tea partiers, the movement grew rapidly, with an estimated 1.2 million people attending tea parties in over 850 locations on tax day, April 15, 2009.

I had the honor of speaking at the New York City tea party, which drew an estimated 12,500 attendees. There, I got to know Kellen Giuda, one of the main organizers. I was impressed by his ability to organize using mediums like Facebook, Twitter, and email. Kellen explained,

> As a new small businessman, it became surreal to think about how government could get away with spending close to a trillion dollars with smokescreens and no accountability to the public. In the private sector, you don't believe people that come to you with smokescreen business plans.
>
> I got increasingly angry and concerned with the Bush administration's spending and stimulus plans. Obama's put me over the top. For the first time, I started publicly expressing my views through Facebook, and started realizing that my concerns and anger were more widespread. And after Rick Santelli's rant, I noticed that people were beginning to organize Tea Parties on Feb 27, 2009. So I organized a protest of my own at City Hall on Feb 27 and 300 people showed up. It was shocking to me—the diversity that was there, every walk of life, different demographics.
>
> After Feb. 27, I wasn't sure where things were going, but it was clear that people wanted more, so much so that they starting getting together on their own. So I started organizing for 4/15. I felt compelled to continue on until our government fundamentally rethinks its relationship with the American people.

Remarkably, like the British in 1773, the elite media today misunderstand and mock the frustration of American tea partiers. Since the elite media believe in big government, big bureaucracy, and high taxes, and since they love the way President Obama is delivering that agenda, they think tea partiers' grievances are unjustified. This bias was perfectly captured in the April 15, 2009, interview of a Chicago tea party attendee by then-CNN reporter Susan Roesgen. As an attendee is responding to a question from Roesgen by explaining Lincoln's thinking on constitutional rights, Roesgen interrupts him and asks, "Sir, what does that have to do with your taxes? Do you realize that you're eligible for a $400 credit?"

This is the same condescending arrogance that the British showed in assuming Americans would accept taxation without representation as long as the East India Company kept tea prices low.

Since the tea party movement is rooted in individual liberty and skepticism of centralized power, it's logical that the movement is evolving differently all over the country. Skeptical of any efforts to be controlled or cajoled by national organizations, personalities, or political parties, the movement is growing stronger and larger as it retains its decentralized structure. While tea party leaders agree on broad principles such as limited government, lower taxes, and individual liberty, they address different issues in different areas.

Through American Solutions (and especially Adam Waldeck, who coordinates American Solutions' activities with tea partiers), I have met with tea party leaders and organizers across the country, listening and learning about what drives them and what they're doing. Here are some examples:

- Contract From America, led by Ryan Hecker of the Tea Party Patriots, is a campaign to ask Americans what policies they want, vote on the best ones, and then present candidates and elected officials with a platform decided upon by the American people. This could help to define the 2010 elections in a way similar to what the House GOP did in 1994.

- The Ohio Liberty Council effort, led in part by Mike Wilson and Chris Littleton in Cincinnati, Ohio, is an alliance of tens of thousands of grassroots Americans and tea partiers across Ohio. Hundreds of people are showing up at neighborhood meetings in bars and restaurants to discuss issues and plan actions.
- Some local organizations, like the Dallas Tea Party, are organizing at the precinct level, registering people to vote by going door to door in their neighborhoods.
- In the Scottsdale, Arizona area, Honey Marques is organizing rallies at her congressman's district offices, while Diane Burnett is learning to create websites to help coordinate tea party efforts across the state.
- In California, tea party leaders are working to break the cycle of public corruption imposed by the bureaucratic government unions that allows them to perpetually fund the legislative machine in Sacramento.

What will be the tea party movement's ultimate impact? We don't know yet, as it is evolving before our eyes. The change we need to save America will not come with one election cycle, but we are beginning to see campaigns, electoral victories, and energetic grassroots action that should give us all hope.

Undoubtedly, the approval of the Democrats' healthcare reform bill was a blow to freedom. But that was an act of politicians, not the people. Note that the bill was not the reform that candidate Obama had endorsed when the people elected him. In fact, he had specifically repudiated a key part of the reform—the individual mandate—during the Democratic primary.

Since Obama's election, the people have rendered their judgment on his policies through the ballot box. The victories of Bob McDonnell in Virginia, Chris Christie in New Jersey, and Scott Brown in Massachusetts all demonstrate a roiling dissatisfaction with the direction Obama is taking this country. These victories are also strong indicators of the influence of the tea party movement, in that the winning messages of these three candidates were rooted in tea party principles of lower taxes, smaller government, and individual liberty.

This is not a movement of any one party. While the recent GOP victories are good for the movement, success will also require moderate, small-government Democrats to beat the secular-socialist machine's candidates in Democratic districts.

The tea party movement is an extraordinary development in the great tradition of American citizen action. It should give us cause for optimism in these dark days. Although we are facing a tenacious opponent, the American people are energized for the fight.

CHAPTER TWENTY-FOUR

American Solutions

The challenges facing America are so fundamental they will shape the very nature of our lives over the next 40–70 years. These challenges include: the growing power of the secular-socialist machine; the importance of scientific and technological innovation; the growing influence of China and India; the nation's ineffective bureaucratic and litigation systems; the need for cultural reaffirmation of American values; and our government's remoteness from and arrogance toward the American people it is supposed to represent and serve.

I encourage every American to engage in active citizenship and that's best done at American Solutions, where I serve as general chairman. As a citizen action network of more than 1.5 million members, including 30,000 small business owners, American Solutions' goal is to unite a majority of Republicans, Democrats, and independents in a tri-partisan coalition to support the next generation of solutions that will ensure the United States remains the safest, freest, and most prosperous country in the world.

In 2010, American Solutions' objectives are three-fold: to stop the radical Obama-Pelosi-Reid agenda; to develop the best solutions at every level of government; and to begin to train candidates and elected officials to implement the kind of real change that is so desperately needed to save America.

The first, easiest step you can take is to visit our website at www.AmericanSolutions.com, where you can:

- Become a member of American Solutions.
- Find links to our Facebook, Twitter, and other social networking sites.
- Join your local American Solutions Real Change chapter.
- Help organize and participate in a Solutions Day/ Town Hall program in your community.
- Participate in our Small Business Program, the Jobs and Prosperity Task Force.
- Provide financial support to continue developing proven solutions to the problems facing America.

American Solutions is dedicated to advocating replacement solutions that work. Denouncing the Left's failed programs and machine politics is important, but it is not enough. If you want to learn about practical alternatives like the ones presented in this book, visit the American Solutions website. It aims to convince you of one thing: there is a better way to create a better future for our children, our grandchildren, and our country.

THE SOLUTIONS ACADEMY

Turning America's current problems into opportunities is the great challenge of our generation. While the frustration is with politics and the problems are with government, we need to focus on a deeper challenge that exists on four levels:

- Intellectual
- Cultural
- Political
- Governmental

We first have to think through what has to be done.

Then we have to learn to communicate our solutions so Americans will support them.

Then we have to win the political struggle to defeat those in both parties who are stuck in old, obsolete, destructive patterns, and to elect people dedicated to the new thinking and new solutions.

Finally, our new coalition of those committed to the right values, the right language, and the right solutions has to translate political victory into profound changes in government.

There are no institutions that work on all four levels of the challenge. Many do a good job at one part or another, but no one puts it all together into one coherent approach.

Until now. To address all four levels of the challenge, American Solutions is working to identify and promote positive solutions that can help create a better America, and to energetically oppose the bad policies that threaten our prosperity. It will take great effort and many citizen leaders to help people remember and understand what has made America great and what it will take to keep her great.

That is where the Solutions Academy comes in.

The Solutions Academy is an online learning and training center for elected officials, candidates, and citizen leaders. While equipping these individuals to more effectively lead, communicate, and persuade, the academy will also advise them how to take specific actions to support the adoption and implementation of policy solutions that will advance America's safety, prosperity, and freedom.

The Solutions Academy will offer individual lessons in subject areas such as the economy, energy, education, corruption, and core values and principles. In the energy section, for instance, you will find lessons on offshore drilling, nuclear power, renewable energy, and the dangers of a cap-and-trade energy tax, just to name a few. Each lesson will include a wide variety of compelling content in the form of video, audio, research, polling data, handouts, and recommended reading.

In addition to the public policy lessons, the Solutions Academy will include lessons on running for office and leading in office that will teach skills such as effective communications, fundraising, social media, and grassroots organizing. Candidates will also be able to listen to podcasts to get advice from candidates and their senior advisors, such as Virginia governor Bob McDonnell and his campaign chairman Ed Gillespie, on what made their campaign successful.

In short, the Solutions Academy is a rich resource to help elected officials formulate legislative solutions, help candidates create campaign platforms, and help citizen leaders stay informed and get the tools to persuade their friends and family about the solutions to advance American prosperity and freedom.*

---

* To learn more about the Solutions Academy, please visit www.AmericanSolutions.com.

Today, the marketplace of ideas is dominated by a left-wing media, academia, and pop culture that equip citizens, either directly or indirectly, with destructive training in bad ideas that run counter to classic and successful American values and principles.

If we are to save America, we need a growing and active group of elected officials at every level of government, candidates for those offices, and citizen leaders who can persuasively communicate the values, principles, and solutions that will ensure a safe, prosperous, and free America.

Citizenship and Saving America

"The land of the free and the home of the brave." There is a reason our national anthem's first verse ends with those words. The generations who created America fought terrible wars against overwhelming odds. They deeply believed freedom required bravery. Unless we were the home of the brave, we would not remain free.

That principle is as true today as it was when Francis Scott Key wrote the words to "The Star Spangled Banner." If the American people do not have the courage to work and fight for their freedom, they will not remain free. Bravery is not just a battlefield phenomenon.

Bravery is a parent protesting a bad policy to her school board.

Bravery is a student challenging his teachers when they propagandize factually incorrect accounts of U.S. history.

Bravery is a politician fighting to reform a powerful bureaucracy.

Bravery is a conservative faculty member risking the loss of tenure and even the loss of her job by standing firm for her beliefs.

Bravery is a businessman risking an audit or worse by speaking out against government intrusion into the private sector.

Bravery is a woman speaking up for life among feminists who will accuse her of being anti-woman.

Bravery is parents deciding to homeschool their child.

Bravery is an entrepreneur deciding to create jobs, not just have one.

Bravery is a reporter ignoring the institutional bias of the mainstream media and insisting on writing the truth.

Bravery is a citizen running for office and accepting all the indignities and frustrations of public life in order to improve his community.

Bravery is a person calling into talk radio and telling the truth as he sees it, even if the host and the audience disagree.

Bravery is crucial, but it is not enough to keep us free. We also need leadership. I'm not saying you have to run for Congress or some other public office (although that is always an option for every citizen). We can all display leadership in our everyday lives.

You lead when you teach positive values to your children and grandchildren.

You lead when you get engaged in civic organizations.

You lead when you assume responsibilities in your religious organization.

You lead when you work in nonprofit and charitable organizations to help people and communities in need.

You lead when you get involved with your local government.

You lead when you mobilize fellow citizens to gather at rallies, demonstrations, and events to voice your objections to government policy.

With brave citizen leaders, the movement to save America will succeed.

Don't think you are powerless because you have no national audience. Politics is primarily local, and that's where we need to focus in order to win—persuading one person at a time, one family at a time, and one community at a time that we have better solutions than the corrupt, collectivist policies now being decreed in Washington. That is how you can contribute to our common cause: be brave, be a leader, and never stop fighting for what's right for America. Together we will bring about a new generation of freedom.

Shortly before this book went to press, the House of Representatives passed the Left's big-government health reform bill, which President Obama quickly signed into law. The vote was the culmination of a shocking series of bribes, thuggish tactics, and lies, all pursued in direct opposition to the clearly expressed wishes of the American people.

The day after the vote could justifiably have been a miserable one for those Americans who spent the last year fighting against the government's takeover of one-sixth of our economy. But it wasn't. The Left's unconscionable power grab simply strengthened their resolve. The spirit of the day was not resignation, but defiance. In op-ed columns and TV programs, in weblogs and Facebook pages, around water coolers and kitchen tables, the bill's approval was met with one word: *repeal.*

That day I wrote in my newsletter, "This is not the end of the fight. It is the beginning." With its corrupt payoffs, legislative tricks, and blatant disregard for the will of the people, the secular-socialist machine has revealed its true nature. Now it's up to us, the American people, to dismantle this machine.

We have the energy and we have the determination to save America. November 2010 will be our first big chance to render judgment on the Left's healthcare bill, and two years later we'll have another opportunity. It's easy to despair, but that energy is better put toward preparing for these elections, which will be the most consequential of our lifetime.

We must speak out, organize, and never forget what's at stake: our livelihood, our freedom, and our precious country.

Acknowledgments

This book is my personal testimony to where we are and what we must do. It is the culmination of fifty-one years of work going back to August 1958, after I watched French paratroopers kill the French Fourth Republic and bring General De Gaulle back to a temporary dictatorship to create a new government. That summer saw the first Berlin crisis with the Soviet Union, the revolution in Iraq, the United States Army (my father's service) go into Lebanon, and a host of other crises that seemed capable of permanently changing our lives.

For more than half a century, I have had an amazing number of friends, colleagues, mentors, and supporters. I hope each of them feels that part of our work together is in this book.

Joe DeSantis has been an invaluable partner in developing *To Save America*. His deep patriotism, love of America, and commitment to intellectual honesty really helped strengthen and reinforce what we are trying to communicate about this great crisis. He is a mainstay of my intellectual and communications work, and this book reflects his hard work and commitment to helping save America.

Brady Cassis is my research assistant at the American Enterprise Institute (AEI) and was vital to the successful completion of *To Save America*. Brady is a young, talented, former College Jeopardy contestant from Yale University who rapidly produced research backgrounders on numerous issues and helped to fact check the final manuscript. I have been working with Brady for less than a year, but have already come to rely on his speed, thoroughness, and professionalism. He led a team of mature and capable interns at AEI including Jay Lucas, Joe Leanza, Francis Baker, and Dave Rodriguez, who assisted him greatly.

Of course, it goes without saying the book would have been incomplete without the efforts of my co-authors on several of the policy chapters in *To Save America*. Over my years in public life I have become known as an "ideas man." I deliberately chose to highlight many co-authors in this book to illustrate that I have gained this reputation largely because I have made it a point to work with very smart people who are developing the policies and proposals that will one day help save America. The work of Peter Ferrara, Dan Varroney, Nancy Desmond, Jim Frogue, David Merritt, Terry Maple, Steve Everley, Fred Asbell, Lisa Graham Keegan, and Nancy Sinnott Dwight certainly fall into that category.

Rick Tyler was not only my co-author on the religious liberty chapter; he is my long time spokesperson and founder of our new organization, Renewing American Leadership (ReAL). Rick's dedication to helping save America and to preserving freedom through faith as central to American liberty is inspirational to all who know him.

As always, I have relied on the advice of my dear friend Steve Hanser, who has been my mentor since my days at West Georgia College before I ran for Congress. He has always pushed me to think carefully and write clearly. He remains one of the most thoughtful and knowledgeable people I have been privileged to work with.

Vince Haley has shown a remarkable range of intellectual capabilities in working with me first at the Center for Health Transformation, then at AEI, and now as policy director at American Solutions. While he was helping with *To Save America*, he was also helping write and develop our new movie, *Nine Days that Changed the World*, about Pope John Paul II's 1979 visit to Poland. He was also preparing the American Solutions Academy described in this book. He is a true polymath of amazing range and dedication. He was very helpful during the editing process in keeping the book's intellectual coherence.

At AEI, the generosity of Ken and Yvonne Hannan have enabled me to build a capable research team that quickly respond to a wide variety of requests for information at all hours of the night. This includes the aforementioned Brady Cassis as well as Emily Renwick, a bright, young researcher with a gift for economics, and Commander John Barrett, a Navy Fellow who works with me on national security issues and whose service to his country in Afghanistan showed amazing skill as a surface naval warrior.

AEI is led by Arthur Brooks, a remarkable man who will release a new book in June called *The Battle: How the Fight Between Free Enterprise and Big Government Will Shape America's Future*. I recommend it highly as a companion piece for *To Save America*. AEI also employs a number of other experts who have been invaluable in the development of the ideas in this book, including Chris

Demuth, David Gerson, Michael Novak, Steve Hayward, Mark McClellan, Kevin Hassett, Danielle Pletka, John Bolton, Salley Satel, Alex Pollock, Peter Wallison, Charles Murray, James Q. Wilson, Karlyn Bowman, and Michael Barone.

Beyond AEI, a number of other scholars and experts were helpful in developing the ideas in this book. These include Herman Pirchner, Walter Isaacson, John Goodman, Cliff May, Grover Norquist, Ed Feulner (the remarkable leader of the Heritage Foundation), Dave Bossie of Citizens United, Craig Shirley (the eminent biographer of Ronald Reagan), Marc Rotterman, Brett Schaefer, David Barton, Attorney General Ed Meese, Andrew McCarthy, and Anne Bayefsky.

Terry Balderson is our general advisor on research. Every day he sends me between 80 and 200 articles from around the world. His hard work has enabled me to remain briefed and up to date on a wide variety of topics. He is simply invaluable.

Kathy Lubbers, my daughter, did a great job representing us in book negotiations. She leads a small but dedicated team at Gingrich Communications, including Matt Scofield and Robbie Gross, our web gurus behind Newt.org; Sylvia Garcia, who runs The Americano, a bilingual news and opinion site for Hispanics; and Michelle Selesky, our media booker and talk radio expert. Gingrich Communications interns Jaime Oliva, Stephen Cord, and Shannon Beattie also assisted in research for *To Save America*.

Jackie Cushman, my younger daughter, has become quite a columnist in her own right, and I am proud to borrow some of her better phrases and to use her insights into how America is evolving.

Marji Ross, president of Regnery Publishing, was a strong believer in this book from the very beginning and was enormously helpful in determining its optimum organization. Jack Langer, our editor, did an extraordinary job under a very tight deadline making the prose as clear and concise as possible. Jeff Carneal, the president of Eagle Publishing, has been a steadfast partner since we first published a book together in 2005, both in the growth and development of my newsletter, the "Newt Gingrich Letter," and for *To Save America*.

As always, Randy Evans and Stefan Passantino brought their considerable legal talents to bear. Randy is the general advisor and strategist for all my activities and his advice is invaluable across a wide range of topics and activities. Stefan is a leading expert on election law and has been counsel to our companies.

Joe Gaylord was my partner in designing the 1994 Contract with America campaign. We worked together for twelve years (1982—1994) to help elect the first House Republican majority in forty years. As the head of American Solutions, Joe brings enormous strategic insight into what we must do to save America and was invaluable in thinking through the ideas in this book.

Dan Varroney and Becky Burkett are doing a great job leading American Solutions on a day to day basis and they helped clarify the ideas around which we must build a new positive majority for solving America's challenges.

Nancy Desmond's leadership of the Center for Health Transformation has been decisive in creating a true collaboration of leaders dedicated to creating a twenty-first century personalized intelligent health system. She is an insightful and thoughtful leader on health and on every other issue we have worked on together. The Center continues to work to get us beyond the current mess in healthcare and to move toward a true transformation with better outcomes at lower costs.

Writing a book while doing everything else we do would be impossible were it not for the leadership of Sonya Harrison and her scheduling team including Bess Kelly and Heather Favors. Without their hard work and Sonya's leadership we would never be able to systematically focus on the many projects we undertake.

Alicia Melvin has become a special assistant of enormous capability helping Callista and me achieve more than we ever could on our own.

Finally, none of this would be possible without my wife, Callista. Her ongoing support and encouragement have been invaluable. With her own responsibilities at Gingrich Productions as a movie producer, co-host, narrator, writer, and photographer, she also spends hours each week as a singer, French hornist, and pianist. In addition, she continually helps me accomplish the key things that make projects like this possible. She has made my life a real joy.

Notes

Chapter 1

1. Walt Bogdanich, "A Disability Epidemic Among a Railroads Retirees," *New York Times*, September 20, 2008; available at: http://www.nytimes.com/2008/09/21/nyregion/21lirr.html?_r=1.

2. Mark Perry, "Cost of Jobs Banks to Big 3 2005–2008: $4,200,000,000," Carpe Diem blog, December 4, 2008; available at: http://mjperry.blogspot.com/2008/12/cost-of-jobs-bank-2005-2008-4200000000.html.

3. Mark Perry, "Post Office Version of the Big Three 'Jobs Bank,'" Carpe Diem blog, October 2, 2009; available at: http://mjperry.blogspot.com/2009/10/post-office-version-of-big-three-jobs.html.

4. Karen Matthews, "New York Teachers Paid To Do Nothing: 700 of Them," *Huffington Post*, June 22, 2009; available at: http://www.huff-

ingtonpost.com/2009/06/22/new-york-teachers-paid-to_n_ 219336.html.

5. Franklin D. Roosevelt, Letter on the Resolution of Federation of Federal Employees Against Strikes in Federal Service, August 16, 1937; available at: http://www.presidency.ucsb.edu/ws/index.php?pid= 15445.

6. See e.g., Duncan Hewitt, "The Shrinking of China," *Newsweek*, October 24, 2009; available at: http://www.newsweek.com/id/219416.

7. "Only 21% Say U.S. Government Has Consent of the Governed," Rasmussen, February 18, 2010; available at: http://www.rasmussenreports. com/public_content/politics/general_politics/february_2010/ only_21_say_u_s_government_has_consent_of_the_governed.

8. "Affidavit: $90,000 found in congressman's freezer," CNN, May 22, 2006; available at: http://www.cnn.com/2006/POLITICS/05/21/ jefferson.search/index.html.

9. "Voters Favor Tort Reform by Two-to-One Margin," Rasmussen Reports, December 2, 2009; available at: http://www.rasmussen reports.com/public_content/politics/current_events/healthcare/ november_2009/voters_favor_tort_reform_by_two_to_one_margi.

10. Copyright _ A.A. World Services, Inc.

Chapter 2

1. "It is impossible to miss the discrimination against...believers," *Salon*; available at: http://mobile.salon.com/news/primary_sources/ 2007/05/21/gingrich_liberty/index2.html.

2. "Colorado Student Files Lawsuit Over Commencement Speech That Mentioned Jesus," FOX News, August 31, 2007; available at: http:// www.foxnews.com/story/0,2933,295432,00.html.

3. "Ninth Circuit sends San Diego Boy Scout case to Cal Supreme Court with 'unprecedented' standing ruling," Boy Scouts of America National Council, December 31, 2008; available at: http:// www.bsalegal.org/.

4. See e.g., Patrick B. Craine, "Supreme Court Takes Up Case of War Memorial Cross in Mojave Desert," *Life Site News*, October 9, 2009; available at: http://www.lifesitenews.com/ldn/2009/oct/09100906.html.

5. "Ten Commandments dispute fouls trial," *St. Petersburg Times* archives, April 16, 1992; available at: http://news.google.com/newspapers?nid=888&dat=19920416&id=byEMAAAAIBAJ&sjid=11wD AAAAIBAJ&pg=5881,134756.

6. Terence Chea, "'Under God' in Pledge of Allegiance Upheld By Court," *Huffington Post*, March 11, 2010; available at: http://www.huffingtonpost.com/2010/03/12/under-god-in-pledge-of-allegiance_n_496255.html.

7. David Horowitz, *Barack Obama's Rules for Revolution: The Alinsky Model* (Horowitz Freedom Center, 2009); available at: http://www.discoverthenetworks.org/Articles/Rules%20for%20Revolution%20(2).pdf.

8. Saul Alinsky, *Rules for Radicals* (NY: Random House, 1971).

9. David Horowitz, *Barack Obama's Rules for Revolution: The Alinsky Model*, 45–46.

10. L. David Alinsky, "Son sees father's handiwork in convention," *Boston Globe*, August 31, 2008; available at: http://www.boston.com/bostonglobe/editorial_opinion/letters/articles/2008/08/31/son_sees_fathers_handiwork_in_convention/.

11. George Orwell, "Politics and the English Language," in *Collected Essays, Journalism, and Letters of George Orwell*, Vol. 4 *In Front of Your Nose* 1945–1950 (Boston, MA: David R. Godine, 2000).

12. George Orwell, "Why I Write," in *Collected Essays, Journalism, and Letters of George Orwell*.

Chapter 3

1. Transcript of Obama's Victory Speech, *New York Times*, November 5, 2008; available at: http://www.nytimes.com/2008/11/04/us/pol-

itics/04text-obama.html?sq=barack%20obama%20victory%20speech&st=cse&scp=4&pagewanted=all.

2. Senator Charles Grassley, letter available at: http://www.c-spanarchives.org/congress/?q=node/77531&appid=595236418.

3. Tim Carney, *Obamanomics* (Washington, D.C.: Regnery, 2009), 50–51.

Chapter 6

1. John Fund, *Stealing Elections: How Voter Fraud Threatens Our Elections* (New York: Encounter Books, 2004).

2. Data available at: http://www.judicialwatch.org/news/2010/mar/obama-justice-department-shut-down-federal-acorn-investigation-according-documents-obt.

3. Data available at: http://www.dispatchpolitics.com/live/content/local_news/stories/2010/03/11/copy/acorn-is-out-of-ohios-elections.html?adsec=politics&sid=101.

Chapter 8

1. Reed Abelson, "Study Raises Questions of Witnesses," *New York Times*, August 4, 2004; available at: http://www.nytimes.com/2004/08/04/business/04lung.html?pagewanted=1.

2. Madison Park, "Medical journal retracts study linking autism to vaccine," CNN, February 2, 2010; available at: http://www.cnn.com/2010/HEALTH/02/02/lancet.retraction.autism/index.html.

3. See e.g., Carla K. Johnson, "1 in 4 parents buys unproven vaccine-autism link," wtop.com, March 1, 2010; available at: http://wtop.com/?nid=106&sid=1900143.

4. Email exchange available at "East Anglia Confirmed Emails from the Climate Research Unit," released November 20, 2009: http://www.eastangliaemails.com/emails.php?eid=1041.

5. Kirk Myers, "Peddling global warming fears puts big money in pockets of climate researchers," *Washington Examiner*, December 23, 2009;

available at: http://www.examiner.com/x-32936-Seminole-County-Environmental-News-Examiner~y2009m12d23-Spreading-global-warming-doom-delivers-big-money-to-climate-researchers.

6. Robert Mendick, "'Climategate' professor Phil Jones awarded £13 million in research grants," *Telegraph*, December 5, 2009; available at: http://www.telegraph.co.uk/earth/copenhagen-climate-change-confe/6735846/Climategate-professor-Phil-Jones-awarded-13-million-in-research-grants.html.

7. Email exchange available at "East Anglia Confirmed Emails from the Climate Research Unit," released November 20, 2009: http://www.eastangliaemails.com/emails.php?eid=1041.

8. Stuart Miller, Robert Muir-Wood, and Auguste Boissonnade, "An exploration of trends in normalized weather-related catastrophe losses," p. 225; available at: http://www.rms.com/Publications/Trends_in_Weather_Related_Cat_loss_Miller_RMW.pdf.

Chapter 9

1. Resolution adopted by the United Nations General Assembly, February 8, 2002; available at: http://www.nyo.unep.org/pdfs/56151.pdf, p. 3.

2. Resolution adopted by the United Nations General Assembly, February 8, 2002; available at: http://www.nyo.unep.org/pdfs/56151.pdf, p. 4.

3. "Fifth Committee Recommends 2008-2009 Budget of $4.17 Billion," General Assembly, December 21, 2007; available at: http://www.un.org/News/Press/docs/2007/gaab3835.doc.htm.

4. Claudia Rosett, "The U.N. Kicks Off Another Season Of Bedlam," *Forbes*, August 20, 2009; available at: http://forbeslife.nl/2009/08/19/united-nations-bribery-muammar-gaddafi-opinions-columnists-claudia-rosett.html?partner=contextstory.

5. Ken Dilanian, "Report: U.N. spent U.S. funds on shoddy projects," *USA Today*, April 15, 2009; available at: http://www.usatoday.com/news/washington/2009-04-14-un-probe_N.htm.

6　"UN wasted $10 mln in Sudan peace mission – audit," *Sudan Tribune*, February 11, 2008; available at: http://www.sudantribune.com/spip.php?article25909.

7.　"Capital Master Plan to Renovate the UN Headquarters," Dialogue on Globalization, October 2008; available at: http://library.fes.de/pdf-files/bueros/usa/05771.pdf.

8.　"UN Renovation and Construction: Issues for Congressional Oversight?" The Heritage Foundation, January 13, 2010; available at: http://blog.heritage.org/2010/01/13/un-renovation-and-construction-issues-for-congressional-oversight/.

9.　Information available at Brett Schaefer, "Suspend UNDP Activities in North Korea, Again," The Heritage Foundation, April 8, 2009; available at: http://www.heritage.org/Research/Reports/2009/04/Suspend-UNDP-Activities-in-North-Korea-Again.

10.　For information, see Brett Schaefer, "United Nations Peacekeeping: The U.S. Must Press for Reform," The Heritage Foundation, September 18, 2008; available at: http://www.heritage.org/Research/Reports/2008/09/United-Nations-Peacekeeping-The-US-Must-Press-for-Reform.

11.　Martin Plaut, "Un troops 'armed DR Congo rebels,'" BBC, April 28, 2008; available at: http://news.bbc.co.uk/2/hi/programmes/panorama/7331077.stm.

12.　"DR Congo: Civilian Cost of Military Operation is Unacceptable," Human Rights Watch, October 13, 2009; available at: http://www.hrw.org/en/news/2009/10/12/dr-congo-civilian-cost-military-operation-unacceptable.

Chapter 11

1.　Alvin and Heidi Toffler, *The Third Wave* (NY: Bantam, 1984).

Chapter 12

1.　Arthur B. Laffer, Stephen Moore, and Peter J. Tanous, *The End of Prosperity* (New York: Simon & Schuster, 2008).

2. Ibid.
3. John Taylor, *Getting Off Track* (Stanford: Hoover Institute Press, 2009).

Chapter 14

1. Ron Haskins, *Work Over Welfare: The Inside Story of the 1996 Welfare Reform Law* (Washington, D.C.: Brookings Institution, 2006), 334.
2. Ibid., 335.

Chapter 15

1. See e.g., "Cash and Counseling Moves into the Mainstream," Alliance for Health Reform, April 2006; available at: http://www.allhealth. org/publications/pub_21.doc.
2. Jack Wennberg, *The Dartmouth Atlas of Healthcare 2006*, Dartmouth Atlas Project; available at: http://www.dartmouthatlas.org
3. Proposal available at: http://intermountainhealthcare.org/About/ News/Documents/deliveryreform.pdf.

Chapter 16

1. Thomson Reuters, "Waste in the U.S. Healthcare System Pegged at $700 Billion in Report from Thomson Reuters," October 26, 2009; available at: http://thomsonreuters.com/content/press_room/tsh/ waste_US_healthcare_system.
2. Government Accountability Office, "High-Risk Series: An Update," January 2009.
3. Congressional Research Service, "Improper Payments Information Act of 2002: Background, Implementation, and Assessment," October 8, 2009.
4. Department of Health & Human Services, Office of Inspector General, "MSIS Data Usefulness for Detecting Fraud, Waste, and Abuse," OEI-04-0-00240, August 26, 2009.
5. Hope Yen, "Report details billions lost in Medicare fraud," *Washington Post*, November 16, 2009; available at: http://www.washingtonpost. com/wp-dyn/content/article/2009/11/15/AR2009111502488.html.

6. "Medicare Fraud: A $60 Billion Crime," CBS News *60 Minutes*, October 25, 2009; video and transcript available at: http://www.cbsnews.com/stories/2009/10/23/60minutes/main5414390.shtml.

7. Associated Press, "Mafia, violent criminals turn to Medicare fraud," October 6, 2009.

8. Associated Press, "32 accused of $60M in Medicare fraud in 3 states," December 15, 2009.

9. Jay Weaver, "Medicare fraud rampant in South Florida," *Miami Herald*, August 3, 2008; available at: http://www.miamiherald.com/2008/08/03/627480/medicare-fraud-rampant-in-south.html.

10. Associated Press, "32 accused of $60M in Medicare fraud in 3 states," December 15, 2009.

11. Jay Weaver, "Fraud suspected in Miami-Dade diabetes care," *Miami Herald*, December 8, 2009; available at: http://www.miamiherald.com/2009/12/07/1370812/fraud-suspected-in-miami-dade.html.

12. Matt Coker, "Dr. George Steven Kooshian Gets Prison, Restitution for AIDS Dosing, Billing Scam," *OC Weekly* blog, February 23, 2010; available at: http://blogs.ocweekly.com/navelgazing/a-clockwork-orange/dr-george-steven-kooshian-sent/.

13. Jay Weaver, "Miami-Dade clinic owner held on Medicare fraud charges," *Miami Herald*, January 5, 2010; available at: http://www.miamiherald.com/2010/01/05/1409485/miami-dade-clinic-owner-held-on.html.

14. Robert Moran, "Couple charged in leading Medicare equipment fraud," *Philadelphia Inquirer*, December 11, 2009; available at: http://www.philly.com/philly/news/20091211_Couple_charged_in_leading_Medicare_equipment_fraud.html.

15. "Businessman pleads guilty to $18.4M Medicare scam," *Chicago Tribune*, September 29, 2009; available at: http://archives.chicagotribune.com/ 2009/sep/29/health/chi-ap-mi-medicarefraud-mic.

16. "Feds want Corvette, Harley that they say were bought with Medicare, Medicaid fraud," *Nashville Business Journal*, December 7, 2009; available at: http://www.nashvillefiles.com/Latest/Feds-want-

Corvette-Harley-that-they-say-were-bought-with-Medicare-Medicaid-fraud.html.

17. Senate Permanent Subcommittee on Investigations Press Release, "Coleman, Levin Investigate Millions in Medicare Payments for Claims Tied to Deceased Doctors," July 8, 2008; available at: http://levin.senate.gov/newsroom/release.cfm?id=300288.

18. Cara Mia DiMassa, Richard Winton, and Rich Connell, "3 Southern California hospitals accused of using homeless for fraud," *Los Angeles Times*, August 7, 2008; available at: http://articles.latimes.com/2008/aug/07/local/me-skidrow7.

19. Clifford J. Levy and Michael Luo, "New York Medicaid Fraud May Reach Into Billions," *New York Times*, July 18, 2005; available at: http://www.nytimes.com/2005/07/18/nyregion/18medicaid.html.

20. "Effective Care," Center for the Evaluative Clinical Sciences, a Dartmouth Atlas Project Topic Brief, available at: http://www.dartmouthatlas.org/topics/effective_care.pdf

21. Kaiser Commission on Medicaid and the Uninsured, "Dual Eligibles: Medicaid Enrollment and Spending for Medicare Beneficiaries in 2005," February 2009; available at: http://www.kff.org/medicaid/7846.cfm.

22. Mark D. Birdwhistell, "The Medicare to Medicaid Crossover: An Open Door to Waste and Fraud," in *Stop Paying the Crooks* (Washington, D.C.: CHT Press, 2009), 149.

23. Government Accountability Office, "Medicaid Third-Party Liability: Federal Guidance Needed to Help States Address Continuing Problems," September 2006; available at: http://www.gao.gov/new.items/d06862.pdf.

24. Craig H. Smith, "South Florida, Ground Zero for Healthcare Fraud," in *Stop Paying the Crooks* (Washington, D.C.: DC CHT Press, 2009), 47.

25. Letter to Congressman Nathan Deal dated February 26, 2010 from Charlene Frizzera, Acting Adminstrator of CMS, in response to a request dated June 17, 2009.

26. Medicare Payment Advisory Commission, "Report to the Congress: Reforming the Delivery System," June 2008; available at: http://www.medpac.gov/documents/Jun08_EntireReport.pdf.

27. The National Supplier Clearinghouse, the Healthcare Integrity and Protection Data Bank, the OIG Exclusion List, and CMS's Medicare Exclusion Database, etc.

28. Gina Kolata, "Patients in Florida Lining Up For All That Medicare Covers," *New York Times*, September 13, 2003; available at: http://www.nytimes.com/2003/09/13/us/patients-in-florida-lining-up-for-all-that-medicare-covers.html?pagewanted=1.

Chapter 17

1. Newt Gingrich and Terry Maple, *A Contract with the Earth* (NY: Plume, 2008), 186.

2. Stuart Butler, "Nuclear power is true 'green' energy," *The Washington Times*, January 29, 2009; available at: http://www.washingtontimes.com/news/2009/jan/29/nuclear-power-is-true-green-energy/.

3. Kevin Trenberth, "More knowledge, less certainty," Nature Reports: Climate Change, Vol. 4, February, pp. 20–21; available at: http://www.nature.com/climate/2010/1002/full/climate.2010.06.html.

4. Nigel Lawson, *An Appeal to Reason: A Cool Look At Global Warming* (London: Gerald Duckworth & Co., Ltd, 2008), 116.

Chapter 18

1. "About Oil Shale," Oil Shale & Tar Sands Programmatic EIS Information Center; available at: http://ostseis.anl.gov/guide/oilshale/index.cfm.

2. "BP reports giant oil discovery in Gulf of Mexico," *Dallas Morning News*, September 3, 2009; available at: http://www.dallasnews.com/sharedcontent/dws/bus/stories/080309dnbusgulfoil.a1444d.html.

3. Elwin Green, "Natural Gas locked in the Marcellus Shale has companies rushing to cash in on possibilities," *Pittsburgh Post-Gazette*, December 6, 2009; available at: http://www.post-gazette.com/pg/09340/1018586-28.stm.

4. "Secretary Chu Announces $3 Billion Investment for Carbon Capture and Sequestration," Department of Energy – National Energy Technology Laboratory, December 4, 2009; available at: http://www.netl.doe.gov/publications/press/2009/09081-Secretary_Chu_Announces_CCS_Invest.html.

5. "James Hansen: Prosecute oil companies, top scientist says," *UK Telegraph*, June 23, 2008; available at: http://www.telegraph.co.uk/news/2177572/James-Hansen-Prosecute-oil-companies-top-scientist-says.html; see also Andrew C. Revkin, "Hansen of NASA Arrested in Coal Country," *New York Times* Dot Earth, June 23, 2009; available at: http://dotearth.blogs.nytimes.com/2009/06/23/hansen-of-nasa-arrested-in-coal-country/.

6. "Rep. Waxman Introduces the 'Moratorium on Uncontrolled Power Plants Act,'" House Oversight Committee, March 11, 2008; available at: http://oversight.house.gov/images/stories/documents/20080311104934.pdf.

7. Otis Port, "Power from the Sunbaked Desert," *Business Week*, September 12, 2005; available at: http://www.businessweek.com/magazine/content/05_37/b3950067_mz018.htm.

8. Todd Woody, "Judge Halts Wind Farm Over Bats," *New York Times* Green Inc, December 10, 2009: available at: http://greeninc.blogs.nytimes.com/2009/12/10/judge-halts-wind-farm-over-bats/.

9. "A Clash of Environmental Ideals in the Mojave Desert: Solar-Energy Project vs. Endangered Desert Tortoises," *Los Angeles Times*, January 4, 2010; available at: http://latimesblogs.latimes.com/unleashed/2010/01/clash-of-environmental-ideals-in-the-mojave-desert-solarenergy-project-vs-endangered-desert-tortoise.html.

10. "RFA Resource Center – Ethanol Facts," Renewable Fuels Association; available at: http://www.ethanolrfa.org/resource/facts/economy/.

11. Adam Waldeck, "Turning Trash into Fuel? It's Happening," American Solutions, June 18, 2009; available at: http://www.

americansolutions.com/energy/2009/06/turning-trash-into-fuel-its-happening.php.

Chapter 22

1. Clayton Christiansen, *The Innovator's Dilemma* (NY: HarperCollins, 2000).
2. "Nuke over U.S. could unleash electromagnetic tsunami," *World Tribune*, December 7, 2005; available at: http://www.worldtribune.com/worldtribune/05/front2453711.9284722223.html.
3. William R. Forstchen, *One Second After* (NY: Forge Books, 2009).
4. See e.g., Gerald Posner, "China's Secret Cyberterrorism," *The Daily Beast*; available at: http://www.thedailybeast.com/blogs-and-stories/2010-01-13/chinas-secret-cyber-terrorism/.
5. See e.g., Joshua Davis, "Hackers Take Down the Most Wired Country in Europe," *Wired* magazine, August 21, 2007; available at: http://www.wired.com/politics/security/magazine/15-09/ff_estonia?currentPage=all.

Chapter 23

1. "Rick Santelli and the 'Rant of the Year,'" CNBC; video available at: http://www.youtube.com/watch?v=bEZB4taSEoA.

Index

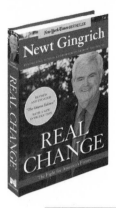
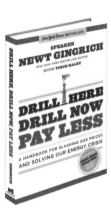
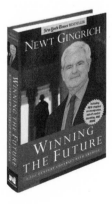